Consolidated Abstracts of the Highway Acts, 1862, 1864; the Locomotive Acts, 1861, 1865, and the Highways and Locomotives (Amendment) Act, 1878, With the Acts in Extenso, Notes and Copious Index

CONSOLIDATED ABSTRACTS

OF THE

HIGHWAY ACTS, 1862, 1864;

THE LOCOMOTIVE ACTS, 1861, 1865,

AND THE

HIGHWAYS AND LOCOMOTIVES (AMENDMENT) ACT, 1878,

WITH THE ACTS IN EXTENSO,

NOTES, AND COPIOUS INDEX.

BY

JAMES A. FOOT, Esq., M.A.,

Of the Middle Temple, Barrister-at-Law.

LONDON :
SHAW & SONS, FETTER LANE AND CRANE COURT,
𝔏𝔞𝔴 𝔓𝔯𝔦𝔫𝔱𝔢𝔯𝔰 𝔞𝔫𝔡 𝔓𝔲𝔟𝔩𝔦𝔰𝔥𝔢𝔯𝔰.

1879.

LONDON: PRINTED BY SHAW AND SONS, FETTER LANE.

PREFACE.

Two objects were had in view in passing the Highways and Locomotives (Amendment) Act, 1878. First, the amendment of the Law relating to Highways in England; and secondly, the amendment of the Locomotive Acts, 1861 and 1865. In carrying out the first of these objects attention appears to have been so much directed to highway districts that, at first sight, it almost seems as though no alteration was contemplated as regards ordinary highway parishes. A closer examination of the Act, however, soon dispels that illusion, and reveals the fact that it makes important alterations in some of the most essential particulars as to the law relating to parish highways, equally with district highways.

Amongst these may be mentioned the provisions with respect to the audit of accounts contained in section 9; those in section 10 as to proceedings for the maintenance and repair of highways; in section 13, as to disturnpiked roads becoming main roads; in section 15, as to declaring ordinary highways to be main roads; in section 23, as to extraordinary traffic; in section 24, as to unnecessary highways; and in section 26, as to bye-laws prohibiting or regulating the use of waggons, &c., with a certain description of wheels, and for other matters. Other sections might be mentioned. But sufficient has been referred to to call attention to the fact that although the Act mainly applies to district parishes, it

nevertheless has an important effect, in many instances, on
ordinary highway parishes, and, therefore, must not be dis-
regarded by highway surveyors.

In preparing the following abstract, however, the difficulty
of dealing with ordinary highway parishes in conjunction
with district parishes was found to be too great to render such
an attempt advisable, and it was therefore decided to take
the Highway Acts, 1862 and 1864 as a model, and to arrange
the Abstract, to a certain extent, in conformity with their
provisions, but with additional headings suitable to the more
careful sub-division of the subject rendered necessary by the
consolidation of the three statutes. It was felt that the most
effectual way of showing the changes effected by the late
Act, was to consolidate its provisions with those of the Acts
of 1862 and 1864, and thereby enable the reader to see at a
glance its effect upon the previous Acts, and the changes
introduced. Of course, such an Abstract cannot possess the
completeness of an Act of Parliament. But it is, at any rate, the
best substitute for it that circumstances permit; and has, at
least, the merit of grouping together subjects which in the
original order followed in the Acts, must necessarily be widely
separated. It is hoped, therefore, that a Consolidated
Abstract, coupled with the Acts themselves, and the notes
which accompany them, will be found of service in showing the
real state of the law with respect to highway districts and the
alterations which have recently been effected in it. The
effect of the late Act upon the general laws of highways is
left for explanation by the notes appended to its various
sections.

One of the leading features of the Highways and Locomotives (Amendment) Act, 1878, is the endeavour to transfer

the management of highways from highway boards to rural sanitary authorities. This is sought to be accomplished by requiring the justices in quarter sessions when forming highway districts or altering their boundaries, to form them, so far as practicable, so as to be coincident in area with rural sanitary districts (section 3), and then giving power to the rural sanitary authorities to apply for an order enabling them to exercise the powers of a highway board within their district (section 4). Upon the making of such an order any existing highway board will be dissolved, and the rural sanitary authority will take their place, with certain exceptions as to the mode of obtaining payment of expenses (section 5). The expenses incurred by a rural sanitary authority in the performance of their duties as a highway board will be payable as general expenses under sections 229, 230 of the Public Health Act, 1875 (*Id.*). The adoption of this power, it will be observed, is quite optional on the part of the rural sanitary authority. But should it be acted upon, the management of highways will devolve upon the board of guardians in addition to their management of the poor, and there will be but one authority having the control of both poor and highways within the union.

Another most important alteration will be found in section 7, providing that after the 25th March, 1879, all expenses incurred by a highway board in maintaining highways will be chargeable on the district fund, instead of to the respective parishes under 27 & 28 Vict. c. 101, s. 32, just as in the case of the maintenance of the poor under the Union Chargeability Act, 1865, 28 & 29 Vict. c. 79, the cost of their relief and other expenses are charged upon the common fund of the union. This alteration will considerably facilitate the adop-

tion by rural sanitary authorities of the powers of highway
boards, as adoption under such circumstances will give them
useful administrative powers without adding to the burthens
on the union.

Following this comes an amended provision as to the audit
of accounts, which applies both to highway districts and
ordinary highway parishes. By section 9 the accounts are
to be made up and balanced to the 25th March in each year,
and the Local Government Board have power to prescribe
the form in which they shall be made up. Shortly after
that date they are to be audited and examined by the poor
law auditor of the district, instead of, as hitherto, by a person
appointed by the board in the case of highway district accounts,
or by justices at special sessions in the case of ordinary highway accounts.

A change of considerable importance is also made by the
10th section respecting the mode of compelling the repair of
highways. Proceedings for this purpose have hitherto been
taken before justices in petty sessions; in the case of parish
highways, under 5 & 6 Will. 4, c. 50, s. 94, and in that of
district highways, under 25 & 26 Vict. c. 61, s. 18. By the
10th section, however, proceedings of a somewhat similar
description are authorized to be taken before the court of
quarter sessions without the intervention of justices in petty
sessions; and looking to the difference between the old and
the new mode of procedure, it would seem that the old law
can no longer be acted upon, but must give place to the
new. But as neither this section, nor any other part of the
Act, repeals the sections above referred to, the question of
their repeal must necessarily be considered doubtful, and one
which it will probably require the intervention of a court of
law to solve.

The introduction of "main roads" is also an innovation which bids fair to have important consequences, though, from the peculiar language of the Act, it is doubtful whether they will be so important as at first sight may appear. By the 13th section certain disturnpiked roads are declared to be main roads, and one half of the expense of their maintenance is to be paid out of the county rate. And by the 15th section, the county authority, on the application of the highway authority, may order that any road which is "a medium of communication between great towns, or a thoroughfare to a railway station, or otherwise," shall be a main road. It may reasonably be presumed that it was the intention of the legislature that the maintenance of all main roads should be treated alike, and that one half of the expense should in all cases be payable out of the county rate. But if that was their intention, it seems very doubtful whether it has been carried out. There is no general provision in the Act charging the county rate with one half of the expense of maintaining main roads, but only a special provision as to disturnpiked roads. So that the simple fact of declaring a road to be a main road (which is all that the Act provides for), does not necessarily carry with it any obligation on the county to contribute to its maintenance. Whether or not that obligation will be inferred from the fact of a road being declared to be a main road, remains to be seen. But certainly, so far as the language of the Act is concerned, there is nothing which necessarily imports it.

Another novelty relates to provision for the expense occasioned by "extraordinary traffic." The 23rd section enacts that where it appears to the road authority by their surveyor's certificate that, "having regard to the average expense of repairing highways in the neighbourhood, extraordinary expenses have been incurred by such authority in repairing any highway by reason of the damage caused by excessive weight passing along the same, or extraordinary traffic thereon, such authority may recover in a summary manner from any person by whose order such weight or traffic has been conducted, the amount of such expenses as may be proved to the satisfaction of the court , , . . to have been incurred by such authority by reason of the damage arising from such weight or traffic as aforesaid." This, no doubt, will in many instances be a very useful provision. But, as pointed out ·in a note, *post*, p. 191, some difficulty will probably be found in carrying it into operation. This consideration, it may be presumed, will furnish a strong ground for inducing road authorities to act liberally in coming to an agreement as to the composition which the same section enables them to accept.

Fresh provisions are also made by section 24 as to the discontinuance of unnecessary highways, which appear to supersede those contained in the 21st section of the Highway Act, 1864, so far as relates to parishes which are situate in a petty sessional division, but leaves them untouched as to other parishes. An entirely new provision is also introduced by the 26th section, enabling the county authority to make bye-laws for prohibiting or regulating the use of waggons, &c., with wheels of which the fellies or tires are not of the prescribed width, and for other matters there mentioned.

The foregoing include the principal changes effected by the Act, so far as regards highways, but by no means exhaust the list. For the others it must suffice to refer the reader to the Act itself, which will be found more fully explained in the notes which accompany it. Coupled with the Consolidated Abstract, there can be little difficulty in ascertaining in what those changes consist.

As regards the amendment of the Locomotive Acts, 1861 and 1865, a similar course has been adopted to that which has been followed in the case of highways. The provisions of those Acts have been incorporated with such of the enactments of the Highways and Locomotives (Amendment) Acts, 1878, as relate to locomotives. And in order to make the Abstract complete in itself, some of the enactments are set out at length, although they are common to both highways and locomotives, and are therefore included in the Highway Abstract also. Although this increases the length of the Abstract to some extent, it dispenses with the necessity for reference to another document, and thereby more than counterbalances the inconvenience arising from the trifling addition to length. By this means also each Abstract contains the whole law on the subject to which it relates, and is perfectly independent of the other.

The principal alterations made with respect to locomotives consist in a re-modelling of the regulations with respect to the weight of locomotives and the construction of their wheels (section 28), an alteration as to the making of bye-laws relating to the hours during which locomotives may pass over turnpike roads and highways (section 31), and the power conferred on the county authority to license locomotives, excepting such as are used solely for agricultural purposes (section 32).

These alterations, however, will only remain in force so long as the Locomotive Act, 1865, continues in force; that is to say, until the 31st December, 1879, or any other date to which that Act may be continued.

In preparing the Abstracts many sections of the Acts which admit of division have been so arranged as to separate the various enactments they contain, and place them before the reader in the form of distinct paragraphs. By this means, it is believed, they will be more readily comprehended than in the statutable form, and many of their provisions which might otherwise escape notice will be brought distinctly under the reader's eye. In addition to this, marginal notes have been added, so as to make the paragraphs more easily intelligible. Many of these notes vary considerably from those contained in the Acts themselves, in consequence of their being so framed as to explain the contents of the various paragraphs, whereas those appended to the Acts, for the most part, merely indicate, in general terms, the subject-matter of the entire section. The precise language of the Acts, too, has been occasionally deviated from, so as to give the provisions of an enactment in more colloquial phraseology, but without altering their import.

In the Acts themselves, where other Acts are referred to, the year and chapter of those Acts are substituted for the fuller and more formal description commonly used.

J. A. F.

10, KING'S BENCH WALK, TEMPLE.
5, *December*, 1878.

CONTENTS.

THE HIGHWAY ACT, 1862, 25 & 26 Vict. c. 61.

Preliminary.

Formation of Highway Districts.

THE HIGHWAY ACT, 1864, 27 & 28 VICT. CAP. 101.

Preliminary.

THE HIGHWAYS AND LOCOMOTIVES (AMENDMENT) ACT, 1878, 41 & 42 Vict. c. 77.

Preliminary.

PART I.

AMENDMENT OF HIGHWAY LAW.

Highway Districts.

THE LOCOMOTIVE ACT, 1861, 24 & 25 Vict. c. 70.

CORRIGENDA

Page 5, line 31, after "to be," add "or to be."

"   "   34, dele "only, only."

Page 44, "   11, after "extent," add "only and in manner."

"   "   14, for "payable," read "repayable."

"   "   21, dele "and be expended by the like persons."

"   lines 23 and 24, for "raised, charged, and expended,"
read "raised and charged."

Page 53, between lines 24 and 25, add heading—
Highways Repairable *ratione tenuræ*, and Private Roads.

Page 80, line 2, dele "and carrying away."

"   "   5, after "working," add "and getting."

TABLE OF CASES.

CONSOLIDATED ABSTRACT

OF

HIGHWAY ACTS, 1862 & 1864,

AND OF

THE HIGHWAYS AND LOCOMOTIVES

(AMENDMENT) ACT, 1878,

SO FAR AS IT RELATES TO HIGHWAYS.

In this Abstract the following abbreviated expressions have been used, viz. :—

Act '62, means "The Highway Act, 1862." (25 & 26 Vict. c. 61.)

Act '64, means "The Highway Act, 1864." (27 & 28 Vict. c. 101.)

Act '78, means "The Highways and Locomotives (Amendment) Act, 1878." (41 & 42 Vict. c. 77.)

PRELIMINARY.

The Act 5 & 6 Will. 4, c. 50, "An Act to consolidate and amend the laws relating to highways in that part of Great Britain called England," is hereinafter distinguished as "the Principal Act." ^{Act '62 s. 4. Principal Act.}

The Act 25 & 26 Vict. c. 62, and the Principal Act and the other Acts amending the Principal Act, are hereinafter included under the expression "The Highway Acts." ^{Highway Acts.}

The Act 25 & 26 Vict. c.62, so far as is consistent with its provisions, is to be construed as one with the Principal Act. ^{Id., s. 42. The Principal Act and 25 & 26 Vict. c. 62, to be construed as one Act.}

B

Act '64, s. 1.
Short titles
of Highway
Acts.

The Acts hereinafter mentioned may be cited for all purposes by the short titles following; that is to say:—

The Act 5 & 6 Will. 4, c. 50, "An Act to consolidate and amend the Laws relating to Highways in that part of Great Britain called England" by the short title of the "Highway Act, 1835."

The Act 25 & 26 Vict. c. 61, by the short title of the "Highway Act, 1862."

The Act 27 & 28 Vict. c. 101, by the short title of the "Highway Act, 1864."

Highway
Acts.

All the above-mentioned Acts, and any Acts passed, or to be passed amending the same, are included under the short title of "The Highway Acts."

Id. s. 2.
Highway
Acts, 1862,
1864, to be
construed as
one Act.

The Act 27 & 28 Vict. c. 101, so far as is consistent with the tenor thereof, is to be construed as one with the "Highway Act, 1862."

Act '78, s. 1.
Short title of
Act, 1878.

The Act 41 & 42 Vict. c. 77, may be cited as "The Highways and Locomotives (Amendment) Act, 1878."

LIMITS OF ACTS.

Act '62, s.1.
Act '78, s.2.

The Acts do not apply to Scotland or Ireland.

APPLICATION OF 41 & 42 VICT. c. 77.

Act '78, . 2.
Exception of
Isle of
Wight, &c.

Save as is therein expressly provided, Part 1 of the 41 & 42 Vict. c. 77, does not apply to the Isle of Wight; nor to any part of the metropolis; nor to any part of a county to which the 23 & 24 Vict. c. 68, "An Act for the better management and control of the highways in South Wales," extends.

DEFINITIONS.

Act '62, s. 2.
County.

The word "County" in the Highway Act, 1862, does not include a "county of a city" or a "county of a town," but where a county, as hereinbefore defined, is divided into ridings or other divisions having a Act'62, s. 2. separate court of quarter sessions of the peace, it means each such division or riding, and not the entire county; and for the purposes of this Act all liberties and franchises, except the liberty of Saint Albans, which is considered a county, and except boroughs as hereinafter defined are considered as forming part of that county by which they are surrounded, or if partly surrounded by two or more counties, then as forming part of that county with which they have the longest common boundary.

"County," includes any division of a county that has Act'64,s.3. County. a separate County Treasurer.

The word "Borough" means a borough as defined Act '62, s. 2. Borough. by 5 & 6 Will. 4, c. 76, "for the regulation of municipal corporations in England and Wales," or any place to which the provisions of the said Act have been or shall hereafter have been extended.

The word "Parish" includes any place maintaining Id. s. 3. Parish. its own highways.

The expressions "highway district" and "highway Highway district. Highway board. board" refer only to highway districts formed and highway boards constituted in pursuance of this Act.

"Poor Law Parish" means a place that separately Act'64. s. 3. Poor Law Parish. maintains its own Poor.

"Highway Parish" means a place that after the con- Highway parish. stitution of a highway district separately maintains its own highways, and is entitled to return a waywarden or waywardens to the highway board of the district.

"Highway Rate" includes any rate, whether poor Highway rate. rate or not, out of the produce of which moneys are payable in satisfaction of precepts of a highway board.

The expression "The Summary Jurisdiction Acts" Act '78, s. 36. The summary juris- diction Acts. means the Act of 11 & 12 Vict. c. 43, "An Act to facilitate the performance of the duties of justices of

Act '78, s.36. the peace out of sessions within England and Wales with respect to summary convictions and orders," inclusive of any Acts amending the same.

Court of summary jurisdiction. The expression "Court of Summary Jurisdiction" means and includes any justice or justices of the peace, metropolitan police magistrate, stipendiary or other magistrate, or officer, by whatever name called, to whom jurisdiction is given by the Summary Jurisdiction Acts: provided that the court, when hearing and determining an information or complaint under the Highways and Locomotives (Amendment) Act, 1878, shall be constituted either of two or more justices of the peace in petty sessions, sitting at a place appointed for holding petty session, or of some magistrate or officer sitting alone or with others at some court or other place appointed for the administration of justice, and for the time being empowered by law to do alone any act authorized to be done by more than one justice of the peace.

Act' 64, s. 18. Provisional and final orders. The expression "Provisional and Final Order," as used in the Highway Act, 1864, means a provisional and final order passed and published in manner provided by that Act and the Highway Act, 1862, with the necessary variations as to notices and otherwise.

INTERPRETATION OF 41 & 42 VICT. c. 77.

In this Act—

Act,'78, s. 38. County. "County" has the same meaning as it has in the Highway Acts, 1862 and 1864, except that every liberty not being assessable to the county rate of the county or counties within which it is locally situate shall, for the purposes of this Act other than those relating to the formation and alteration of highway districts, and the transfer of the powers of a highway board, be deemed to be a separate county.

"County authority" means the justices of a county in general or quarter sessions assembled.

"Borough" means any place for the time being subject to 5 & 6 Will. 4, c. 76, "An Act to provide for the regulation of Municipal Corporations in England and Wales," and the Acts amending the same

"Highway district" means a district constituted in pursuance of the Highway Act, 1862, and the Highway Act, 1864, or one of such Acts.

"Highway board" means the highway board having jurisdiction within a highway district.

"Highway parish" means a parish or place included or capable of being included in a highway district in pursuance of the Highway Acts, 1862 and 1864, or one of such Acts.

"Highway authority" means as respects an urban sanitary district the urban sanitary authority, and as respects a highway district the highway board, and as respects a highway parish the surveyor or surveyors or other officers performing similar duties.

"Rural sanitary district" and "rural sanitary authority" mean respectively the districts and authorities declared to be rural sanitary districts and authorities by the Public Health Act, 1875.

"Urban sanitary district" and "urban sanitary authority" mean respectively the districts and authorities declared to be urban sanitary districts and authorities by the Public Health Act, 1875, except that for the purposes of this Act, no borough having a separate court of quarter sessions, and no part of any such borough shall be deemed to be included in any such district, and where part of a parish is included in such district for the purpose only of the repairs of the highways only, only such part shall be deemed to be included in the district for the purposes of this Act.

[Marginal notes:] Act '78, s. 36. County authority. Borough. Highway district. Highway board. Highway parish. Highway authority. Rural sanitary district. Rural sanitary authority. Urban sanitary district. Urban sanitary authority.

Act '78, s. 8.
___
Metropolis.   " The Metropolis " means the parishes and places mentioned in the Schedules A., B., and C., annexed to the Metropolis Management Act, 1855, and any parish to which such Act may be extended by Order in Council in manner in the said Act provided; also the city of London and the liberties of the said city.

Quarter
sessions.   " Quarter sessions " includes general sessions.

Petty ses-
sional
division.   " Petty sessional division " means any division for the holding a special sessions formed, or to be formed under the provisions of 9 Geo. 4, c. 43, or any Act amending the same; also any division of a county, or of a riding, division, parts, or liberty of a county, having a separate commission of the peace, in and for which petty sessions or special sessions are usually held, whether in one or more place or places, in accordance with any custom, or otherwise than under the said last-mentioned Act; but does not include any city, borough, town corporate, or district constituted a petty sessional division by 12 & 13 Vict. c. 18, " An Act for the holding of petty sessions of the peace in boroughs, and for providing places for the holding of such petty session in counties and boroughs."

Person.   " Person " includes a body of persons corporate or unincorporate.

———

PLACES SEPARATELY MAINTAINING HIGHWAYS.

Act '62, s. 32.
Extra-
parochial
places.   Where in pursuance of 20 Vict. c. 19, " An Act for the Relief of the Poor in extra-parochial places," any place is declared to be a parish, or where overseers of the poor are appointed for any place, such

place shall for the purposes of the Highway Act, 1862, Act '62, s. 32. be deemed to be a parish separately maintaining its own highways; and where in pursuance of the same Act any place is annexed to any adjoining parish, or to any district in which the relief of the poor is administered under a local Act, such place shall for the purposes of the Highway Act, 1862, be deemed to be · annexed to such parish or district for the purposes of the maintenance of the highways, as well as for the purposes in the said Act mentioned.

Where part of a parish is not contiguous to the *Id.* s. 33. Outlying part of parish parish of which it is apart, such outlying part may at the discretion of the justices be annexed to a district, and, when so annexed, it shall, for all the purposes of the Highway Acts, be deemed to be a parish separately maintaining its own highways.

Any parish, township, tithing, hamlet or other place Act '64, s. b. Places in which highways are not repaired out of highway rate. having a known legal boundary in which there are no highways repairable at the expense of the place, or in which the highways are repaired at the expense of any person, body politic or corporate, by reason of any grant, tenure, limitation, or appointment of any charitable gift, or otherwise howsoever than out of a highway rate or other general rate, shall, for the purposes of the Highway Acts, be deemed to be a place separately maintaining its own highways.

Where part of a parish is, in pursuance of the Local Government Act, 1858, Amendment Act, 1861, sect. 9, treated as forming part of a district constituted under the Local Government Act, 1858, for all purposes connected with the repair of highways and the payment of highway rates, but for no other purpose, such part, for the purposes of the Highway Acts, 1862, and

Act '64, s. 5. 1864, is deemed to be a place separately maintaining its own highways, and capable of being included in a highway district, without requiring the consent of the local board to be given.

Where the highways of one part of a parish are, in pursuance of a private Act of Parliament, repairable out of a different rate from that out of which the highways of the other part are repairable, each of such parts, for the purposes of the Highway Acts, is deemed to be a place separately maintaining its own highways.

HIGHWAY DISTRICTS.
FORMATION.

Act '62, s. 5. Five justices may require clerk of the peace to send notice of proposal, &c. Any five or more justices of a county may by writing under their hands require the clerk of the peace to add to or send with the notice required by law to be given of the holding of courts of general or quarter sessions a notice in the form marked (A.) *post*, p. 120, in the schedule, or as near thereto as circumstances admit, that at the court therein mentioned a proposal will be made to the justices to divide the county or some part thereof into highway districts, or to constitute the whole or some part thereof a highway district, and also require the clerk of the peace to send by post in a prepaid letter notices in the aforesaid form to the churchwardens or overseers of every parish mentioned in the said notice.

Justices in quarter sessions may make provisional order. Upon such requisition being complied with the justices assembled at the court of general or quarter sessions mentioned in the notice may entertain such proposal, and make a provisional order dividing their county or some part thereof into highway districts, or constituting the whole or some part of their county a

highway district, for the more convenient manage- Act '62, s. 5.
ment of highways, but such order shall not be of any Order not
validity unless it is confirmed by a final order of the confirmed
justices assembled at some subsequent court of general order.
or quarter sessions.

When it is proposed that only part of a county is to Act '64, s. 6.
be constituted a highway district, not less than two constitute
out of the five justices making such proposal shall be part of
resident in the said district, or acting in the petty highway
sessional division in which such district or some part district.
thereof is situate.

In forming any highway districts, or in altering Act '78, s. 3.
the boundaries of any highway districts, the county be made so
authority shall have regard to the boundaries of the sible coinci-
rural sanitary districts in their county, and shall, so rural sani-
far as may be found practicable, form highway dis- tary districts.
tricts so as to be coincident in area with rural sanitary
districts, or wholly contained within rural sanitary
districts.

All powers and jurisdictions vested in justices by Act '64, s. 17.
the Highway Act, 1862, and the Highway Act, powers of
1864, or either of such Acts, may from time to time justices.
be exercised in relation to highway districts, highway
boards, and highway parishes already formed, as well
as upon the occasion of forming new highway districts, boards, or parishes.

REGULATIONS AS TO MAKING, ETC., OF ORDERS.

The following regulations apply to the making, confirmation, and approval of the orders of justices for
forming highway districts.

1. The justices making a provisional order under Act '66, s. 6.
   the Highway Act, 1862, must appoint some provisional
   subsequent court of general or quarter sessions, sequent court
   to be held within a period of not more than six pointed for

months, for the taking into consideration the confirmation of the provisional order by a final order.

2. The clerk of the peace must add to or send with the notice required by law to be given of the holding of courts of general or quarter sessions a notice in the form marked (B.) *post*, p. 120, in the schedule hereto, or as near thereto as circumstances admit, of the appointment so made by the justices in relation to the confirmation of the provisional order :

3. The justices assembled at the appointed court of general or quarter sessions may make a further order quashing the provisional order, or confirming it with or without variations, or respiting the consideration of such provisional order to some subsequent court of general or quarter sessions, provided—

Firstly, that where the variations made extend to altering the parishes constituting any highway district or districts as formed in the provisional order, the order shall be deemed to be provisional only, and shall be dealt with accordingly :

Secondly, that where a respite is made to any subsequent general or quarter sessions, the clerk of the peace shall give notice of such respite in manner in which he is required to give notice in respect of sessions at which a provisional or final order is proposed to be made :

4. The provisional order shall state the parishes to be united in each district, the name by which the district is to be known, and the number of

waywardens (such number to be at least one) Act '62, s. 6.
which each parish is to elect. name of district, and number of waywardens.

Where more highway districts than one are com- Act '64, s. 4.
prised in any order of justices, whether provisional or Construction of order including more than one district.
final, and whether made before or after the passing of
the Highway Act, 1864, the formation of each of such
districts is to be deemed independent of the formation
of any other district, and the order shall for all purposes be construed and take effect as if a separate
order had been made in respect of each district; and
any variation in a provisional order altering the
parishes in any one or more districts comprised in that
order shall make that order provisional only as to the
particular district or districts in which the alterations
are made, and not as to any other district or districts
included in the same order.

Contiguous places situate in different counties and Id. s. 13. Jurisdiction of justices as to union of parishes in different counties.
places situate partly in one county and partly in
another county or counties shall, for the purpose of
being united in one highway district, be deemed to be
subject to the jurisdiction of the justices of any county,
who may make a provisional and final order constituting them an highway district, in the same manner as
if all such places or parts of places were situate in
such last-mentioned county; subject to this proviso,
that the provisional and final orders of the justices of
the said county shall be of no validity unless provisional and final orders to the same effect are passed
either concurrently with or subsequently to the first-
mentioned provisional and final orders by the justices
of every other county in which any of the said places
or parts of places are situate.

The first meeting of the highway board after the Id. s. 10. First meeting of board
formation of a district shall be held at such time as
may be appointed by the provisional or final order of

Act '64, s. 10. the justices, so that the time appointed be not more
to be held at than seven days after the expiration of the time
time
appointed limited by law for the election of waywardens, or, in
by pro-
visional or the case of a special day being appointed for such
final order. election as hereinafter mentioned, be not more than
twenty-one days after that day.

Day ap-   The day appointed for the first meeting of the board
pointed for
first meeting shall for all the purposes of the Highway Acts be
deemed day
of formation deemed to be the day of the formation of the district; and
of district.
the surveyor for the time being of every parish within
the district shall continue in office until seven days after
the appointment of the district surveyor, and no longer.

Id. s. 11.   In forming a highway district under the Highway
Justices may
appoint day Act, 1862, the justices may, for the purpose of avoid-
for first
election of ing delay in bringing the Act into operation, appoint
waywardens.
by their final order a day on which the first election
of waywardens as members of the highway board is to
take place in the district.

Waywardens   On the day appointed for the election waywardens
to be elected
on appointed shall be elected in every parish in the district entitled
day.
to elect such officers by the same persons and in the
same manner by and in which waywardens are elected
under the Highway Act, 1862, and all the provisions of the Highway Acts relating to the qualifications of surveyors or waywardens, and to the appointment of surveyors and waywardens by justices in the
event of no election taking place, shall apply accordingly : but the waywardens elected under this section
Continuance shall continue in office only until the time at which
in office.
the next annual election of surveyors would have
taken place in the several parishes of the district if the
same had not been constituted a highway district, and
at that time new waywardens shall be elected in
manner provided by the Highway Acts.

Notwithstanding anything in the Highway Acts, waywardens continue in office till the 30th day of April in the year following the year in which they were elected, and on that day their successors come into office.

Act '78, s. 11.
Duration of
office of
waywarden.

If any highway board make default in holding its first meeting in pursuance of the Highway Act, 1862, such board shall not thereupon become disqualified from acting, but the justices in general or quarter sessions shall, on the application of any persons liable to pay highway rates within the district, make such order as they think fit for the holding of such board at some other time, and any order so made shall be deemed to be an order capable of being removed into the Court of Queen's Bench, in pursuance of the Act 12 & 13 Vict. c. 45, and may be enforced accordingly, and the costs of any application to the court of quarter sessions in puruance of this section shall be defrayed out of the district fund of the board.

Id. s. 40.
If board fail
to hold first
meeting,
quarter ses-
sions may
order board
to be held at
some other
time.

Costs of
application
to be de-
frayed out of
district fund.

6. Notice of the provisional and final orders shall as soon as possible after the making thereof be given by the clerk of the peace, by publishing a copy in the *London Gazette* and in one or more newspapers circulating in the county, or if the whole county is not affected by such order in one or more newspapers circulating in the district affected by such orders, and by sending a copy by post in a prepaid letter to the overseers of every parish within the pro- posed highway district, and there shall be added to the notice of the provisional order the date of the sessions at which the confirmation of such order will be considered.

Id. s. 6.
Orders to be
published in
Gazette and
county
newspaper.

Copy to be
sent to over-
seers.

RESTRICTIONS ON FORMATION.

Act '82, s. 7.

The following restrictions are imposed with respect to the formation of highway districts in pursuance of the Highway Act, 1862;

Firstly, there shall not be included in any highway district formed in pursuance of that Act any of the following places; that is to say,

Prohibition against including places to which 23 & 24 Vict. c. 68, extends.

Any part of a county to which 23 & 24 Vict. c. 68, An Act for the better Management and Control of the Highways in South Wales, extends:

Isle of Wight.

The Isle of Wight:

Districts under Public Health Act, 1848, and Local Government Act, 1858.

Any district constituted under the Public Health Act, 1848, and the Local Government Act, 1858, or either of such Acts:

Parishes within limits of metropolis.

Any parish or place within the limits of the metropolis as defined by 18 & 19 Vict. c. 120, An Act for the better Local Management of the Metropolis:

Parishes under local Acts.

Any parish or place, or part of a parish or place, the highways whereof are maintained under the provisions of any local Act of Parliament:

Parishes within the limits of a borough.

Secondly, there shall not be included in any highway district formed in pursuance of the Highway Act, 1862, any parish or place, or part of a parish or place, within the limits of a borough without the consent, firstly, of the council of such borough, and, secondly, of the vestry of the parish which, or part of which, is proposed to be included:

As to parishes in several counties.

Thirdly, where any parish separately maintaining its own highways is situate in more than one county, the whole of such parish shall, for the purposes of the Highway Act, 1862, be deemed Act '62, s. 7. to be within the county within which the church of such parish, or (if there be no church) the greater part of such parish, is situate:

Lastly, where a parish separately maintaining its Combination of townships, &c. own poor is divided into townships, tithings, hamlets, or places, each of which separately maintains its own highways, it shall be lawful for the justices, if they think fit, in their provisional order to combine such townships, tithings, hamlets, and places,

And to declare that no separate waywardens shall be elected for such townships, tithings, hamlets, and places, and that such parish shall be subject to the same liabilities in respect of all the highways within it which were before maintained by such townships, tithings, hamlets, and places separately, as if all their several liabilities had attached to the whole parish; and that a waywarden or waywardens shall be elected for such parish as a whole;

And where such order is made, all the provisions herein contained in relation to parishes within the meaning of the Highway Act, 1862, are applicable to the parish formed by such combination.

The power given by section 7 of the Highway Act '64, s. 7. Power to combine townships extends to two or more. Act, 1862, of combining townships, tithings, hamlets, or places separately maintaining their own highways, and situate in a poor law parish, extends to combining any two or more of such townships, tithings, hamlets, or places, and any combination so formed shall for all the purposes of the Highway Acts be deemed to be a highway parish.

Where a township, tithing, hamlet, or other place Parts of townships, &c., may be combined with parish. separately maintaining its own highways is situate in two or more poor law parishes, each part of

Act '64, s. 7. such township, tithing, hamlet, or other place may be combined with the parish in which that part is situate.

Poor law parish may be declared to be a highway parish. The justices may, by their provisional and final order, declare that any poor law parish within their jurisdiction, or residue of a poor law parish, after excluding such part, if any, as is prohibited by the Highway Act, 1862, either wholly or without the consent of the governing body, from being included in the highway district, shall henceforward become a highway parish.

Power to return waywardens to highway board. And upon such declaration being made such poor law parish, or residue of a poor law parish, shall thereafter be a highway parish entitled to return a waywarden or waywardens to the highway board of the district in which it is included; and no rate shall be separately levied for the maintenance of the highways, and no separate waywardens be elected in any township, tithing, hamlet, or other subdivision of such poor law parish or residue of a poor law parish.

Provision for election of waywardens in certain parishes. Where, previously to the passing of the provisional order forming a highway district, no surveyors or waywardens have been elected within any highway parish in that district, and where the mode of electing a waywarden or waywardens in such parish is not provided by the Highway Act, 1864, or the Highway Act, 1862, the justices must, by their provisional and final orders constituting the district, or by any subsequent provisional and final orders, make provisions for the annual election of a waywarden or waywardens for such parish.

Id. s. 8. Outlying part of parish partly within and partly without a Where a parish or place separately maintaining its own highways is situate partly within and partly without the limits of a borough, the justices may by their provisional and final orders include in a highway dis-

trict the outlying part of such parish or place; and Act '64, s. 8.
where the outlying part of a parish or place situate as borough may be included in highway district.
aforesaid has been, previously to the passing of this
Act, or may be hereafter, included in a highway district, each part of such parish or place shall for all the
purposes of the Highway Acts be deemed to be a
place separately maintaining its own highways; and a
waywarden or waywardens shall be elected by the
ratepayers in each such part at such time and in such
manner as may be provided by the said justices.

Justices in petty sessions may appoint overseers or Id. s. 9. Justices may constitute any extra-parochial place a highway parish.
otherwise deal with any extra-parochial place with a
view to constituting it a highway parish or part of a
highway parish, in the same manner as they may
deal with such place for the purpose of constituting it
a place or part of a place maintaining its own poor, in
pursuance of the powers for that purpose given by the
Act 20 Vict. c. 19.

ALTERATION OF DISTRICTS.

Any highway district formed under the Highway Act '62, s. 39. Districts may be altered by addition or subtraction of parishes and new districts may be formed by union of existing districts,&c.
Act, 1862, may from time to time be altered by the
addition of any parishes in the same or in any adjoining county, or the subtraction therefrom of any
parishes, and new highway districts may be formed by
the union of any existing highway districts in the
same or in any adjoining county, or any parishes form-
ing part of any existing highway districts, or any or district may be dissolved.
highway district may be dissolved.

But any such alteration of existing districts, or for- Alterations &c., to be by provisional and final orders, and other provisions relating to formation of
mation of new districts, or dissolution of any district,
shall be made by provisional and final orders of the justices; and all the provisions of the Highway Act, 1862,
with respect to the formation of highway districts and

provisional and final orders of justices, and the notices to be given of and previously to the making of such orders and all other proceedings relating to the formation of highway districts, shall, in so far as the same are applicable, extend to such alteration of existing or formation of new districts, or dissolution of districts, as is mentioned in this section.

And in addition thereto provision shall be made, if necessary, in any orders of justices made under this section for the adjustment of any matters of account arising between parishes or parts of districts in consequence of the exercise of the powers given by this section.

Final order
not to be
confirmed
until after
approval of
provisional
order by jus-
tices of
county with
which
union, &c.,
is to be
made. Where any parish is added to or any district united with any district in another county, the final order of the justices of the county in which such parish or district is situate shall not be confirmed by them until they shall have received the approval of their provisional order for such addition or union from the s-tices of the county in which the district is situate to or with which such addition or union is to be made.

Upon disso-
lution, &c.,
of district
highways to
be main-
tained as if
they had
never been
included in
the district. Where any highway district is dissolved, or where any parish is excluded from any highway district, the highways in such parish or district shall be maintained, and the provisions of the Principal Act in relation to the election of surveyors and to all other matters shall apply to the said highways, in the same manner as if such highways had never been included within the limits of a highway district.

Act '64 s. 14.
Approval to
be testified
by provi-
sional and
final orders. The approval of the justices of any county to any provisional order made by the justices of another county affecting any place in such first mentioned county, in pursuance of the Highway Act, 1862, s. 39, must be testified by provisional and final orders of the justices of the said first-mentioned county.

The powers conferred on justices by the Highway Act, 1862, s. 39, shall be deemed to extend to the separation of any townships, tithings, hamlets, or places separately maintaining their own highways which may have been consolidated by any previous order of the justices, and to an alteration in the number of waywardens of any parish. Act '64, s.14. Separation of townships, &c., consolidated by previous order.

Where, after the formation of an highway district, an application is made by any parish in that district to any court of general or quarter sessions, praying that the said parish may be removed from that district, all costs incidental to or consequential on such application and the removal of the said parish shall, unless the court otherwise directs, be paid by the parish that has made the application in such manner as the said court may direct. The amount of such costs shall be raised in the same manner as if they were expenses incurred in maintaining and keeping in repair the highways of that parish. Id. s. 15. Costs of application to be removed from district, to be paid by parish making the application.

Where an alteration is made in part only of a highway district the residue of that district shall not be affected thereby, but shall continue subject to the Highway Acts in the same manner as if no such alteration had been made. Id. s. 17. Residue of district not affected by alteration of part.

VALIDITY AND EVIDENCE OF ORDER OF FORMATION.

No objection can be made at any trial or in any legal proceeding to the validity of any orders or proceedings relating to the formation of a highway district, after the expiration of three calendar months from the date of the publication in the *Gazette* of the order under which the district is formed. Act '62, s. 8. No objection available after three months from publication in *Gazette*.

c 2

Act '62, s. 8.
Copy of *Gazette* evidence of formation, &c.
And the production of a copy of the *London Gazette* containing a copy of the order of justices forming a highway district is receivable in all courts of justice, and in all legal proceedings, as evidence of the formation of the district and of the matters in the said order mentioned.

Act '64, s. 12.
Orders not invalidated by non-publication in *Gazette*.
No order of the justices forming a highway district shall be invalidated by reason of its not being published in the *London Gazette*.

Date of final order substituted for date of publication in *Gazette*.
And where any reference is made in any section of the Highway Act, 1862, to the date of the publication in the *Gazette* of the order, such section shall be construed as if the date of the making of the final order under which the district is formed were substituted for " the date of the publication in the *Gazette* of the order under which the district is formed."

Certified copy receivable as evidence.
And any copy of the provisional or final order of the justices forming a highway district, certified under the hand of the clerk of the peace to be a true copy, shall be receivable in all courts of justice and in all legal proceedings as evidence of the formation of the district and of the matters in the said order mentioned.

Id. s. 16.
Order not avoided by including place not lawfully included therein.
No order of the justices forming a highway district, whether made before or after the passing of the Highway Act, 1864, shall be void by reason that it includes in such district a place which the justices are not entitled to include under the provisions of this Act or the Highways Act 1862, or one of such Acts; and any order containing such prohibited place shall be construed and take effect as if that place had not been mentioned therein.

Expenses incurred in defending order, payable out of county rate.
All expenses properly incurred by the justices of any county in maintaining the validity of any provisional or final order made by them shall be payable out of the county rate of that county.

HIGHWAY BOARD.

With respect to the constitution of the highway board, the following provisions are enacted:— *Constitution of Board.*

(1.) The highway board shall consist of the way-wardens elected in the several places within the district, in manner hereinafter mentioned, and of the justices acting for the county and residing within the district: *Board consists of way-wardens and justices.*

(2.) The board shall be a body corporate, by the name of the highway board of the district to which it belongs, having a perpetual succession and a common seal, with a power to acquire and hold lands for the purposes of the Highway Acts, without any license in mortmain: *Is a body corporate.*

(3.) No act or proceeding of the board shall be questioned on account of any vacancy or vacancies in their body: *No act to be questioned on account of vacancy.*

(4.) No defect in the qualification or election of any person or persons acting as members or member of the board or committee of a board shall be deemed to vitiate any proceedings of such board in which he or they have taken part in cases where the majority of members parties to such proceedings are duly entitled to act: *No defect in qualification, &c., to vitiate proceedings.*

(5.) Any minute made of proceedings at meetings of the board or of committees of the board, if signed by any person purporting to be the chairman of the board or committee of the board, either at the meeting of the board or committee of the board at which such proceedings took place, or at the next ensuing meeting of the board or committee of the board, shall be receivable in evidence in all legal proceedings without further proof: *Minute of proceedings signed by chairman, evidence without further proof.*

And until the contrary is proved every meeting of
the board or committee of the board in respect
of the proceedings of which minutes have
been so made shall be deemed to have been
duly convened and held, and all the members
thereof to have been duly qualified :

(6.) No member of a board, by being party to, or
executing in his capacity of member, any contract or other instrument on behalf of the
board, or otherwise lawfully exercising any of
the powers given to the board, shall be subject
to be tried or prosecuted, either individually
or with others, by any person whomsoever :

And the bodies or goods or lands of the members
shall not be liable to execution of any legal
process by reason of any contract or other
instrument so entered into, tried, or executed
by them, or by reason of any other lawful
act done by them in execution of any of the
powers of the board :

And the members of the board may apply any
moneys in their hands for the purpose of indemnifying themselves against any losses,
costs, or damages they may incur in execution of the powers granted to them :

A justice of the peace acting for the county in which
a highway district is situate, if he is resident in any
place which is prohibited either altogether or without the
consent of the local authority from being included in a
highway district by sect. 7 of the Highway Act,
1862, and which is surrounded by or adjoins in
any part such highway district, is by virtue of his
office a member of the highway board of such district,
subject to this qualification, that if in pursuance of

this section he would be entitled to be a member of ^{Act '64, s. 29} two or more highway boards in the same county, he shall, by letter under his hand, addressed to the clerk of the highway board for which he elects to act, and by him to be transmitted to the clerk of the peace of the county, declare of which of the said highway boards he elects to be a member, and having made that election he is bound thereby, and is not entitled by virtue of his office of justice to be a member of any other of the said boards.

The board for all the purposes of the Principal Act, ^{Act '62, s. 43 (3).} except that of levying highway rates, is deemed to be ^{Board successor of parish surveyor.} the successor in office of the surveyor of every parish within the district.

The 46th section of the Highway Act, 1835, does ^{Act '64, s. 20. Board not affected by s. 46 of Principal Act.} not apply to the highway board or to any parish within any highway district.

The proceedings of the board are subject to the following regulations :—

(1.) The board shall meet for the despatch of ^{Id. s. 27, and Sched 1. Proceedings of board.} business, and shall from time to time make such regulations with respect to the summoning, notice, place, management, and adjournment of such meetings, and generally with respect to the transaction and management of business, including the quorum at meetings of the board, as they think fit, subject to the following conditions :

(a.) The first meeting after the formation of the district shall be held at the time and place fixed by the order of the justice* in that behalf; *Sic.

(b.) One ordinary meeting shall be held in each period of four months, and of such meetings one shall be held on some day between the seventh and fourteenth days of April;

(c.) An extraordinary meeting may be summoned
at any time on the requisition of three members of the board addressed to the clerk of
board ;

(d.) The quorum as be fixed by the board shall
consist of not less than three members ;

(e.) Every question shall be decided by a majority
of votes of the members voting on that question ;

(f.) The names of the members present at a meeting shall be recorded.

(2.) The board shall at the first meeting, and afterwards from time to time at their first meeting after each annual appointment of members
of the board as hereafter mentioned, appoint
one of their members to be chairman and one
other of their members to be a vice-chairman
for the year following such choice :

(3.) If any casual vacancy occur in the office of chairman or vice-chairman, the board shall, as soon
as they conveniently can after the occurrence
of such vacancy, choose some member of their
number to fill such vacancy ; and every such
chairman or vice-chairman so elected as last
aforesaid shall continue in office so long only
as the person in whose place he may be so
elected would have been entitled to continue
if such vacancy had not happened :

(4.) If at any meeting the chairman is not present
at the time appointed for holding the same,
the vice-chairman shall be the chairman of the
meeting; and if neither the chairman nor vice-
chairman shall be present, then the members
present shall choose some one of their number to be a chairman of such meeting :

(5.) In case of an equality of votes at any meeting the chairman for the time being of such meeting shall have a second or casting vote: Act '64, s. 27. and sched 1.

(6.) All orders of the board for payment of money, and all precepts issued by the board, shall be deemed to be duly executed if signed by two or more members of the board authorized to sign them by a resolution of the board, and counter-signed by the clerk; but it shall not be necessary in any legal proceeding to prove that the members signing any such order or precept were authorized to sign them, and such authority shall be presumed until the contrary is proved.

Any notice in respect of which no other mode of service is provided by the highway board in pursuance of powers in that behalf conferred on them, and any precept, summons, or order issued by the highway board, may be served,— Id. s. 28. Service of notices, &c., by highway board.

By delivery of the same personally on the party required to be served; or

By leaving the same at the usual or last known place of abode of such party as aforesaid; or

By forwarding the same by post as a prepaid letter addressed to the usual or last known place of abode of such party.

In proving service of a document by post it shall be sufficient to prove that the document was properly directed, and that it was put as a prepaid letter into the post office; and in serving notice on the overseers or the waywardens (if more than one) of any parish it shall be sufficient to serve the same on any one of such officers in a parish. Proof of service by post.

Service on overseers or way- wardens.

WAYWARDENS.

Act '62, s. 10.

Regulations as to elections.

The following regulations shall be observed with respect to the election of waywardens in highway districts :—

One or more to be elected annually for ensuing year.

In every parish forming part of a highway district there shall be elected every year for the year next ensuing a waywarden or such number of waywardens as may be determined by order of the justices :

Election to be at the meeting, &c., at which surveyor would have been chosen.

Such waywarden or waywardens shall be elected in every parish forming part of a highway district at the meeting and time and in the manner and subject to the same qualification and the same power of appointment in the justices, in the event of no election taking place, or in the event of a vacancy, at, in, and subject to which a person or persons to serve the office of surveyor would have been chosen or appointed if this Act had not passed :

Provisional order to provide for election in places where no surveyor previously elected.

The justices shall in their provisional order make provision for the election of a waywarden or waywardens in places where no surveyor or surveyors were elected previously to the place forming part of a highway district :

To continue to act until successor appointed.

A waywarden shall continue to act until his successor is appointed, and shall be re-eligible.

Act, '78. s. 11. Duration of office.

Notwithstanding anything in the Highway Acts, waywardens continue in office till the 30th day of April in the year following the year in which they were elected, and on that day their successors come into office.

Act '64, s. 19. To produce certificate of appo ntment signe

Every waywarden before taking his seat as a member of a highway board must produce a certificate of his having been duly elected or appointed a waywarden and such certificate, in the case of an elected waywarden, must be signed by the chairman of the vestry or other meeting at which he was elected; and in the case of a waywarden appointed by justices, must be signed by the justices making the appointment. *Act '64, s. 19.*

by chairman of vestry, &c.

A waywarden may sit as such for more places than one, but he shall be entitled to one vote only as waywarden. *May sit for several places, but has only one vote.*

No waywarden can directly or indirectly, in his own name or in the name of any other person or persons, contract for the repair of any road, or for any other work to be executed under the provisions of the Highway Act, 1862, within the parish for which he is elected waywarden, or within any other parish in the same district, under the pain of forfeiting £10, with full costs of suit, to any person or persons who shall sue for the same by action for debt in any county court within the jurisdiction of which the parish in which the roads to be repaired or the other work so contracted for, is situate. *26 & 27 Vict. c. 61, s. 1. Waywardens not to be concerned in contracts within their own districts.*

It is unlawful for any highway board to pay knowingly for any repair or work so contracted for; and any money paid by any board under any such contract is recoverable by them with full costs from the person or persons to whom it has been paid, by action of debt in any of Her Majesty's Courts of Record at Westminster, if it amounts to above £50, or in any county court, as aforesaid, if below that amount; and the balance so recovered, after paying all expenses, is to be placed to the credit of the district fund. *Id. s. 2. Board not to pay for repair or work so contracted for; and may recover back money so paid.*

This Act is to be construed with and held to be part of the Highway Act, 1862. *Id. s. 3.*

Act '64, s. 20.
Waywardens may contract for supply or cartage of materials, with license of two justices.

Notwithstanding anything contained in 26 & 27 Vict. c. 61, or in any other Act, any waywarden may contract for the supply or cartage of materials within the parish for which he is waywarden, with the license of two justices assembled at petty sessions, such license to be granted on the application of the clerk of the highway board, who must be authorized to make such application by a resolution of his board assembled, at a meeting of which notice has been given.

Id. s. 31.
May appoint paid collectors of highway rates with consent of ratepayers.

The power of appointing paid collectors of highway rates with the consent of the inhabitants in vestry assembled, which is vested in a surveyor by the Highway Act, 1835, and all the provisions of that Act relating to such appointment, are vested in and extend to any waywarden required to levy rates in pursuance of the Highway Act, 1862, and the Highway Act, 1864, or either of them; and for the purposes of the Highway Act, 1864, any meeting of ratepayers entitled to elect a waywarden or waywardens is deemed to be included under the expression "inhabitants in vestry assembled," as used in this section, and the Highway Acts.

CONSEQUENCES OF FORMATION.

Act, '62, s. 11.
All property belonging to surveyor of any parish in the district vests in board.

At and after the first meeting in any district of the board of such district the following consequences ensue:—

All such property, real and personal, including all interests, easements, and rights in, to, and out of property, real and personal, and including things in action, as belong to or are vested in, or would but for the Highway Act, 1862, have belonged to or been vested in, any surveyor or surveyors of any parish forming part of the district, pass to and

vest in the highway board of that district for all Act,'62, s. 11.
the estate and interest of such surveyor or surveyors as aforesaid, but subject to all debts and liabilities affecting the same:

All debts and liabilities incurred in respect of any Debts may be enforced against board.
property transferred to the highway board may be enforced against the board to the extent of the property transferred:

All such powers, rights, duties, liabilities, capacities, All powers, &c. (except that of making, &c., rates) attaching to parish surveyors, vest in board.
and incapacities (except the power of making, assessing, and levying highway rates) as are vested in or attached to, or would but for the Highway Act, 1862, have become vested in or attached to, any surveyor or surveyors of any parish forming part of the district, vest in and attach to the highway board:

All property by the Highway Act, 1862, transferred All property transferred to board to be held upon trust for parish to which it belongs &c.
to the board will be held by them upon trust for the several parishes or places maintaining their own highways within their district to which such property belongs, or for the benefit of which it was held previously to the formation of the district.

On the formation of a district the following regula- Act '62, s. 43.
tions are enacted with respect to the surveyors and the highway board:— No surveyor to be appointed for any parish in the district.

1. No surveyor shall be appointed under the Principal Act for any parish within such district:

2. The outgoing surveyor of every parish within the Outgoing parish surveyor to continue in office until seven days after appointment of district surveyor.
district shall continue in office until seven days after the appointment of the district surveyor by the board of the district of such outgoing surveyor, and no longer; and he may recover any highway rate made and then remaining May recover unpaid rates.
unpaid, in the same manner as if the High-

Act '62, s. 42.

Application of moneys recovered.

way Act, 1862, had not been passed, and the money so recovered shall be applied, in the first place, in re-imbursing any expenses incurred by him as such surveyor and in discharging any debts legally owing by him on account of the highways within his jurisdiction, and the surplus (if any) shall be paid by him to the treasurer of the board; and he shall be entitled to receive from the board any sum which on the allowance of his account shall be found to be due to him as such surveyor after the collection and expenditure of the whole of the highway rate made in such parish during the last year:

Board deemed successor in office of parish surveyor.

3. The board, for all the purposes of the Principal Act, except that of levying highway rates, is deemed to be the successor in office of the surveyor of every parish within the district.

APPLICATION OF PRINCIPAL ACT.

Act '62, s. 42. Principal Act and 25 & 26 Vict. c. 61 to be construed as one Act.

The following regulations are to be observed with respect to the construction of the Principal Act and the Highway Act, 1862:—

1. The Highway Act, 1862, so far as is consistent with its provisions, is to be construed as one with the Principal Act:

Sect. 9 of Principal Act, as to aid surveyor, not to apply.

2. The 9th section of the Principal Act, whereby it is enacted that a surveyor may be appointed by the inhabitants of a parish with a salary, is not to apply to any parish within any district formed under the Highway Act, 1862:

Sect. 10 of Principal Act, as to outgoing surveyor delivering name, &c., of

3. The 10th section of the Principal Act, whereby it is enacted that the surveyor or surveyors at the time of passing his or their accounts as therein mentioned shall deliver to the justices a statement

in writing of the name and residence of the ^{Act '62, s. 42.} person or persons appointed to succeed him or successor not to apply. them as a surveyor or surveyors, is not to apply to any parish within any district formed under the Highway Act, 1862:

4. The 13th, 14th, 15th, 16th, and 17th sections of ^{Provisions of Principal} the Principal Act, providing for the formation of ^{Act as to} parishes into districts, and the 18th and 19th ^{formation of parishes into} sections of the Principal Act, providing for the ^{districts, &c.,} appointment of a board in large parishes, is not ^{&c., not to apply.} to apply to any parish within any district formed under the Highway Act, 1862:

5. The penalty imposed by sect. 20 of the Principal ^{Penalty on surveyor for} Act on the surveyor for neglect of duty is not to ^{neglect of duty not to} apply to a highway board constituted under the ^{apply.} Highway Act, 1862:

6. Any summons or notice, or any writ or any ^{Service of} proceeding, at law or in equity, requiring to be ^{summons, &c., on} served upon the board, may be served by the ^{board.} same being left at or transmitted through the post in a pre-paid letter directed to the office of the board or being given personally to the district surveyor or clerk of the board:

7. The 35th section of the Principal Act, whereby ^{Sect. 35 of Principal} it is provided that the ratepayers of any parish ^{Act, as to ratepayers} may divide amongst themselves the carriage ^{dividing carriage of} of materials in manner therein mentioned, is ^{materials} not to apply to any parish within any district ^{not to apply.} formed under the Highway Act, 1862.

8. The 39th, 40th, 43rd, 44th, and 45th sections ^{Provisions of Principal} of the Principal Act, relating to the accounts ^{Act as to surveyor's} of surveyors, are not to apply to the highway ^{accounts not} board of any district formed under the High- ^{to apply.} way Act, 1862.

(*c.*) An extraordinary meeting may be summoned at any time on the requisition of three members of the board addressed to the clerk of board;

(*d.*) The quorum to be fixed by the board shall consist of not less than three members;

(*e.*) Every question shall be decided by a majority of votes of the members voting on that question;

(*f.*) The names of the members present at a meeting shall be recorded.

(2.) The board shall at the first meeting, and afterwards from time to time at their first meeting after each annual appointment of members of the board as hereafter mentioned, appoint one of their members to be chairman and one other of their members to be a vice-chairman for the year following such choice:

(3.) If any casual vacancy occur in the office of chairman or vice-chairman, the board shall, as soon as they conveniently can after the occurrence of such vacancy, choose some member of their number to fill such vacancy; and every such chairman or vice-chairman so elected as last aforesaid shall continue in office so long only as the person in whose place he may be so elected would have been entitled to continue if such vacancy had not happened:

(4.) If at any meeting the chairman is not present at the time appointed for holding the same, the vice-chairman shall be the chairman of the meeting; and if neither tho chairman nor vice-chairman shall be present, then the members present shall choose some one of their number to be a chairman of such meeting:

(5.) In case of an equality of votes at any meeting the chairman for the time being of such meeting shall have a second or casting vote: Act '64, s. 27. and sched 1.

(6.) All orders of the board for payment of money, and all precepts issued by the board, shall be deemed to be duly executed if signed by two or more members of the board authorized to sign them by a resolution of the board, and counter-signed by the clerk; but it shall not be necessary in any legal proceeding to prove that the members signing any such order or precept were authorized to sign them, and such authority shall be presumed until the contrary is proved.

Any notice in respect of which no other mode of service is provided by the highway board in pursuance of powers in that behalf conferred on them, and any precept, summons, or order issued by the highway board, may be served,— Id. s. 26. Service of notices, &c., by highway board.

By delivery of the same personally on the party required to be served; or

By leaving the same at the usual or last known place of abode of such party as aforesaid; or

By forwarding the same by post as a prepaid letter addressed to the usual or last known place of abode of such party.

In proving service of a document by post it shall be sufficient to prove that the document was properly directed, and that it was put as a prepaid letter into the post office; and in serving notice on the overseers or the waywardens (if more than one) of any parish it shall be sufficient to serve the same on any one of such officers in a parish. Proof of service by post. Service on overseers or way- wardens.

WAYWARDENS.

Act '62, s. 10.

Regulations as to elections.

The following regulations shall be observed with respect to the election of waywardens in highway districts :—

One or more to be elected annually for ensuing year.

In every parish forming part of a highway district there shall be elected every year for the year next ensuing a waywarden or such number of waywardens as may be determined by order of the justices :

Election to be at the meeting, &c., at which surveyor would have been chosen.

Such waywarden or waywardens shall be elected in every parish forming part of a highway district at the meeting and time and in the manner and subject to the same qualification and the same power of appointment in the justices, in the event of no election taking place, or in the event of a vacancy, at, in, and subject to which a person or persons to serve the office of surveyor would have been chosen or appointed if this Act had not passed :

Provisional order to provide for election in places where no surveyor previously elected.

The justices shall in their provisional order make provision for the election of a waywarden or waywardens in places where no surveyor or surveyors were elected previously to the place forming part of a highway district :

To continue to act until successor appointed.

A waywarden shall continue to act until his successor is appointed, and shall be re-eligible.

Act, '78. s. 11. Duration of office.

Notwithstanding anything in the Highway Acts, waywardens continue in office till the 30th day of April in the year following the year in which they were elected, and on that day their successors come into office.

Act '64. s. 19. To produce certificate of appointment signed

Every waywarden before taking his seat as a member of a highway board must produce a certificate of his having been duly elected or appointed a waywarden

and such certificate, in the case of an elected waywarden, Act '64, s. 19.
must be signed by the chairman of the vestry or other by chairman
of vestry, &c.
meeting at which he was elected ; and in the case of a
waywarden appointed by justices, must be signed by
the justices making the appointment.

A waywarden may sit as such for more places May sit for
several
than one, but he shall be entitled to one vote only as places, but
has only one
waywarden. vote.

No waywarden can directly or indirectly, in his own 26 & 27 Vict.
c. 61, s. 1.
name or in the name of any other person or persons, Waywardens
not to be
contract for the repair of any road, or for any other concerned in
contracts
work to be executed under the provisions of the High- within their
way Act, 1862, within the parish for which he is own dis-
tricts.
elected waywarden, or within any other parish in the
same district, under the pain of forfeiting £10, with
full costs of suit, to any person or persons who shall
sue for the same by action for debt in any county court
within the jurisdiction of which the parish in which the
roads to be repaired or the other work so contracted
for, is situate.

It is unlawful for any highway board to pay know- *Id.* s. 2.
Board not to
ingly for any repair or work so contracted for ; pay for
repair or
and any money paid by any board under any such work so
contracted
contract is recoverable by them with full costs from for: and
the person or persons to whom it has been paid, by may
recover
action of debt in any of Her Majesty's Courts of back money
so paid.
Record at Westminster, if it amounts to above £50, or
in any county court, as aforesaid, if below that
amount; and the balance so recovered, after paying all
expenses, is to be placed to the credit of the district
fund.

This Act is to be construed with and held to be part *Id.* s. 3.
of the Highway Act, 1862.

Waywardens may contract for supply or cartage of materials, with license of two justices. Notwithstanding anything contained in 26 & 27 Vict. c. 61, or in any other Act, any waywarden may contract for the supply or cartage of materials within the parish for which he is waywarden, with the license of two justices assembled at petty sessions, such license to be granted on the application of the clerk of the highway board, who must be authorized to make such application by a resolution of his board assembled, at a meeting of which notice has been given.

Id. s. 31. **May appoint paid collectors of highway rates with consent of ratepayers.** The power of appointing paid collectors of highway rates with the consent of the inhabitants in vestry assembled, which is vested in a surveyor by the Highway Act, 1835, and all the provisions of that Act relating to such appointment, are vested in and extend to any waywarden required to levy rates in pursuance of the Highway Act, 1862, and the Highway Act, 1864, or either of them; and for the purposes of the Highway Act, 1864, any meeting of ratepayers entitled to elect a waywarden or waywardens is deemed to be included under the expression " inhabitants in vestry assembled," as used in this section, and the Highway Acts.

CONSEQUENCES OF FORMATION.

Act, '62, s. 11. **All property belonging to surveyor of any parish in the district vests in board.** At and after the first meeting in any district of the board of such district the following consequences ensue :—

All such property, real and personal, including all interests, easements, and rights in, to, and out of property, real and personal, and including things in action, as belong to or are vested in, or would but for the Highway Act, 1862, have belonged to or been vested in, any surveyor or surveyors of any parish forming part of the district, pass to and vest in the highway board of that district for all the estate and interest of such surveyor or surveyors as aforesaid, but subject to all debts and liabilities affecting the same:

All debts and liabilities incurred in respect of any property transferred to the highway board may be enforced against the board to the extent of the property transferred: *Debts may be enforced against board.*

All such powers, rights, duties, liabilities, capacities, and incapacities (except the power of making, assessing, and levying highway rates) as are vested in or attached to, or would but for the Highway Act, 1862, have become vested in or attached to, any surveyor or surveyors of any parish forming part of the district, vest in and attach to the highway board: *All powers, &c. (except that of making, &c., rates) attaching to parish surveyors, vest in board.*

All property by the Highway Act, 1862, transferred to the board will be held by them upon trust for the several parishes or places maintaining their own highways within their district to which such property belongs, or for the benefit of which it was held previously to the formation of the district. *All property transferred to board to be held upon trust for parish to which it belongs &c.*

On the formation of a district the following regulations are enacted with respect to the surveyors and the highway board:— *Act '62, s. 43.*

1. No surveyor shall be appointed under the Principal Act for any parish within such district: *No surveyor to be appointed for any parish in the district.*

2. The outgoing surveyor of every parish within the district shall continue in office until seven days after the appointment of the district surveyor by the board of the district of such outgoing surveyor, and no longer; and he may recover any highway rate made and then remaining unpaid, in the same manner as if the High- *Outgoing parish surveyor to continue in office until seven days after appointment of district surveyor. May recover unpaid rates.*

Act '78, s. 5.

All powers, &c., of highway board (except obtaining payment of expenses, or making, &c., highway rates) vest in rural sanitary authority.

All such powers, rights, duties, liabilities, capacities, and incapacities (except the power of obtaining payment of their expenses by the issue of precepts in manner provided by the Highway Acts, or the power of making, assessing, and levying highway rates) as are vested in or attached to or would but for such order have become vested in or attached to the highway board, or any surveyor or surveyors of any parish forming part of the district, vest in and attach to the rural sanitary authority:

All property transferred, to be held on trust for parishes for which it was previously held.

All property by the Highways and Locomotives (Amendment) Act, 1878, transferred to the rural sanitary authority will be held by them on trust for the several parishes for the benefit of which it was held previously to such transfer.

On alteration of boundaries, powers of rural sanitary authority to be exercised within altered district.

(2.) If at any time after a rural sanitary authority has become invested with the powers of a highway board in pursuance of this Act, the boundaries of the district of such authority are altered, the powers and jurisdiction of such authority in their capacity of highway board shall be exercised within such altered district; and on the application of any authority or

Local Government Board may provide for adjustment of accounts or settlement of differences.

person interested the Local Government Board may by order provide for the adjustment of any accounts, or the settlement of any doubt or difference so far as relates to highways consequent on the alteration of the boundaries of such rural sanitary district.

Expenses to be deemed general expenses under Public Health Act, 1875.

(3.) All expenses incurred by a rural sanitary authority in the performance of their duties as a highway board shall be deemed to be general expenses of such authority within the meaning of the Public Health Act, 1875.

MAINTENANCE AND REPAIR OF HIGHWAYS.

DUTIES AND POWERS OF HIGHWAY BOARD.

The highway board shall maintain in good repair the highways within their district, and shall, subject to the provisions of the Highway Act, 1862, as respects the highways in each parish within their district, perform the same duties, have the same powers, and be liable to the same legal proceedings as the surveyor of such parish would have performed, had, and been liable to if this Act had not passed. *Act '62, s. 17. Board to maintain highways*

It shall be the duty of the district surveyor to submit to the board at their first meeting in every year an estimate of the expenses likely to be incurred during the ensuing year for maintaining and keeping in repair the highways in each parish within the district of the board, and to deliver a copy of such estimate as approved or modified by the board so far as the same relates to each parish to the waywarden of such parish. *Estimate of expenses to be submitted to board by district surveyor, and copy given to waywarden of each parish.*

Where complaint is made to any justice of the peace that any highway within the jurisdiction of the highway board is out of repair, the justice shall issue two summonses, the one addressed to the highway board and the other to the waywarden of the parish liable to the repair of such highway, requiring such board and waywarden to appear before the justices at some petty sessions, in the summons mentioned, to be held in the division where such highway is situate; *Id. s. 18. Where roads are out of repair justice to issue summons to board and waywarden.*

And at such petty sessions, unless the board undertake to repair the road to the satisfaction of the justices, or unless the waywarden deny the liability of *Sessions to require board to appear at subsequent sessions, and*

Act '62, s. 18. appoint person to view. the parish to repair, the justices shall direct the board to appear at some subsequent petty sessions to be then named, and shall either appoint some competent person to view the highway, and report to them on its state at such other petty sessions, or fix a day, previous to such petty sessions, at which two or more of such justices will themselves attend to view the highway.

If justices satisfied that highway not in complete repair they shall make order. At such last-mentioned petty sessions, if the justices are satisfied, either by the report of the person so appointed, or by such view as aforesaid, that the highway complained of is not in a state of complete repair, it shall be their duty to make an order on the board limiting a time for the repair of the highway complained of; and if such highway is not put in complete and effectual repair by the time limited in the order, the justices in petty sessions shall appoint some person to put the highway into repair, and shall by order direct that the expenses of making such repairs, together with a reasonable remuneration to the person appointed for superintending such repairs, and amounting to a sum specified in the order, together with the costs of the proceedings, shall be paid by the board: and any order made for the payment of such costs and expenses may be removed into the Court of Queen's Bench, in the same manner as if it were an order of general or quarter sessions, and be enforced accordingly.

If highway not repaired by time limited in order justices to appoint person to put it into repair, and make order on board for payment of expenses and costs.

Expenses deemed to have been incurred in repairing highway. All expenses so directed to be paid by the board in respect of the repairs of any highway shall be deemed to be expenses incurred by the board in repairing such highway, and shall be recovered accordingly.

Board may appear at sessions by district surveyor, &c. The highway board may appear before the justices at petty sessions by their district surveyor or clerk, or any member of the board.

When on the hearing of any such summons respect- Act '62, s. 19.
ing the repair of any highway, the liability to repair If liability to repair is
is denied by the waywarden on behalf of his parish, or denied by
by any party charged therewith, the justices shall waywarden justices to
direct a bill of indictment to be preferred, and the direct indict-ment to be
necessary witnesses in support thereof to be sub- preferred.
pœnaed, at the next assizes to be holden in and for the
said county, or at the next general quarter sessions of
the peace for the county, riding, division, or place
wherein such highway is situate, against the inhabitants of the parish, or the party charged therewith, for
suffering and permitting the said highway to be out of
repair; and the costs of such prosecution shall be paid Costs of prosecution
by such party to the proceedings as the court before to be paid as court shall
whom the case is tried shall direct, and if directed to direct.
be paid by the parish shall be deemed to be expenses
incurred by such parish in keeping its highways in
repair, and shall be paid accordingly.

The highway board may contract for purchasing, Act '64, s. 52. Board may
getting, and carrying the materials required for the contract for
repair of the highways, and for maintaining and keep- materials re-quired for
ing in repair all or any part of the highways of any repairing highways for
parish within their highway district, for any period three years.
not exceeding three years.

The highway board of any district may from time Id. s. 22. Board may
to time contract for any time not exceeding three contract to
years with any person or body of persons, corporate or repair high-ways for the
unincorporate, to repair any highways, turnpike roads, repair of which other
or roads over county or other bridges, or any part parties are liable.
thereof, for the repairing of which such persons or
body of persons are liable; and any persons or body of
persons liable to repair any roads may contract with
the highway board for the repairing any highways,
inclusive as aforesaid, or any part thereof, which the
highway board is liable to make or repair; and the

Act'62,s. 15. copies, as the case may require, of the meetings, acts, orders, resolutions, proceedings and correspondence of such board, and shall keep all books, papers, and documents committed to his charge, and shall perform all such other duties as the board may direct.

Id. s. 16.
Duties of
district sur-
veyor.
The district surveyor shall act as the agent of the board in carrying into effect all the works and performing all the duties by this Act required to be carried into effect or to be performed by the board, and he shall in all respects conform to the orders of the board in the execution of his duties, and the assistant surveyor, if any, shall perform such duties as the board may require, under the direction of the district surveyor.

Act '78. s. 6.
Boards may
combine to
appoint a
district sur-
veyor.
Any two or more highway boards may unite in appointing and paying the salary of a district surveyor who shall in relation to the district of each of the boards by whom he is appointed have all the powers and duties of a district surveyor under the Highway Acts.

Act'62, s.37.
Surveyor of
highway
board ex-
empted from
turnpike
tolls
No toll shall be demanded by virtue of any Act of Parliament on any turnpike road from the surveyor of a highway board when executing or proceeding to execute his duties as such surveyor, and all provisions applicable to the exemptions in the Act of 3 Geo. 4, c. 126, shall apply to the case of the exemptions conferred by this enactment.

Id. s.31.
Officers to
account to
board when
required, and
pay over
money re-
maining in
their hands.
All officers appointed by the highway board shall, as often as required by them, render to them or to such persons as they appoint a true, exact, and perfect account in writing under their respective hands, with the proper vouchers, of all moneys which they may respectively to the time of rendering such accounts have received and disbursed on account or by reason f their respective offices, and in case any money so re-

-ceived by any such officer remains in his hands, the
same shall be paid to the board, or to such person or
persons as they in writing under their hands empower
to receive the same;

And if any officer refuses or wilfully neglects to
render and give such account, or to deliver up such
vouchers, or for the space of fourteen days after being
thereunto required by the board, refuses or wilfully
neglects to give up to them or to such person or
persons as they appoint all books, papers, writings,
tools, and things in his hands, custody, or power relating to the execution of his office, it shall be lawful
for any justice of the peace for the county where the
officer so making default is or resides, upon application
made to him for that purpose by or on behalf of the
board, to make inquiry of and concerning any such
default as aforesaid in a summary way, as well by the
confession of the party as by the testimony of any
credible witness or witnesses upon oath, and by
warrant under his hand and seal to cause such money
as may appear to him to be due and unpaid to be
levied by distress and sale of the goods and chattles of
such officer, rendering to him the overplus (if any), on
demand, after payment of the money remaining due
and deducting the charges and expenses of making
such distress and sale;

If officer re-
fuses, &c.,
any justice,
&c., may in-
quire con-
cerning such
default and
cause unpaid
money tobe
levied by
distress.

And if sufficient distress cannot be found, or if it
appears to any such justice in manner aforesaid that
any such officer has refused or wilfully neglected to
give such account, or to deliver up all books, papers,
writings, tools, matters, and things in his custody or
power relating to the execution of his office, the justice
shall commit him to the house of correction or common
gaol of the county where such offender is or resides,
there to remain without bail until he gives a true and

If no suffi-
cient distress,
or if officer
has refused,
&c., to ac-
count or de-
liver up
books, &c.,
justice
will commit
him until he
gives true
account, &c.,
and pays the
money re-
maining in

Act '62, s. 31. perfect account and verifies the same in manner afore-
his hands, or said, and produces and delivers up the vouchers relating
delivers up
books, &c. thereto, and pays the money (if any) remaining in his
hands as aforesaid according to the direction of the
board, or has compounded with the board for such
money and paid such composition (which composition
the board are hereby empowered to make and receive),
or until he delivers up such books, papers, and writings,
tools, matters, and things as aforesaid, or has given
satisfaction to the board concerning the same;

No officer
can be de-
tained in But no officer who may be committed on account of
prison more his not having sufficient goods and chattels as aforesaid
than six
months. shall be detained in prison by virtue of this Act for
any longer time than six calendar months.

RURAL SANITARY AUTHORITY.

Act '78, s. 4. Where a highway district, whether formed before or
Application
of rural sani- after the passing of the Highways and Locomotives
tary autho-
rity of (Amendment) Act, 1878, is or becomes coincident in
district co-
incident with area with a rural sanitary district, the rural sanitary
highway
district to authority of such district may apply to the county
exercise
powers of authority, stating that they are desirous to exercise the
highway
board. powers of a highway board under the Highway Acts
within their district.

County
authority On such application the county authority may, if
may declare they see fit, by order declare that from and after a day to
that rural
sanitary be named in the order (in this Act called the commence-
authority
shall exercise ment of the order) such rural sanitary authority shall
powers of
highway exercise all the powers of a highway board under the
board. Highway Acts; and as from the commencement of
the order the existing highway board (if any) for the
district shall be dissolved, and waywardens or surveyors
shall not hold office or be elected for any parish in the
district.

An order made under this section may be amended, altered, or rescinded by a subsequent order of the county authority.

Act '78. s. 4.

Order may be amended, &c.

Where a highway district, being coincident in area with a rural sanitary district, is situate in more than one county, an order under this section may be made by the county authority of any county in which any part of such district is situate, but such order, and any order amending, altering, or rescinding the same, shall not be of any force or effect until it has been approved by the county authority or authorities of the other county or counties in which any part of such district is situate.

Districts situate in more than one county.

Consequences of Rural Sanitary Authority Exercising Powers of Highway Board.

(1.) From and after the commencement of the order declaring a rural sanitary authority entitled to exercise the powers of a highway board within their district, the following consequences ensue :—

All such property, real or personal, including all interests, easements, and rights in to and out of property, real and personal, and including things in action, as belongs to or is vested in, or would but for such order have belonged to or been vested in the highway board or any surveyor or surveyors of any parish forming part of the district, passes to and vests in the rural sanitary authority for all the estate and interest of the highway board, or of such surveyor or surveyors, but subject to all debts and liabilities affecting the same:

Id. s. 5.

All property belonging to highway board, &c., vests in rural sanitary authority, subject to debts, &c.

All debts and liabilities incurred in respect of any property transferred to the rural sanitary authority may be enforced against that authority to the extent of the property transferred :

Debts, &c., may be enforced against rural sanitary authority.

Act '78, s. 5.

All powers, &c., of highway board (except obtaining payment of expenses, or making, &c., highway rates) vest in rural sanitary authority.

All such powers, rights, duties, liabilities, capacities, and incapacities (except the power of obtaining payment of their expenses by the issue of precepts in manner provided by the Highway Acts, or the power of making, assessing, and levying highway rates) as are vested in or attached to or would but for such order have become vested in or attached to the highway board, or any surveyor or surveyors of any parish forming part of the district, vest in and attach to the rural sanitary authority:

All property transferred, to be held on trust for parishes for which it was previously held.

All property by the Highways and Locomotives (Amendment) Act, 1878, transferred to the rural sanitary authority will be held by them on trust for the several parishes for the benefit of which it was held previously to such transfer.

On alteration of boundaries, powers of rural sanitary authority to be exercised within altered district.

(2.) If at any time after a rural sanitary authority has become invested with the powers of a highway board in pursuance of this Act, the boundaries of the district of such authority are altered, the powers and jurisdiction of such authority in their capacity of highway board shall be exercised within such altered district; and on the application of any authority or person interested the Local Government Board may by order provide for the adjustment of any accounts, or the settlement of any doubt or difference so far as relates to highways consequent on the alteration of the boundaries of such rural sanitary district.

Local Government Board may provide for adjustment of accounts or settlement of differences.

Expenses to be deemed general expenses under Public Health Act, 1875.

(3.) All expenses incurred by a rural sanitary authority in the performance of their duties as a highway board shall be deemed to be general expenses of such authority within the meaning of the Public Health Act, 1875.

MAINTENANCE AND REPAIR OF HIGHWAYS.

DUTIES AND POWERS OF HIGHWAY BOARD.

The highway board shall maintain in good repair the highways within their district, and shall, subject to the provisions of the Highway Act, 1862, as respects the highways in each parish within their district, perform the same duties, have the same powers, and be liable to the same legal proceedings as the surveyor of such parish would have performed, had, and been liable to if this Act had not passed.

Act '62, s. 17.
Board to maintain highways

It shall be the duty of the district surveyor to submit to the board at their first meeting in every year an estimate of the expenses likely to be incurred during the ensuing year for maintaining and keeping in repair the highways in each parish within the district of the board, and to deliver a copy of such estimate as approved or modified by the board so far as the same relates to each parish to the waywarden of such parish.

Estimate of expenses to be submitted to board by district surveyor, and copy given to waywarden of each parish.

Where complaint is made to any justice of the peace that any highway within the jurisdiction of the highway board is out of repair, the justice shall issue two summonses, the one addressed to the highway board and the other to the waywarden of the parish liable to the repair of such highway, requiring such board and waywarden to appear before the justices at some petty sessions, in the summons mentioned, to be held in the division where such highway is situate;

Id. s. 18.
Where roads are out of repair justice to issue summons to board and waywarden.

And at such petty sessions, unless the board undertake to repair the road to the satisfaction of the justices, or unless the waywarden deny the liability of

Sessions to require board to appear at subsequent sessions, and

Act '62, s. 18.
appoint person to view.

the parish to repair, the justices shall direct the board to appear at some subsequent petty sessions to be then named, and shall either appoint some competent person to view the highway, and report to them on its state at such other petty sessions, or fix a day, previous to such petty sessions, at which two or more of such justices will themselves attend to view the highway.

If justices satisfied that highway not in complete repair they shall make order.

At such last-mentioned petty sessions, if the justices are satisfied, either by the report of the person so appointed, or by such view as aforesaid, that the highway complained of is not in a state of complete repair, it shall be their duty to make an order on the board limiting a time for the repair of the highway com-

If highway not repaired by time limited in order justices to appoint person to put it into repair, and make order on board for payment of expenses and costs.

plained of; and if such highway is not put in complete and effectual repair by the time limited in the order, the justices in petty sessions shall appoint some person to put the highway into repair, and shall by order direct that the expenses of making such repairs, together with a reasonable remuneration to the person appointed for superintending such repairs, and amounting to a sum specified in the order, together with the costs of the proceedings, shall be paid by the board: and any order made for the payment of such costs and expenses may be removed into the Court of Queen's Bench, in the same manner as if it were an order of general or quarter sessions, and be enforced accordingly.

Expenses deemed to have been incurred in repairing highway.

All expenses so directed to be paid by the board in respect of the repairs of any highway shall be deemed to be expenses incurred by the board in repairing such highway, and shall be recovered accordingly.

Board may appear at sessions by district surveyor, &c.

The highway board may appear before the justices at petty sessions by their district surveyor or clerk, or any member of the board.

When on the hearing of any such summons respect- Act '62, s. 19.
ing the repair of any highway, the liability to repair If liability to repair is
is denied by the waywarden on behalf of his parish, or denied by
by any party charged therewith, the justices shall waywarden justices to
direct a bill of indictment to be preferred, and the direct indict-ment to be
necessary witnesses in support thereof to be sub- preferred.
poenaed, at the next assizes to be holden in and for the
said county, or at the next general quarter sessions of
the peace for the county, riding, division, or place
wherein such highway is situate, against the inhabitants of the parish, or the party charged therewith, for
suffering and permitting the said highway to be out of
repair; and the costs of such prosecution shall be paid Costs of prosecution
by such party to the proceedings as the court before to be paid as
whom the case is tried shall direct, and if directed to court shall direct.
be paid by the parish shall be deemed to be expenses
incurred by such parish in keeping its highways in
repair, and shall be paid accordingly.

The highway board may contract for purchasing, Act '64, s. 52. Board may
getting, and carrying the materials required for the contract for materials re-
repair of the highways, and for maintaining and keep- quired for repairing
ing in repair all or any part of the highways of any highways for three years.
parish within their highway district, for any period
not exceeding three years.

The highway board of any district may from time Id. s. 22. Board may
to time contract for any time not exceeding three contract to repair high-
years with any person or body of persons, corporate or ways for the repair of
unincorporate, to repair any highways, turnpike roads, which other
or roads over county or other bridges, or any part parties are liable.
thereof, for the repairing of which such persons or
body of persons are liable; and any persons or body of
persons liable to repair any roads may contract with
the highway board for the repairing any highways,
inclusive as aforesaid, or any part thereof, which the
highway board is liable to make or repair; and the

Act '64, s. 22. money payable under any contract made in pursuance of this section shall be raised in the same manner and be paid out of the same rates as would have been applicable to defray the expenses of the repair of such highways if no contract had been made in respect thereto.

Act '62, s. 46.
Board may permit land-owner to erect fences without incurring liability to repair highway.
No person through whose land a highway passes, which is to be repaired by the parish, shall become liable for the repair of such highway by erecting fences between such highway and the adjoining land, if such fences are erected with the consent in writing of the highway board of the district within which such highway is situate in the case of a place within the jurisdiction of a highway board, and in the case of any other place with the consent of the surveyor or other authority having jurisdiction over the highway.

DEFAULT BY HIGHWAY AUTHORITY.

Act '78, s. 10.
On complaint of default in maintaining, &c., highways, county authority may make order on defaulting authority.
Where complaint is made to the county authority that the highway authority of any highway area within their jurisdiction has made default in maintaining or repairing all or any of the highways within their jurisdiction, the county authority, if satisfied after due inquiry and report by their surveyor that the authority has been guilty of the alleged default, shall make an order limiting a time for the performance of the duty of the highway authority in the matter of such complaint.

On non-compliance with order, county authority to appoint some person to perform the duty, and make order on
If such duty is not performed by the time limited in the order, and the highway authority fail to show to the county authority sufficient cause why the order has not been complied with, the county authority may appoint some person to perform such duty, and shall by order direct that the expenses of performing the same,

together with the reasonable remuneration of the person Act'78, s. 10. appointed for superintending such performance, shall defaulting authority for payment of expenses and costs. be paid by the authority in default, and any order made for payment of such expenses and costs may be removed into the High Court of Justice, and be enforced in the same manner as if the same were an order of such court.

Any person appointed under this section to perform Person appointed, to have the power of defaulting authority, except making rates, &c. the duty of a defaulting highway authority shall, in the performance and for the purpose of such duty, be invested with all the powers of such authority other than the powers of making rates or levying contributions by precept, and the county authority may from time to time, by order, change any person so appointed.

Where an order has been made by a county autho- On notice to clerk of peace that defaulting authority declines to comply with order until their liability has been determined, county authority shall either cancel or modify the order, or submit the question of liability to a jury. rity for the repair of a highway on a highway authority alleged to be in default, if such authority, within ten days after service on them of the order of the county authority, give notice to the clerk of the peace that they decline to comply with the requisitions of such order until their liability to repair the highway in respect to which they are alleged to have made default has been determined by a jury, it, shall be the duty of the county authority either to satisfy the defaulting authority by cancelling or modifying in such manner as the authority may desire the order of the county authority, or else to submit to a jury the question of the liability of the defaulting authority to repair the highway.

If the county authority decide to submit the question If question submitted to jury indictment to be preferred to next practicable assizes. Order suspended until conclusion to a jury they shall direct a bill of indictment to be preferred to the next practicable assizes to be holden in and for their county, with a view to try the liability of the defaulting authority to repair the highway. Until the trial of the indictment is concluded the order

Act '78, s. 10. of the county authority shall be suspended. On the
of trial: to conclusion of the trial, if the jury find the defendants
come into
force if guilty, the order of the county authority shall forth-
defendants
found guilty, with be deemed to come into force; but if the jury
or to become acquit the defendants the order of the county authority
void if
defendants shall forthwith become void.
acquitted.

Costs to be The costs of the indictment and of the proceedings
paid as
court may consequent thereon shall be paid by such parties to the
direct. proceedings as the court before whom the case is tried

Out of what may direct. Any costs directed to be paid by the
funds
payable. county authority shall be deemed to be expenses properly incurred by such authority, and shall be paid
accordingly out of the county rate; and any costs directed to be paid by the highway authority shall be
deemed to be expenses properly incurred by such
authority in maintenance of the roads within their
jurisdiction, and shall be paid out of the funds applicable to the maintenance of such roads.

Id. s. 14. The following areas are deemed to be highway areas
Description
of highway for the purposes of the Highways and Locomotives
areas. (Amendment) Act, 1878; that is to say:—

　　(1.) Urban sanitary districts:
　　(2.) Highway districts:
　　(3.) Highway parishes not included within any
　　　　highway district or any urban sanitary dis-
　　　　trict.

MAIN ROADS.

Id. s. 13. For the purposes of the Highways and Locomotives
Disturn-
piked roads (Amendment) Act, 1878, and subject to its provisions,
to become
main roads. any road which has, within the period between the
31st December, 1870, and the date of the passing of
that Act (16th August, 1878), ceased to be a turnpike road, and any road which, being at the time
of passing of that Act a turnpike road, may afterwards

cease to be such, shall be deemed to be a main road; and Act '78. s. 13.
one half of the expenses incurred from and after the One-half the expense of
29th September, 1878, by the highway authority in maintenance
the maintenance of such road shall, as to every part to be paid out of
thereof which is within the limits of any highway area, county rate.
bepaid to the highway authority of such area by the
county authority of the county in which such road is
situate, out of the county rate, on the certificate of the
surveyor of the county authority or of such other person or persons as the county authority may appoint to
the effect that such main road has been maintained to
his or their satisfaction.

Provided that no part of such expenses shall be
included in—

(1.) Any precept or warrant for the levying or col- Proviso as to metro-
lection of county rate within the metropolis, polis and municipal
subject and without prejudice to any provision corporations.
to be hereafter made; or

(2.) Any order made on the council of any borough
having a separate court of quarter sessions
under sect. 117 of the Municipal Corporation Act, 1835.

The term "expenses" in this section shall mean the Definition of expenses
cost of repairs defrayed out of current rates, and shall
not include any re-payment of principal moneys borrowed, or of interest payable thereon.

Where it appears to any highway authority that any Id. s. 15.
highway within their district ought to become a main County authority
road by reason of its being a medium of communica- may order ordinary
tion between great towns, or a thoroughfare to a rail- highway to be a main
way station, or otherwise, such highway authority may road.
apply to the county authority for an order declaring
such road, as to such parts as aforesaid, to be a main
road; and the county authority, if of opinion that there
is probable cause for the application, shall cause the

road to be inspected, and, if satisfied that it ought to be a main road, shall make an order accordingly.

A copy of the order so made shall be forthwith deposited at the office of the clerk of the peace of the county, and shall be open to the inspection of persons interested at all reasonable hours ; and the order so made shall not be of any validity unless and until it is confirmed by a further order of the county authority made within a period of not more than six months after the making of the first-mentioned order.

If it appears to a county authority that any road within their county which, within the period between the 31st December, 1870, and the date of the passing of the Act (16th August, 1878), ceased to be a turnpike road, ought not to become a main road in pursuance of the Highways and Locomotives (Amendment) Act, 1878, such authority must, before the 1st of February, 1879, make an application to the Local Government Board for a provisional order declaring that such road ought not to become a main road.

Subject as aforesaid, where it appears to a county authority that any road within their county which has become a main road in pursuance of this Act ought to cease to be a main road and become an ordinary highway, such authority may apply to the Local Government Board for a provisional order declaring that such road has ceased to be a main road and become an ordinary highway.

The Local Government Board, if of opinion that there is probable cause for an application under this section, shall cause the road to be inspected, and if satisfied that it ought not to become or ought to cease to be a main road and become an ordinary highway, shall make a provisional order accordingly, to be confirmed as hereinafter mentioned.

All expenses incurred in or incidental to the making or confirmation of any order under this section must be defrayed by the county authority applying for such order. Act '78, s. 16. Expenses to be defrayed by county authority.

Where a turnpike road subject to one trust extends into divers counties, such road, for the purposes of the Highways and Locomotives (Amendment) Act, 1878, must be treated as a separate turnpike road in each county through which it passes. Id. s. 17. Turnpike road in several counties.

Every highway authority must keep, in such form as may be directed by the county authority, a separate account of the expenses of the maintenance of the main roads within their jurisdiction, and must forward copies thereof to the county authority at such time or times in every year as may be required by the county authority, and the accounts so kept shall, where the accounts of the highway authority are audited under the Highways and Locomotives (Amendment) Act, 1878, or under sect. 247 of the Public Health Act, 1875, be audited in the same manner as the other accounts of such authority, and where the accounts of the highway authority are not so audited shall be subject to such audit as the county authority may direct. Id. s. 18. Accounts of expenses of maintenance of main roads to be kept by highway authority, and audited.

If any highway authority makes default in complying with the provisions of this section, or with any directions given in pursuance thereof by the county authority, the county authority may withhold all or any part of the contribution payable by them under this Act towards the expenses of the maintenance of main roads by such highway authority for the year in which such default occurs. In case of default, county authority may withhold contribution.

Where a highway district is situate in more than one county, the provisions of the Highways and Locomotives (Amendment) Act, 1878, with respect to the expenses of the maintenance of main roads shall apply Id. s. 19. Highway district situate in more than one county.

Act '78, s. 19. as if the portion of such district situate in each county were a separate highway district in that county.

Id. s. 20. In the case of main roads over bridges, county authority may order them to be repairable either by county or hundred. Notwithstanding the provisions of the Highways and Locomotives (Amendment) Act, 1878, in the case of any county in which certain of the bridges within the county are repairable by the county at large, and others are repairable by the several hundreds within the county in which they are situate, it shall be lawful for the county authority from time to time, by order, to declare any main road or part of a main road within their county to be repairable to the extent provided by sect. 13 of that Act either by the county or by the hundred in which such main road or part is situate, as *Expense of repairing main roads over hundred bridges, repayable out of separate rate, as in case of repairs of such bridges.* they think fit; and where a main road or part thereof is declared to be repairable by a hundred, the expense of repairing the same shall, to the extent to which but for this section the expense or any contribution towards the expense of repairing the same would be payable out of the county rate, be repayable out of a separate rate, which shall be raised and charged in the like manner, and be expended by the like persons as the expenses of repairing the hundred bridges in the same hundred would have been raised, charged and expended.

BRIDGES.

Id. s. 21. Existing bridges erected without superintendence of county surveyor may be accepted by county authority. Any bridge erected before the passing of the Highways and Locomotives (Amendment) Act, 1878, in any county without such superintendence as is provided in the statute 43 Geo. 3, c. 59, s. 5, and which is certified by the county surveyor or other person appointed in that behalf by the county authority to be in good repair and condition, shall, if the county authority see fit so to order, become and be deemed to be a bridge which the inhabitants of the county shall be liable to maintain and repair.

The county authority may make such contribution as it sees fit out of the county rates towards the cost of any bridge to be hereafter erected after the same has been certified in accordance with the provisions of the statute 43 Geo. 3, c. 59, s. 5, as a proper bridge to be maintained by the inhabitants of the county; so always that such contribution shall not exceed one half the cost of erecting such bridge.

Act '78, s. 22.
County authority may contribute out of county rates not exceeding one half the cost of erecting bridges.

EXTRAORDINARY TRAFFIC.

Where by a certificate of their surveyor it appears to the authority which is liable or has undertaken to repair any highway, whether a main road or not, that having regard to the average expense of repairing highways in the neighbourhood, extraordinary expenses have been incurred by such authority in repairing such highway by reason of the damage caused by excessive weight passing along the same, or extraordinary traffic thereon, such authority may recover in a summary manner from any person by whose order such weight or traffic has been conducted the amount of such expenses as may be proved to the satisfaction of the court having cognizance of the case to have been incurred by such authority by reason of the damage arising from such weight or traffic as aforesaid.

Id. s. 23.
Power of road authority to recover expenses of extraordinary traffic.

Provided, that any person against whom expenses are or may be recoverable under this section may enter into an agreement with such authority as is mentioned in this section for the payment to them of a composition in respect of such weight or traffic, and thereupon the persons so paying the same shall not be subject to any proceedings under this section.

Persons from whom such expenses are recoverable may agree for payment of a composition.

E

DISCONTINUANCE OF UNNECESSARY HIGHWAYS.

Act '64, s. 21.

Board may direct surveyor to apply to justices to view unnecessary highway.

Like proceedings to be had as under Highway Act, 1835, for stopping up highway.

Order to direct that highway shall cease to be one which parish is liable to repair.

When any highway board consider any highway unnecessary for public use, they may direct the district surveyor to apply to two justices to view the same, and thereupon the like proceedings shall be had as where application is made under the "Highway Act, 1835," to procure the stopping up any highway, save only that the order to be made thereupon, instead of directing the highway to be stopped up, shall direct that the same shall cease to be a highway which the parish is liable to repair, and the liability of the parish shall cease accordingly; and for the purpose of such proceedings under this enactment, such variation shall be made in any notice, certificate, or other matter preliminary to the making of such order as the nature of the case may require:

Court of quarter sessions may at any time thereafter direct that the liability of the parish to repair shall revive.

Provided that if at any time thereafter, upon application of any person interested in the maintenance of such highway, after one month's previous notice in writing thereof to the clerk of the highway board for the district in which such highway is situated, it appear to any court of general or quarter sessions of the peace that from any change of circumstances since the time of the making of any such order as aforesaid under which the liability of the parish to repair such highway has ceased the same has become of public use, and ought to be kept in repair by the parish, they may direct that the liability of the parish to repair the same shall revive from and after such day as they may name in their order, and such liability shall revive accordingly as if the first-mentioned order had not been made; and the said court may by their order

Expenses of application to be paid as court see fit.

direct the expenses of and incident to such application to be paid as they may see fit.

If any authority liable to keep any highway in repair is of opinion that so much of such highway as lies within any parish situate in a petty sessional division is unnecessary for public use, and therefore ought not to be maintained at the public expense, such authority (in this section referred to " as the applicant authority ") may apply to the court of summary jurisdiction of such petty sessional division to view by two or more justices, being members of the court, the highway to which such application relates, and on such view being had, if the court of summary jurisdiction is of opinion that the application ought to be proceeded with, it shall by notice in writing to the owners or reputed owners and occupiers of all lands abutting upon such highway, and by public notice appoint a time and place, not earlier than one month from the date of such notice, at which it will be prepared to hear all persons objecting to such highway being declared unnecessary for public use, and not repairable at the expense of the public.

Any authority liable to keep highway in repair may apply to court of summary jurisdiction to view.

If court of opinion that the application should proceed, it shall by notices appoint a time and place at which it will hear objections to highway being declared unnecessary.

On the day and at the place appointed, the court shall hear any persons objecting to an order being made by the court that such highway is unnecessary for public use and ought not to be repairable at the public expense, and shall make an order either dismissing the application or declaring such highway unnecessary for public use, and that it ought not to be repaired at the public expense.

On appointed day court to hear objections and make order dismissing application or declaring highway unnecessary.

If the court make such last-mentioned order as aforesaid, the expenses of repairing such highway shall cease to be defrayed out of any public rate.

Public notice of the time and place appointed for hearing a case under this section shall be given by the applicant authority as follows: that is to say :—

Public notice of hearing to be given by applicant by advertisement in local

   (1.) By advertising a notice of the time and place

Act '73, s. 24.

ewspaper
and affixing
copy to
church and
chapel doors.

appointed for the hearing and the object of the hearing, with a description of the highway to which it refers in some local newspaper circulating in the district in which such highway is situate once at least in each of the four weeks preceding the hearing; and

(2.) By causing a copy of such notice to be affixed at least fourteen days before the hearing to the principal doors of every church and chapel in the parish in which such highway is situate, or in some conspicuous position near such highway.

And the application shall not be entertained by the court until the fact of such public notice having been given is proved to its satisfaction.

Court of
quarter ses-
sions may at
any time
thereafter
direct that
the liability
of such high-
way to be
maintained
at public
expense
shall revive.

If at any time after an order has been made by a court of summary jurisdiction under this section, upon application of any person interested in the maintenance of the highway in respect of which such order has been made, after one month's previous notice in writing thereof to the applicant authority, it appears to the court of quarter sessions that from any change of circumstances since the time of the making of any such order as aforesaid such highway has become of public use, and ought to be maintained at the public expense, the court of quarter sessions may direct that the liability of such highway to be maintained at the public expense shall revive from and after such day as they may name in their order, and such highway shall thenceforth be maintained out of the rate applicable to payment of the expenses of repairing other highways repairable by the applicant authority; and the said court of quarter sessions may by their order direct the expenses of and incident to such application to be paid as they may see fit.

Expenses of
application
to be paid as
court see fit.

Any order of a court of summary jurisdiction under this section shall be deemed to be an order from which an appeal lies to a court of quarter sessions.

Act '78, s. 24.

Appeal to quarter sessions lies against order of court of summary jurisdiction.

IMPROVEMENTS.

A highway board may make such improvements as are hereinafter mentioned in the highways within their jurisdiction, and may, with the approval of the justices in general or quarter sessions assembled, borrow money for the purpose of defraying the expenses of such improvements :

Act '64, s. 47. Board may make improvements and borrow money for them with approval of quarter sessions.

Previously to applying for the approval of the justices the highway board must cause an estimate of the expense of the improvements to be made, and two months at the least before making their application must give notice of their intention so to do.

Estimate must be made, and two months' notice given, before application for justices' approval.

The notice must state the following particulars :—

Contents of notice.

(1.) The nature of the work, the estimated amount of expense to be incurred, and the sum proposed to be borrowed :

(2.) The parish or parishes within the district by which the sum borrowed and the interest thereon is to be paid, and in case of more parishes than one being made liable to pay the principal and interest the annual amounts to be contributed by each parish towards the payment thereof :

(3.) The number of years within which the principal moneys borrowed are to be paid off, not exceeding twenty years, and the amount to be set apart in each year for paying off the same :

(4.) The sessions at which the application is to be made

Notice must be given as follows :—

Act '61, s. 47.
Service and
publication
of notice.

(1.) By transmitting a copy to the clerk of the peace for the county or division :

(2.) By placing a copy of such notice for three successive *Sundays* on the church door of every church of the parish ' or parishes on behalf of which such works are to be done, or, in the case of any place not having a church, in some conspicuous position in such place.

Application
may be
opposed by
any person.

Upon the hearing of the application any person or persons may oppose the approval of the justices being given, and the justices may give or withhold their approval, with or without modification, as they think just.

Moneys borrowed to be
a first charge
on highway
rates after
payment of
sums due to
board.

All moneys borrowed in pursuance of this Act, together with the interest thereon, shall be a first charge on the highway rates of each parish liable to contribute to the payment thereof, after paying the sums due to the highway board on account of the district fund, in the same manner, so far as the creditor is concerned, as if the money had been borrowed on account of each parish alone ; and the sums

Sums required for
repayment
recoverable
like expenses
of keeping
highways in
repair.

necessary to repay the said borrowed moneys, with interest, shall in each such parish be recoverable in the same manner as if they were expenses incurred by the board in keeping in repair the highways of that parish.

But it shall be the duty of the highway board, in case of any one parish paying more than its share of such borrowed money, or of the interest thereon, to make good to that parish the excess so paid out of the rates of the other parishes liable to contribute thereto.

General
orders as

The justices may from time to time make general orders in relation to the mode in which applications are to be made to them for their consent under this Act to the borrowing of any moneys.

The following works are deemed to be improvements of highways :—

(1.) The conversion of any road that has not been stoned into a stoned road :

(2.) The widening of any road, the cutting off the corners in any road where land is required to be purchased for that purpose, the levelling roads, the making any new road, and the building or enlarging bridges :

(3.) The doing of any other work in respect of highways beyond ordinary repairs essential to placing any existing highway in a proper state of repair.

Any parish may, with the consent of its waywarden, contribute to any improvements made in another parish, whether situate or not in the same district, if such first-mentioned parish consider such improvements to be for its benefit; and any highway board may contribute to any improvements made in another district if such improvements are, in the opinion of the highway board of the first-mentioned district, for the benefit of their district. The contribution to be made by one parish to another shall be payable in the same manner as if such contributions were moneys due from the contributing parish in respect of expenses incurred in keeping in repair the highways of that parish, and moneys contributed by one district to another district shall be payable out of the common fund of the contributing district.

The clauses of "The Commissioners Clauses Act, 1847," with respect to mortgages to be created by the commissioners shall form part of and be incorporated

Act'64, s. 50. with this Act, and any mortgagee or assignee may
respect to enforce payment of his principal and interest by
mortgages,
incor- appointment of a receiver.
porated.

In the construction of the said clauses " the commissioners " shall mean " the highway board."

Mortgages, Mortgages and transfers of mortgages shall be valid
&c., valid
if made in if made in the forms prescribed by the last-mentioned
prescribed
form. Act, or in the forms appearing in the second schedule
annexed to this Act (*post*), or as near thereto as circumstances admit.

Id. s. 53. A highway board, for the purpose of improving the
Highway
board may highways within their district, may purchase such
purchase
lands for im- lands or easements relating to lands as they may re-
provements. quire; and "The Lands Clauses Consolidation Act,
1845," and the Act 23 & 24 Vict. c. 106, amending the
same, are incorporated with the Highway Act, 1864,
with the exception of the clauses relating to the purchase of land otherwise than by agreement.

In the construction of the Highway Act, 1864, and
the said incorporated Acts, the Highway Act, 1864, is
deemed to be the special Act, and the board are
deemed to be the promoters of the undertaking, and
the word " land " or " lands" include any easement in
or out of lands.

Act '62, s. 34. Where any highway which any body politic or cor-
Act '64, s. 23.
Board may porate or person is liable to repair by reason of tenure
direct sur-
veyor to of any land, or otherwise howsoever, shall be adjudged
repair high-
way ad- in manner provided by the Highway Act, 1862, to be
judged to be
out of repair out of repair, the highway board of the district in
which any
party is which such highway is situate may, if they see fit,
liable to
repair direct their surveyor to repair the same, and the ex-
ratione
tenuræ. penses to be incurred in such repair shall be paid by
the party liable to repair as aforesaid.

Any justice, upon the application of any person authorized in this behalf by the highway board, may summon the party liable to pay such expenses to appear before two justices at a time and place to be named in such summons, and upon the appearance of the parties, or in the absence of either of them, it shall be lawful for such justices to hear and determine the matter, and make such order, as well as to costs or otherwise, as to them may seem just.

Act '62, s. 34.
Party liable to expenses may be summoned.

Justices may determine the matter, and make order as to costs.

Where any person or corporation is liable, by reason of tenure of lands or otherwise, to repair any highway situate in a highway district, the person or corporation so liable may apply to any justice of the peace for the purpose of making such highway a highway to be repaired and maintained by the parish in which the same is situate; and such justice shall thereupon issue summonses requiring the waywarden of such parish, the district surveyor, and the party so liable to repair such highway as aforesaid, to appear before two or more justices in petty sessions assembled:

Id. s. 35.
Party liable to repair highway *ratione tenuræ* may apply to have it repaired by parish.

Waywarden, district surveyor, and party liable to repair, to be summoned before justices.

And the justices at such petty sessions shall proceed to examine and determine the matter, and shall, if they think fit, make an order under their hands that such highway shall thereafter be a highway to be thereafter repaired and maintained by the parish, and shall in such order fix a certain sum to be paid by such person or corporation to the highway board of the district in full discharge of all claims thereafter in respect of the repair and maintenance of such highway; and in default of payment of such sum the board may proceed for the recovery thereof in the same manner as for the recovery of penalties or forfeitures recoverable under the Highway Act, 1862:

Justices may order highway to be maintained by parish, and fix sum to be paid by party in discharge of future claims.

Recoverable like a penalty.

Act '62, s. 35.

Sums exceeding £50 to be invested in name of highway board, and interest applied towards maintenance of highways within the parish. Smaller sums to be applied in like manner.

Provided always, that when the sum so fixed to be paid in full discharge of all claims thereafter in respect of the repair and maintenance of such highway exceeds £50, the same, when received, shall be invested in the name of the highway board of the district in some public Government securities, and the interest and dividends arising therefrom shall be applied by such board towards the repair and maintenance of the highways within the parish in which such highway is situate; but when such sum does not exceed £50 the same or any part thereof, at the discretion of such highway board, shall from time to time be applied by such board towards the repair and maintenance of the highways within such parish :

Appeal to quarter sessions upon written notice within 14 days after order, and recognizance 7 days before sessions to try appeal and abide judgment and pay costs.

Provided that any person aggrieved by any order of justices made in pursuance of this section may appeal to a court of general or quarter sessions holden within four months from the date of such order ; but no such appeal shall be entertained unless the appellant has given to the other party to the case a notice in writing of such appeal, and of the matter thereof, within fourteen days after such order, and seven clear days at the least before such sessions, and has entered into a recognizance, with two sufficient sureties, before a justice of the peace, conditioned to appear at the said sessions, and to try such appeal, and to abide the judgment of the court thereupon, and to pay such costs as may be by the court awarded ; and upon such notice being given, and such recognizance being entered into, the court at such sessions shall hear and determine the matter of the appeal, and shall make such order thereon, with or without costs to either party, as to the court may seem meet :

After order, &c., high-

From and after the making of such order by the justices, or by the court on appeal, as the case may require, such highway shall be repaired in like manner _{Act '62, s. 35.} and at the like expense as highways which a parish is way repair-able by liable to repair. parish.

The highway board may apply, under sect. 35 of _{Act '64, s. 4.} the Highway Act of 1862, for the purpose of making apply to make high-any highway to which that section refers a highway to way repair-be repaired and maintained by the parish in which the *tenure* re-same is situate, and upon such application being made pairable by parish. the same proceedings may be had as upon the applica-tion of the person or corporation liable to repair the same.

Where the inhabitants of any parish are desirous of _{Act '62, s.26.} Upon appli-undertaking the repair or maintenance of any driftway, cation of dis-trict sur-or any private carriage or occupation road, within veyor, at re-quest of their parish, in return for the use thereof, the district vestry and with written surveyor may, at the request of the inhabitants of such consent of owner and parish assembled in a vestry duly convened for the occupier, justices in purpose, and with the consent in writing of the owner petty ses-and occupier of every part thereof, apply to the justices sions may declare in petty sessions to declare such driftway or road to be driftway, &c., to be a a public highway to be repaired at the expense of the public car-riage road, parish ; and upon such application being made it shall &c. be lawful for the justices to declare the same to be a public carriage road to be repaired at the expense of the parish.

BYE-LAWS.

A county authority may from time to time make, _{Act '78, s.26.} County au-with respect to all or any main roads or other high- thority may make, alter, ways within any highway area in their county, and and repeal when made alter or repeal bye-laws for all or any of bye-laws. the purposes following ; that is to say :

    (1.) For prohibiting or regulating the use of any
           waggon, wain, cart or carriage drawn by
           animal power, and having wheels of which

the fellies or tires are not of such width
in proportion to the weight carried by,
or to the size of, or to the number of wheels
of such waggon, wain, cart or carriage, as
may be specified in such bye-laws; and

(2.) For prohibiting or regulating the use of any
waggon, wain, cart or other carriage drawn
by animal power not having the nails on its
wheels countersunk in such manner as may
be specified in such bye-laws, or having on
its wheels bars or other projections forbidden
by such bye-laws; and

(3.) For prohibiting or regulating the locking of the
wheel of any waggon, wain, cart, or carriage
drawn by animal power when descending a hill, unless there is placed at the
bottom of such wheel during the whole time
of its being locked a skidpan, slipper, or shoe,
in such manner as to prevent the road from
being destroyed or injured by the locking of
such wheel; and

(4.) For prohibiting or regulating the erection of
gates across highways and prohibiting gates
opening outwards on highways.

(5.) For regulating the use of bicycles.

Fines not
exceeding
£2 for each
offence may
be imposed.

Fines, to be recovered summarily, may be imposed
by any such bye-laws on persons breaking any bye-
law made under this section, provided that no fine exceeds for any one offence the sum of two pounds, and
that the bye-laws are so framed as to allow of the
recovery of any sum less than the full amount of the
fine.

Id. s. 35.
Confirmation
by Local

A bye-law made under the Highways and Locomotives (Amendment) Act, 1878, and any alteration

made therein and any repeal of a bye-law will not be of any validity until it has been submitted to and confirmed by the Local Government Board.

Act '78, s. 35.
Government Board.

A bye-law made under that Act shall not, nor shall any alteration therein or addition thereto or repeal thereof be confirmed until the expiration of one month after notice of the intention to apply for confirmation of the same has been given by the authority making the same in one or more local newspapers circulating in their county or district.

Months' notice to be given previous to confirmation.

LOCAL GOVERNMENT BOARD.

If at any time after a rural sanitary authority has become invested with the powers of a highway board, the boundaries of such authority are altered, the Local Government Board, on the application of any authority or person interested, may by order provide for the adjustment of any accounts, or the settlement of any doubt or difference so far as relates to highways consequent on the alteration of the boundaries of such rural sanitary authority.

Act' 78, s. 5 (2).
Order for adjustment of accounts or, settlement of difference, on alteration of boundaries of rural sanitary authority.

The Local Government Board may direct what remuneration the auditor of accounts of highway districts and parishes shall receive.

Id. s. 9. Auditor's remuneration.

The Local Government Board may make a provisional order that any road which has ceased to be a turnpike between the 31st December, 1870, and the 16th August, 1878, ought not to become a main road; or that any road which has become a main road ought to cease to be a main road and become an ordinary highway.

Id. s. 16. Provisional orders as to roads.

The Local Government Board may submit any provisional order made by them under the Highways and Locomotives (Amendment) Act, 1878, to Parliament

Id. s. 34. Confirmation of provisional orders.

for confirmation, and without such confirmation no provisional order will be of any validity.

No bye-law made under the Highways and Loco-motives (Amendment) Act, 1878, nor any alteration made therein, nor any repeal of a bye-law will be of any validity until it has been submitted to and confirmed by the Local Government Board.

DISTRICT FUND, AND EXPENSES OF HIGHWAY BOARD.

EXPENSES—HOW CHARGED.

The salaries of the officers appointed for each district, and any other expenses incurred by any highway board for the common use or benefit of the several parishes within such district, shall be annually charged to a district fund to be contributed by and charged upon the several highway parishes within such district in proportion to the rateable value of the property in each parish, but the expenses of maintaining and keeping in repair the highways of each highway parish within the
district, and all other expenses legally payable by the highway board in relation to such parish, including any sums of money that would have been payable out of the highway rates of such parish if the same had not become part of a highway district, except such expenses as are in the Highway Act, 1864, authorized to be charged to the district fund, shall be a separate charge on each parish.

The rateable value of the property in each parish shall be ascertained according to the valuation list or other estimate for the time being in force in such parish for the purposes of the poor rate, or if no such valuation list or estimate be in force, then in such manner as may Act '64, s. 32. be determined by the justices in petty sessions, subject to an appeal by any person aggrieved to the next general or quarter sessions.

All expenses incurred by any highway board in main- Act '78, s. 7. After 25th March, 1879, the mainte- nance of highways, and all other expenses in- curred by board, to be charged on district fund. taining and keeping in repair the highways of each parish within their district, and all other expenses legally incurred by such board, shall, notwithstanding anything contained in the Highway Acts, on and after the 25th day of March, 1879, be deemed to have been incurred for the common use or benefit of the several parishes within their district, and shall be charged on the district fund: Provided, that if a highway board think it just, by reason of natural differences of soil or locality, or other exceptional circumstances, that any parish or parishes within their district should bear the expenses of maintaining its or their own highways, they may (with the approval of the county authority, or authorities of the county or counties within which their district, or any part thereof, is situate) divide Board may divide district, and charge maintenance of highways on each part. their district into two or more parts, and charge exclusively on each of such parts the expenses payable by such highway board in respect of maintaining and keeping in repair the highways situate in each such part; so, nevertheless, that each such part shall consist of one or more highway parish or highway parishes.

All moneys borrowed by a highway board after the Id. s. 8. After 25th March, 1879, all borrowed moneys to be charged on district fund. 25th day of March, 1879, under the Highway Acts, shall be charged on the district fund, but nothing in the Highways and Locomotives (Amendment) Act, 1878, shall affect the security, chargeability, or repayment of any moneys borrowed before that day.

MODE OF OBTAINING PAYMENT.

Act '64, s. 33.

Precepts to be issued to waywardens or overseers requiring them to pay the amount of contribution to the treasurer.

For the purpose of obtaining payment from the several highway parishes within their district of the sums to be contributed by them, the highway board shall order precepts to be issued to the waywardens or overseers of the said parishes according to the provisions hereinafter contained, stating the sum to be contributed by each parish, and requiring the officer to whom the precept is addressed, within a time to be limited by the precept, to pay the sum therein mentioned to the treasurer of the board.

Precept to be addressed to waywarden of parish not separately maintaining its own poor, &c.; in other cases to overseers.

Where a highway parish is not a parish separately maintaining its own poor, or where in any highway parish it has, for a period of not less than seven years immediately preceding the passing of the Highway Act, 1862, been the custom of the surveyor of highways for such parish to levy a highway rate in respect of property not subject by law to be assessed to poor rates, the precept of the highway board shall be addressed to the waywarden of the parish, and in all other cases it shall be addressed to the overseers.

Where precept addressed to waywarden, he must pay required sum out of separate rate assessed and levied as herein provided.

Where the precept is addressed to a waywarden he shall pay the sum thereby required out of a separate rate, and such separate rate shall, in the case of a parish in which for such period aforesaid it has been the custom of the surveyor of highways to levy a highway rate in respect of property not subject by law to be assessed to poor rate, be assessed on and levied from the persons and in respect of the property on, from, and in respect of which the same has been assessed and levied during such period as aforesaid; and in all other cases such rate shall be assessed on and levied from the persons and in respect of the property on, from, and in respect of which a poor rate would be assessable and leviable if the parish of which he is waywarden were a place separately maintaining its own poor.

No rate leviable by a waywarden under this Act shall be payable until the same has been published in manner in which rates for the relief of the poor are by law required to be published.

A waywarden shall account to the highway board for the amount of all rates levied by him, and at the expiration of his term of office shall pay any surplus in his hands arising from any rate so levied, above the amount for which the rate was made, to the treasurer of the highway board, to the credit of the parish within which such rate was made, and such surplus shall go in reduction of the next highway rate that may be leviable in such parish.

Where the precept is addressed to the overseers they shall pay the sum thereby required out of a poor rate to be levied by them, or out of any moneys in their hands applicable to the relief of the poor.

No contribution required to be paid by any parish at any one time in respect of highway rates shall exceed the sum of tenpence in the pound, and the aggregate of contributions required to be paid by any parish in any one year in respect of highway rates shall not exceed the sum of two shillings and sixpence in the pound, except with the consent of four-fifths of the ratepayers of the parish in which such excess may be levied present at a meeting specially called for the purpose, of which ten days' previous notice has been given by the waywarden of such parish, and then only to such extent as may be determined by such meeting.

All sums of money payable in pursuance of the precepts of a highway board shall, whether they are or not payable by the overseers of the poor, be subject to

Act '64, s. 33.
which high-
way rates are
subject. all charges to which ordinary highway rates are subject by law.

Id. s. 34.
Waywardens
and overseers
to have same
powers, &c.,
for assessing,
&c., rates, as
in case of
poor rates.

All waywardens and overseers to whom precepts of a highway board are hereby directed or authorized to be issued shall within their respective parishes have the same powers, remedies, and privileges, for and in respect of assessing and levying any rates required to be levied for making payments to a highway board, in the case of overseers, as they have in assessing and levying ordinary rates for the relief of the poor, and in the case of waywardens, as they would have if the parish of which they are waywardens were a place separately maintaining its own poor, and they were overseers thereof, and the rate to be levied by them were a duly authorized poor rate.

Id. s. 35.
In case of
nonpayment
by overseers
or way-
warden
justice may
summon
them to
show cause
why pay-
ment has not
been made.

Justices at
petty ses-
sions may
cause
amount in
arrear, with
costs, to be
levied from
overseers or
waywarden
as in case of
poor rate.

If any payment required to be made by the overseers, or waywardens of any parish of moneys due to a highway board is in arrear, it shall be lawful for any justice, on application under the hand of the chairman for the time being, or by the clerk of such board, to summon the said overseers or waywardens to show cause at petty sessions why such payment has not been made; and the justices at such petty sessions, after hearing the complaint preferred on behalf of the board, may, if they think fit, cause the amount of payment in arrear, together with the costs occasioned by such arrear, to be levied and recovered from the said overseers or waywardens, or any of them, in like manner as moneys assessed for the relief of the poor may be levied and recovered, and the amount of such arrear, together with the costs aforesaid, when levied and recovered, to be paid to the said board.

ACCOUNTS AND AUDIT.

Act '78, s. 9.

The accounts of the highway authority of every highway district and highway parish shall be made up in such form as the Local Government Board shall from time to time prescribe, and shall be balanced to the 25th day of March in each year, and as soon as conveniently may be after such day the said accounts shall be audited and examined by the auditor of accounts relating to the relief of the poor for the audit district in which the highway district or highway parish, or the greater part thereof in rateable value, is situate.

Every such auditor shall (as nearly as may be) have in relation to the accounts of the highway authority of a highway district or highway parish and of their officers, the same powers and duties as he has in the case of accounts relating to the relief of the poor; and any person aggrieved by the decision of the auditor shall have the same rights and remedies as in the case of such last mentioned audit.

The auditor shall receive such remuneration as the Local Government Board direct; and such remuneration, together with the expenses incident to the audit, shall be paid by the highway authority of the highway district or highway parish out of the fund or rate applicable to the repair of highways within such district or parish; and such remuneration and expenses may, in default of payment, be recovered in a summary manner.

Within thirty days after the completion of the audit under the Highways and Locomotives (Amendment) Act, 1878, sect. 9, the board shall cause a statement showing the receipt and expenditure in respect of each parish, and the apportioned part of expenditure

Marginal notes:
Accounts of highway districts and parishes to be made up and balanced to the 25th March, and audited by the auditor of the poor law district.

Auditor has same powers and duties as in case of poor law accounts; and any person aggrieved by his decision has same rights as in case of poor law audit.

Auditor's remuneration to be fixed by Local Government Board and paid by highway authority, and recoverable summarily in default of payment.

Act '64 s. 36.
Act '78 s. 9.
35 & 36 Vict. c. 79, s. 36.
Statement of receipt and expenditure of each parish, and

F 2

Act '64, s. 36.
Act '75, s. 9.
35 & 36 Vict.
c. 72, s. 36.
of appor-
tioned part
chargeable
thereto, &c.,
to be sent to
each member
of the board
and to over-
seers of
every parish.
Clerk of
board to fur-
nish copy to
any rate-
payer or
owner on
payment.
Books of
account open
to inspection
of ratepayers

chargeable thereto in respect of the district fund, and such other particulars and in such form as the Local Government Board may direct, to be printed, and sent by post or otherwise to each member of the board, and to the overseers of every parish within the district having overseers; and the clerk of the board shall furnish a copy of such statement to any ratepayer or owner of property situate within the district, on his application, and on the payment of a sum not exceeding one penny.

The books of account of the board shall at all seasonable times be open to the inspection of any ratepayer of any highway parish within the district of the board.

APPEAL TO SPECIAL SESSIONS.

Act '64, s. 37.
Persons
aggrieved
by rates
levied,
on the
ground of
incorrectness
in valuation,
&c., may
appeal to
justices in
special
sessions.

If any person feels aggrieved by any rate levied on him for the purpose of raising moneys payable under a precept of a highway board, on the ground of incorrectness in the valuation of any property included in such rate, or of any person being put on or left out of such rate, or of the inequality or unfairness of the sum charged on any person or persons therein, he may appeal to the justices in special sessions in manner provided by the Act 6 & 7 Will. 4, c. 96, ss. 6, 7, and all the provisions of the said sections shall be applicable to such appeal.

APPEAL TO QUARTER SESSIONS.

Id. s. 38.
Waywarden
or ratepayer
may appeal
in respect of
order for
repair of
highways,
&c., or of
items of

Where any waywarden of a highway parish of a district, or any ratepayer of such parish, feels aggrieved in respect of the matters following:—

    (1.) In respect of any order of the highway board for the repair of any highway in his parish

on the ground that such highway is not ^{Act' 64, s. 80-}
legally repairable by the parish, or in respect ^{expense and}
of any other order of the board on the ground ^{&c.}
that the matter to which such order relates
is one in regard to which the board have no
jurisdiction to make an order;

(2.) In respect of any item of expense charged to
the separate account of his parish on the
ground that such item of expense has not in
fact been incurred or has been incurred in
respect of a matter upon which the board
have no authority by law to make any expenditure whatever;

(3.) In respect of any item of expenditure charged
to the district fund on the ground that such
item of expense has not in fact been incurred,
or has been incurred in respect of a matter
upon which the board has no authority by
law to make any expenditure whatever;

(4.) In respect of the contribution required to be
made by each parish to the district fund on
the ground that such amount, when com-
pared with the contribution of other parishes
in the district, is not according to the proportion required by the Highway Act, 1864;

he may, upon the complying with the conditions mentioned in sect. 39 of the Highway Act, 1864, appeal
to the court of general or quarter sessions having jurisdiction in the district;

But no appeal shall be had in respect of any exercise
of the descretion of the board in matters within their
discretion; and no appeal shall be had except in respect

Act '64, s. 39. of the matters and upon the grounds hereinbefore-mentioned.

Conditions of appeal.

No appeal can be entertained by any court of general or quarter sessions in pursuance of the Highway Act, 1864, unless the following conditions have been complied with :—

Notice of appeal must be served on clerk of the board within two months after order, or within one month after statement of account.

(1.) Notice of the intention of appeal must be served by the appellant on the clerk of the highway board in the case of an appeal against an order within two months after the order, and in the case of an appeal in respect of any item of expense or contribution within one month after the statement of the account of the board has been sent to each member of the board as mentioned in sect. 36 of the Highway Act, 1864 :

Notice must state ground of appeal.

(2.) The notice must state the matter appealed against, and the ground of the appeal.

Board may serve counter notice requiring appellant to appear and support appeal.

On the receipt of the notice the board may serve a counter notice on the appellant, requiring him to appear in person or by his agent at the next meeting of the board, and support his appeal. On hearing the appellant the board may rectify the matter complained of,

Board may rectify matter complained of; and on tender of costs of attendance, appellant cannot proceed with appeal.

and if they do so to a reasonable extent, and tender to the appellant a reasonable sum for the costs of his attendance, it shall not be lawful for the appellant to proceed with his appeal. In any other case the appellant may proceed with his appeal, and the reasonable costs of his attendance on the board shall be deemed part of the costs of the appeal.

On proceeding with appeal costs of attendance on board deemed costs of appeal.

If at any time after notice of appeal has been given it appears to the court of general or quarter sessions, on the application of either party in the presence of or-after notice has been given to the other party, that the Act '64, s. 40. matter in question in such appeal consists wholly or in If the matter in question consists of mere matter of account, &c., court may order it to be referred to arbitration. part of matters of mere account which cannot be satisfactorily tried by the court, it shall be lawful for such court to order that such matters, either wholly or in part, be referred to the arbitration of one or more persons, to be appointed by the parties, or in case of disagreement, by the court; and the award made on Award enforceable like order of court. such arbitration shall be enforceable by the same process as the order of the court of quarter sessions.

The provisions of "The Common Law Procedure Id. s. 41. Provisions of 17 & 18 Vict. c. 125, relating to compulsory references, incorporated. Act, 1854," relating to compulsory references, shall be deemed to extend to arbitrations directed by the court of quarter sessions; and the word "court" in the said Act shall be deemed to include the court of quarter sessions.

If upon the hearing of the appeal it appears to the Id. s. 42. If question in dispute involves inquiry as to whether road is or is not a highway, &c., &c., court may decide the question, or empanel a jury, and submit such questions as they think fit. Verdict conclusive as to questions submitted to jury. court that the question in dispute involves an inquiry as to whether a road is or is not a highway repairable by the public, or an inquiry as to any other important matter of fact, the court may either themselves decide such question, or may empanel a jury of twelve disinterested men out of the persons returned to serve as jurymen at such quarter sessions, and submit to such jury such questions in relation to the matters of fact in dispute as the court think fit; and the verdict of such jury, after hearing the evidence adduced, shall be conclusive as to the questions submitted to them.

The questions so submitted shall be in the form and Questions to be submitted in the form of feigned issues. shall be tried as nearly as may be in the manner in which feigned issues are ordinarily tried; and the court shall decide the parties to be plaintiffs and defendants in such trials.

Subject as aforesaid, the court may, upon the hearing Cou t may confirm, &c.,

of any appeal under this Act, confirm, reverse, or modify any order of the highway board, or rectify any account appealed against.

Id. s. 43.
If appellant
successful,
costs to be
paid by
board and
charged to
parishes
within their
jurisdiction
other than
parish to
which appel-
lant belongs.
If the appellant is successful, the costs shall, unless the court otherwise orders, be paid by the board, and shall be charged to the parishes within the jurisdiction of the board other than the parish to which the appellant belongs in the same proportions in which such parishes contribute to the common fund of the board.

If appellant
unsuccessful,
board may
charge costs
to parish to
which ap-
pellant, if a
waywarden,
belongs.
If the appellant is unsuccessful, the board, if the waywarden be the appellant, may charge the costs of the appeal to the parish to which the appellant belongs, in the same manner as if they were expenses incurred in repairing the roads in such parish, and may levy the sum accordingly, and may carry the sum so levied to the account of the several parishes within the jurisdiction of the board, other than the parish to which the appellant waywarden belongs, in the same manner as if they were expenses contributed by such parishes to the common fund of the board; but if some ratepayer

If appellant
be a rate-
payer other
than the
waywarden,
court may
order costs to
be paid by
appellant.
other than the waywarden is the appellant, the court may order the costs of the appeal to be paid by such appellant; and such costs shall be recoverable in he same manner as a penalty is recovered under "The Highway Act, 1862."

Id. s. 44.
Places
situate in
different
counties,
&c., when
united in one
highway
district, are
for matters
relating to
appeals
against
accounts,
deemed to
be subject to
jurisdiction
Places situate in different counties, and places situate partly in one county and partly in another county, when united in one highway district, shall, for all matters connected with the provisions of the Highway Act, 1864, relating to appeals to quarter sessions against accounts, be deemed to be subject to the jurisdiction of the justices of the county in which the district is situate to which such places shall have been united by any provisional and final order or orders, or to which after the passing of that Act any such district shall be de-

clared to be subject by the orders constituting the same, in the same manner as if all such places or parts of places were situate in such county.

Act '64, s. 44.
of justices
of county in
which dis-
trict is
situate.

JURISDICTION OF JUSTICES.

No justice of the peace shall act as such in any matter in which he has already acted as a member of the highway board, and in which the decision of such board is appealed against.

Act '62, s. 38.
Limitation.

All powers and jurisdictions vested in justices by the Highway Act, 1862, and the Highway Act, 1864, or either of such Acts, may from time to time be exercised in relation to highway districts, highway boards, and highway parishes already formed, as well as upon the occasion of forming new highway districts, boards, or parishes.

Act '64, s. 17.
Powers, &c.,
may be
exercised in
relation to
existing and
future high-
way dis-
tricts, &c.

The justices assembled in petty sessions at their usual place of meeting may exercise any jurisdiction which they are authorized under the Highway Acts or any of them to exercise in special sessions;

Id. s. 46.
Justices in
petty sessions
may exer-
cise same
jurisdiction
as in special
sessions.

And no justice of the peace shall be disabled from acting as such at any petty or special or general quarter sessions in any matter merely n the ground that he is by virtue of his office a member of any highway board complaining, interested, or concerned in such matter, or has acted as such at any meeting of such board.

No justice
disabled
from acting
merely on
ground of
being *ex
officio*
member of
highway
board.

RECOVERY OF PENALTIES, AND APPEALS.

UNDER HIGHWAY ACT, 1862.

All penalties under the Highway Act, 1862, and all moneys recoverable as penalties, may be recovered summarily before any two or more justices in the manner directed by the Act 11 & 12 Vict. c. 43, and any Act amending the same; but where any sum adjudged to be paid under this Act in respect of such penalties or moneys exceeds five pounds, an appeal may be had by any person aggrieved to a court of general or quarter sessions in manner provided by the 110th section of the Act 24 & 25 Vict. c. 96, An Act to consolidate and amend the Statute Law of England and Ireland relating to Larceny and other similar Offences.

UNDER HIGHWAYS AND LOCOMOTIVES (AMENDMENT) ACT, 1878.

All offences, fines, and expenses under the Highways and Locomotives (Amendment) Act, 1878, or any byelaw made in pursuance of that Act, may be prosecuted, enforced, and recovered before a court of summary jurisdiction in manner provided by the Summary Jurisdiction Acts.

If any party thinks himself aggrieved by any conviction or order made by a court of summary jurisdiction on determining any information or complaint under this Act, the party so aggrieved may appeal therefrom, subject to the conditions and regulations following :—

(1.) The appeal shall be made to the next practicable court of quarter sessions for the county or place where the decision appealed from was ^{Act '78, s.87.} given, holden not less than twenty-one days ^{sions holden not less than} after the decision of the court from which the ^{21 days after decision.} appeal is made; and

(2.) The appellant shall, within ten days after the ^{Written notice to be} pronouncing by the court of the decision ap- ^{given within 10 days to} pealed from, give notice to the other party ^{the other} and to the court of summary jurisdiction of ^{party and to court of} his intention to appeal and of the ground ^{summary jurisdiction,} thereof; such notice of appeal shall be in ^{of intention to appeal} writing signed by the person or persons ^{and of the ground} giving the same, or by his, her, or their ^{thereof, signed by} solicitor on his, her, or their behalf; and ^{appellant or solicitor.}

(3.) The appellant shall, within three days after such ^{Within 3 days after} notice, enter into a recognizance before a jus- ^{notice, appellant to} tice of the peace, with two sufficient sureties, ^{enter into recognizance} conditioned personally to try such appeal, and ^{with two sureties, or} to abide the judgment of the court thereon, ^{give other security by} and to pay such costs as may be awarded ^{deposit of money, &c.} by the court, or give such other security by deposit of money or otherwise as the justice may allow; and

(4.) Where the appellant is in custody the justice ^{Appellant may be} may, if he think fit, on the appellant entering ^{liberated from custody} into such recognizance or giving such other ^{on entering into recog-} security as aforesaid, release him from ^{nizance, &c.} custody:

(5.) The court of appeal may adjourn the appeal ^{Court may adjourn ap-} and upon the hearing thereof they may con- ^{peal, and confirm, &c.,} firm, reverse, or modify the decision of the ^{the decision} court of summary jurisdiction, or remit the ^{or remit the matter to} matter to the court of summary jurisdiction ^{court of summary} with the opinion of the court of appeal ^{jurisdiction}

Act '78, s. 26.

with opinion of court of appeal, &c.

If matter remitted, court of summary jurisdiction to re-hear and decide according to opinion of court of appeal. Court of appeal may make order as to costs.

thereon, or make such other order in the matter as the court thinks just, and if the matter be remitted to the court of summary jurisdiction the said last-mentioned court shall thereupon re-hear and decide the information or complaint in accordance with the opinion of the said court of appeal. The court of appeal may also make such order as to costs to be paid by either party as the court thinks just.

MISCELLANEOUS PROVISIONS.

Act '62, s. 44. Provisions of Principal Act to be applicable to Highways under local or personal Acts.

All the provisions of the Principal Act for widening, diverting, and stopping up highways shall be applicable to all highways which now are or may hereafter be paved, repaired, or cleansed under or by virtue of any local or personal Act or Acts of Parliament, or which may be situate within the limit of any such Act or Acts, except highways which any railway company, or the owners, conservators, commissioners, trustees, or undertakers of any canal, river, or inland navigation, are liable by virtue of any Act of Parliament relating to such railway, canal, river, or inland navigation to make, maintain, repair, or cleanse.

Id. s. 45. Enabling councils of certain boroughs to adopt parish roads and highways and to apply rates for their repair.

Whereas there are in certain boroughs in England and Wales roads and highways that are now and have heretofore been repaired by the inhabitants of the several parishes or townships within which such roads and highways are situated, and who also contribute and pay to the general rates levied for the repair of the public streets, roads, and highways maintained and kept in repair by the council of such boroughs, by reason whereof a great burthen is imposed upon the ratepayers of the said parishes and townships ; and it being doubtful whether the council of such boroughs have the power to adopt such parish roads and highways, or to apply the rates collected in such boroughs in repairing the same, be it enacted that it shall and may be lawful for the council of every such borough in England and Wales, upon the petition of the majority of the ratepayers of such parishes or townships present at a public meeting duly convened, to to adopt all or any of such parish roads and highways as the council shall in its discretion consider advisable, and to apply the rates levied and collected by the said council for the repair of the public streets, roads, and highways within such borough in repairing and maintaining such parish roads and highways : Provided always, that it shall be competent for such council, previous to adopting such parish roads and highways, to require the provisions contained in any local Act applying to the public streets, roads, and highways of such borough to be complied with.

The 74th section of the Highway Act, 1835, shall be repealed, and instead thereof be it enacted, if any horse, mare gelding, bull, ox, cow, heifer, steer, calf, mule, ass, sheep, lamb, goat, kid, or swine is at any time found straying on or lying about any highway, or across any part thereof, or by the sides thereof (except on such parts of any highway as pass over any common or waste or uninclosed ground) the owner or owners thereof shall, for every animal so found straying or lying, be liable to a penalty not exceeding five shillings, to be recovered in a summary manner, together with the reasonable expense of removing such animal from the highway where it is found to the

[marginal note: Act '62. s. 45.]

[marginal note: Act, 64, s. 25. Sect. 74 of 5 & 6 W. 4. c. 50, repealed, and other provisions made as to cattle found straying, &c. on highways.]

Act '64, s. 25. fields or stable of the owner or owners, or to the common pound (if any) of the parish where the same shall be found, or to such other place as may have been provided for the purpose: Provided always, that no owner of any such animal shall in any case pay more than the sum of thirty shillings, to be recovered as aforesaid, over and above such reasonable expenses as aforesaid, including the usual fees and charges of the authorized keeper of the pound: Provided also, that nothing in this Act shall be deemed to extend to take away any right of pasturage which may exist on the sides of any highway.

Id. s. 51.
As to en-
croachment
on highways.

From and after the passing of the Highway Act, 1864, if any person shall encroach by making or causing to be made any building, or pit, or hedge, ditch, or other fence, or by placing any dung, compost, or other materials for dressing land, or any rubbish, on the side or sides of any carriageway or cartway within fifteen feet of the centre thereof, or by removing any soil or turf from the side or sides of any carriageway or cartway, except for the purpose of improving the road, and by order of the highway board, or, where there is no highway board, of the surveyor, he shall be subject on conviction for every such offence to any sum not exceeding forty shillings, notwithstanding that the whole space of fifteen feet from the centre of such carriageway or cartway has not been maintained with stones or other materials used in forming highways; and it shall be lawful for the justices assembled at petty sessions, upon proof to them made upon oath, to levy the expenses of taking down such building, hedge, or fence, or filling up such ditch or pit, and removing such dung, compost, materials, or rubbish, as aforesaid, or restoring the injury caused by the removal

of such soil or turf, upon the person offending : Pro- Act '64, s. 51.
vided always, that where any carriageway or cartway
is fenced on both sides no encroachment as aforesaid shall be allowed whereby such carriageway or
cartway shall be reduced in width to less than
thirty feet between the fences on each side.

Whereas doubts have arisen whether a surveyor of Act '78. s. 25. Removal of
highways can be appointed, in pursuance of the High- doubt as to appointment
way Act, 1835, for a parish which does not maintain any of surveyors in certain
highway : be it therefore enacted, that it shall be lawful parishes.
for the inhabitants in vestry assembled of any parish
or place having a known legal boundary (notwithstanding that the inhabitants at large are not for the time
being liable to maintain any highway or to contribute
to any rate applicable to the maintenance of highways),
or on the neglect or refusal of such inhabitants for the
justices at a special sessions for the highways or in
petty sessions assembled, at any time to exercise all the
powers of the Highway Acts with respect to the election
or appointment of a surveyor of highways with or
without a salary for such parish or place : and any
surveyor so elected or appointed shall have all the
powers and duties (including the power of making,
assessing, and levying of highway rates) of a surveyor
under the Highways Acts.

Notwithstanding anything contained in sect. 68 of Id. s. 27. Application
the Public Health Act, 1848, or in sect. 149 of the of 7 & 8 Geo.
Public Health Act, 1875, all mines and minerals of 4, c. 24, s. 18, with respect
any description whatsoever under any disturnpiked road to minerals, to disturn-
or highway which has or shall become vested in an piked roads and to high
urban sanitary authority by virtue of the said sections, ways.
or either of them, shall belong to the person who
would be entitled thereto in case such road or highway
had not become so vested, and the person entitled to

Act '78, s. 27. any such mine or minerals shall have the same powers of working and of getting and carrying away the same or other minerals as if the road or highway had not become vested in the urban sanitary authority, but so nevertheless that in such working no damage shall be done to the road or highway.

This section extends to the Isle of Wight and to South Wales, as defined by the said Act of 23 & 24 Vict. c. 68, " An Act for the better management and control of the highways in South Wales."

HIGHWAY ACT, 1862.

25 & 26 VICT. c. 61.

An Act for the better Management of Highways in England *(a).* [29th July, 1862.]

WHEREAS it is expedient to amend the law relating to highways in *England;* Be it enacted by the Queen's most Excellent Majesty, by and with the advice and consent of the Lords spiritual and temporal, and Commons, in this present Parliament assembled, and by the authority of the same, as follows :—

PRELIMINARY.

1. This Act shall not extend to *Scotland* or *Ireland.* Limits of Act.

2. The word " county" in this Act shall not include a "county of a city" or " a county of a town," but where a county, as hereinbefore defined, is divided into ridings or other divisions having a separate court of quarter sessions of the peace, it shall mean each such division or riding, and not the entire county ; and for the purposes of this Act all liberties and franchises, except the liberty of *Saint Albans,* which shall be considered a county, and except boroughs as hereinafter defined, shall be considered as forming part of that county by which they are surrounded *(b),* or if partly surrounded by two or more counties, then as forming part of that county with

Definition of " county" and " borough."

(a) This Act, so far as is consistent with its provisions, is to be construed as one with 5 & 6 Will. 4, c. 50 (sect. 42, sub-sect. 1). And the Highway Act, 1864, so far as is consistent with the tenor thereof, is to be construed as one with this Act. (27 & 28 Vict. c. 101, s. 2).

G

Act '62, s. 2. which they have the longest common boundary; the
word "borough" shall mean a borough as defined by
the Act 5 & 6 Will. 4, c. 76, "for the Regulation of
Municipal Corporations in *England* and *Wales*," or any
place to which the provisions of the said Act have
been or shall hereafter have been extended.

(*b*) In *Giles* v. *Glubb*, 30 J. P. 38, it was held that L., an ancient
borough, separately maintaining its own poor and highways,
which had charters with non-intromittant clauses, and was entirely surrounded by the county of C., was properly included by
the justices of the county within a highway district under sect. 5,
notwithstanding the non-intromittant clause: and further, that
the justices of the county of C. had jurisdiction to enforce payment of a contribution under a precept from the highway board,
and also that in an order including the parish or place of L., the
"borough of L." was sufficiently described.

Definition
of "parish,"
"highway
district,"
and "high-
way board."
   3. The word "parish" shall include any place maintaining its own highways (*c*); the expressions "highway district" and "highway board" shall refer only to
highway districts formed and highway boards constituted in pursuance of this Act.

(*c*) See *Giles* v. *Glubb*, 30 J. P. 38, *supra*, that the borough
of L. is a parish within this definition. See also 27 & 28 Vict.
c. 101, s. 3, as to definitions of "poor law parish," "highway
parish," "highway rate" and "county." See also sects. 32 & 33
(*infra*), and 27 & 28 Vict. c. 101, s. 5, as to what places shall be
considered as separately maintaining their own highways.

Definition of
Principal
Act" and
"Highway
Acts"
   4. The Act 5 & 6 Will. 4, c. 50, *An Act to consolidate and amend the Laws relating to highways in
that Part of* Great Britain *called* England, is hereinafter distinguished as "the Principal Act;" and this
Act and the Principal Act, and the other Acts amending
the Principal Act, are hereinafter included under the
expression "the Highway Acts."

FORMATION OF HIGHWAY DISTRICTS.

Power to
justices, in
   5. Any five or more justices of a county may by
writing under their hands require the clerk of the

peace to add to or send with the notice required by law Act '62, s. 5.
to be given of the holding of courts of general or quarter
sessions a notice in the Form marked (A.) in the
.Schedule, or as near thereto as circumstances admit,
that at the court therein mentioned a proposal will be
made to the justices to divide the county or some part
thereof into highway districts, or to constitute the whole
-or some part thereof a highway district, and also require the clerk of the peace to send by post in a prepaid
letter notices (*d*) in the aforesaid form to the churchwardens or overseers of every parish mentioned in the
-said notice; and upon such requisition being complied
with the justices assembled at the court of general or
-quarter sessions mentioned in the notice may entertain
such proposal, and make a provisional order dividing
their county or some part thereof into highway districts, or constituting the whole or some part of their
-county a highway district, for the more convenient
management of highways (*e*), but such order shall not
be of any validity unless it is confirmed by a final
order of the justices assembled at some subsequent
court of general or quarter sessions (*f*).   *   *

(*d*) It is a condition precedent to the formation of a district
that notice be first sent to all parishes proposed to be included;
and the order is bad if any parish has been omitted (*Reg.* v. *JJ.
of Sussex*, 28 J. P. 469).

(*e*) The 39th section (*infra*) provides for the alteration of districts by the addition or subtraction of parishes, and the union of
existing districts, &c., and 27 & 28 Vict. c. 101, s. 14, extends the
powers conferred by that section to the separation of any
consolidated townships, &c. All provisions with respect to
the formation of districts, &c., &c., extend to such alterations.

(*f*) The proviso to this section is repealed by 27 & 28
Vict. c. 101, s. 6 (*post*, p. 124), and other provisions made in
lieu of it.

As regards the union of parishes in different counties, see 27 & 28
Vict. c. 101, s. 13.

Act '62, s. 6.
Regulations
as to the
making, &c.,
of orders
of justices.
* *Sic.*

6. The following regulations shall be enacted as to the making, confirmation, and approval of the orders of justice* for forming highway districts :—

  1. The justices making a provisional order under this Act shall appoint some subsequent court of general or quarter sessions, to be held within a period of not more than six months, for the taking into consideration the confirmation of the provisional order by a final order :

  2. The clerk of the peace shall add to or send with the notice required by law to be given of the holding of courts of general or quarter sessions a notice in the Form marked (B.) in the Schedule hereto, or as near thereto as circumstances admit, of the appointment so made by the justices in relation to the confirmation of the provisional order :

  3. The justices assembled at the appointed court of general or quarter sessions may make a further order quashing the provisional order, or confirming it with or without variations, or respiting the consideration of such provisional order to some subsequent court of general or quarter sessions, provided—

    Firstly, that where the variations made extend to altering the parishes constituting any highway district or districts as formed in the provisional order, the order shall be deemed to be provisional only, and shall be dealt with accordingly (*g*) :

    Secondly, that where a respite is made to any subsequent general or quarter sessions, the clerk of the peace shall give notice of such respite in manner in which he is required to give notice in respect of sessions at which a provisional or final order is proposed to ^{Act '62, s.} be made:

4. The provisional order shall state the parishes to be united in each district, the name by which the district is to be known, and the number of waywardens (such number to be at least one) which each parish is to elect (*h*):

5. (*i*) * * * * * *

6. Notice of the provisional and final orders shall (*j*) as soon as possible after the making thereof be given by the clerk of the peace, by publishing a copy in the *London Gazette* and in one or more newspapers circulating in the county, or if the whole county is not affected by such order in one or more newspapers circulating in the district affected by such orders, and by sending a copy by post in a prepaid letter to the overseers of every parish within the proposed highway district, and there shall be added to the notice of the provisional order the date of the sessions at which the confirmation of such order will be considered.

(*g*) Where more districts than one are comprised in the same order the formation of each district is to be deemed independent of the formation of any other, and the order is to take effect as if a separate order had been made for each district; and any variation in a provisional order altering the parishes in any one or more districts makes the order provisional only as to the particular district in which the alterations are made (27 & 28 Vict. c. 101. s. 4).

(*h*) In *Reg.* v. *JJ. of Yorkshire, W. R.*, 29 J. P. 440, 34 L. J. m, 227. A provisional order included the township of A. (which maintained its own poor) and assigned to it one waywarden: the township, however, consisted of three hamlets, B., C. and D., each of which maintained its own highways, but no separate waywarden was assigned to each. And it was *held* that the order was bad, as the justices had not made any order combining these hamlets, and in default of such combination, each of them, by sect. 3, was a separate parish. (See also *Ex parte Kay*, 29 J. P. 259).

Act '82, s. 6. (*i*) This sub-section is repealed by 27 & 28 Vict. c. 101, s. 10,. (*post*, p. 126,) and other provisions substituted for it.

(*j*) But by 27 & 28 Vict. c. 101, s. 12, no such order shall be invalidated by reason of its not being published in the *London Gazette*..

Restrictions on formation of highway districts.   **7.** The following restrictions shall be imposed with respect to the formation of highway districts in pursuance of this Act :—

     Firstly, there shall not be included in any highway district formed in pursuance of this Act any of the following places; that is to say :

         Any part of a county to which the Act 23 & 24. Vict. c. 68, *An Act for the better Management and Control of the Highways in* South. Wales, extends :

         The *Isle of Wight* (*k*):

         Any district constituted under the Public Health Act, 1848, and the Local Government Act,. 1858, or either of such Acts (*l*) :

         (*m*)   *   *   *   *   *   *

         Any parish or place within the limits of the metropolis as defined by the Act 18 & 19 Vict.. c. 120, *An Act for the better Local Management of the Metropolis:*

         Any parish or place, or part of a parish or place,. the highways whereof are maintained under the provisions of any Local (*n*) Act of Parliament:

     Secondly, there shall not be included in any highway district formed in pursuance of this Act any: parish or place, or part of a parish or place, within the limits of a borough, without the consent, firstly,. of the council of such borough, and, secondly, of: the vestry of the parish which, or part of which,. is proposed to be included (*o*) :

     Thirdly, where any parish separately maintaining its. own highways is situate in more than one county the whole of such parish shall, for the purposes of ^{Act '68, s. 7.} this Act, be deemed to be within the county within which the church of such parish, or (if there be no church) the greater part of such parish, is situate (*p*) :

Lastly, where a parish separately maintaining its own poor is divided into townships, tithings, hamlets, or places, each of which separately maintains its own highways, it shall be lawful for the justices, if they think fit, in their provisional order to combine such (*q*) townships, tithings, hamlets, and places, and to declare that no separate waywardens shall be elected from such townships, tithings, hamlets, and places, and that such parish shall be subject to the same liabilities in respect of all the highways within it which were before maintained by such townships, tithings, hamlets, and places separately, as if all their several liabilities had attached to the whole parish; and that a waywarden or waywardens shall be elected for such parish as a whole; and where such order is made, all the provisions herein contained in relation to parishes within the meaning of this Act shall be applicable to the parish formed by such combination (*r*).

(*k*) The repair of roads and highways in the Isle of Wight is provided for by the local Act 53 Geo. 3, c. xcii.

(*l*) But where part of a parish is, in pursuance of the Local Government Act, 1858, Amendment Act, 1861, sect. 9, treated as forming part of a district constituted under the Local Government Act, 1858, for all purposes connected with the repair of highways and the payment of highway rates, but for no other purpose, such part, for the purposes of the Highway Acts, 1862 and 1864, is deemed to be a place separately maintaining its own highways, and capable of being included in a highway district, without requiring the consent of the local board to be given (27 & 28 Vict. c. 101, s. 5).

And where any local government district or any other place is

Act '62, s. 7. surrounded by or adjoins a highway district constituted under the Highway Acts, the first mentioned district or other place, for the purpose of any meeting of the highway board, is deemed to be within the highway district (26 & 27 Vict. c. 17, s. 6).

(*m*) This paragraph, prohibiting the inclusion of certain parishes, &c., under the superintendence of a board established under 5 & 6 Will. 4, c. 50, s. 18, is repealed by 41 & 42 Vict. c. 77, s. 12.

(*n*) "Local Act," as here used, does not include turnpike Acts (26 & 27 Vict. c. 94, s. 1).

(*o*) But see 27 & 28 Vict. 101, s. 8, as to places partly within and partly without a borough.

(*p*) But see 27 & 28 Vict. c. 101, s. 13, as to union of places in different counties.

(*q*) Or any two or more of such townships, &c., and any combination so formed is, for all purposes of the Highway Acts, deemed to be a highway parish (27 & 28 Vict. c. 101, s. 7).

(*r*) But if no such order is made, each township, &c., must be treated as a separate parish, and have a waywarden assigned to it (*Reg. v. JJ. of Yorkshire, W. R.*, 29 J. P. 440, 34 L. J. *m*, 227, note (*h*), p. 85, *supra*).

LEGAL OBJECTIONS TO FORMATION OF DISTRICT.

Rules as to objections and evidence.

8. No objection shall be made at any trial or in any legal proceeding to the validity of any orders or proceedings relating to the formation of a highway district, after the expiration of three calendar months from the date of the publication in the Gazette of the order under which the district is formed (*s*) ; and the production of a copy of the *London Gazette*, containing a copy of the order of justices forming a highway district (*t*) shall be receivable in all courts of justice, and in all legal proceedings, as evidence of the formation of the district and of the matters in the said order mentioned.

(*s*) The words, "the date of the publication in the Gazette of the order under which the district is formed," are virtually repealed by 27 & 28 Vict. c. 101, s. 12, and the words, "the date of the making of the final order under which the district is formed," are substituted for them. It appears from *Reg.* v. *JJ. Lindsey*, 30 J. P. 86, that where the order is objected to, it is sufficient to obtain a rule for a *certiorari* within three months from the date of the final order.

Act '64, s. 8.

(*t*) And by 27 & 28 Vict. c. 101, s. 12, any copy of the provisional or final order of the justices forming a highway district, certified under the hand of the clerk of the peace to be a true copy, is receivable in evidence in all respects, as a copy of the *London Gazette* is receivable under this section.

HIGHWAY BOARD.

9. There shall be enacted, with respect to the constitution of the highway board in each highway district, the provisions following (that is to say):— Constitution of highway board.

> (1.) The highway board shall consist of the waywardens elected in the several places within the district, in manner hereinafter mentioned, and of the justices acting for the county and residing within the district (*u*):

> (2.) The board shall be a body corporate, by the name of the highway board of the district to which it belongs, having a perpetual succession and a common seal, with a power to acquire and hold lands (*v*) for the purposes of the Highway Acts, without any license in mortmain:

> (3.) No act or proceeding of the board shall be questioned on account of any vacancy or vacancies in their body (*x*):

> (4.) No defect in the qualification or election of any person or persons acting as members or member of the board or committee of a board shall be deemed to vitiate any proceedings of such board in which he or they have taken part in cases where the majority of members parties to such proceedings are duly entitled to act:

> (5.) Any minute made of proceedings at meetings of the board or of committees of the board, if signed by any person purporting to be

the chairman of the board or committee of the board, either at the meeting of the board or committee of the board at which such proceedings took place, or at the next ensuing meeting of the board or committee of the board, shall be receivable in evidence in all legal proceedings without further proof; and until the contrary is proved every meeting of the board or committee of the board in respect of the proceedings of which minutes have been so made shall be deemed to have been duly convened and held, and all the members thereof to have been duly qualified :

(6.) No member of a board, by being party to, or executing in his capacity of member, any contract or other instrument on behalf of the board, or otherwise lawfully (y) exercising any of the powers given to the board, shall be subject to be tried or prosecuted, either individually, or with others, by any person whomsoever; and the bodies or goods, or lands of the members shall not be liable to execution of any legal process by reason of any contract or other instrument so entered into, tried or executed by them, or by reason of any other lawful Act done by them in execution of any of the powers of the board; and the members of the board may apply any moneys in their hands for the purpose of indemnifying themselves against any losses, costs, or damages they may incur in execution of the powers granted to them :

(7.) (z)   *   *   *   *   *   *

(*u*) In addition to the parties here mentioned justices acting for the county and resident in any place which is prohibited by the 7th section from being included in a district, and is surrounded by or adjoins in any part a highway district, are *ex officio* members of the highway board of such district, subject to certain qualifications (27 & 21 Vict. c. 101, s. 29).

(*v*) They may purchase such lands, or easements relating to lands, as they require for the purpose of improving the highways within their district (27 & 28 Vict. c. 101, s. 53).

(*x*) The proceedings of the board are regulated by the provisions contained in the 1st schedule to 27 & 28 Vict. c. 101.

(*y*) In *Mill* v. *Hawker*, L. R. 9 Ex. 309, the Court of Exchequer (Kelly, C. B., dissenting) held that in the case of an illegal resolution requiring the plaintiff to remove a lock from a gate placed across a path running through land in his occupation, and of a subsequent removal of the lock by the surveyor by order of the board, the members of the board who concurred in the resolution were personally responsible; and that the fact that the surveyor was by 25 & 26 Vict. c. 61, s. 16, bound to obey the orders of the board, did not excuse him if in obeying their orders he did an unlawful act. On appeal, it was held by the Exchequer Chamber that the surveyor was liable, but, no opinion was expressed as to the liability of the members of the board (10 Ex. (Ex. Ch.) 92).

(*z*) This sub-section, providing that the rules contained in the schedule should be observed, is repealed by the Statute Law Revision Act, 1875. The schedule containing the rules of proceedings of the board had been previously repealed by 27 & 28 Vict. c. 101, s. 27, which also provided that the proceedings of the board should be subject to the regulations in the 1st schedule to that Act, *post*, p. 161.

ELECTION OF WAYWARDENS.

10. The following regulations shall be observed with respect to the election of waywardens in highway districts :—

In every parish (*a*) forming part of a highway district there shall be elected (*b*) every year for the year next ensuing a waywarden or such number of waywardens as may be determined by order of the justices (*c*):

Such waywarden or waywardens shall be elected in every parish forming part of a highway district at the meeting and time and in the manner and subject to the same qualification and the same power of appointment in the justices in the event of no election taking place, or in the event of a vacancy, at, in, and subject to which a person or persons to serve the office of surveyor would have been chosen or appointed if this Act had not passed (*d*):

The justices shall in their provisional order make provision for the election of a waywarden or waywardens in places where no surveyor or surveyors were elected previously to the place forming part of a highway district (*e*):

A waywarden shall continue to act until his successor is appointed, and shall be re-eligible.

(*a*) This applies to every township or hamlet, &c., within the parish maintaining its own highways, unless combined by an order under sect. 7 (See *Reg.* v. *JJ. of Yorkshire, W. R.*, 29 J. P. 440; 34 L. J. *m*, 227, note (*h*), *ante*, p. 85, and *Ex parte Kay*, 29 J. P. 259.)

(*b*) In *Reg.* v. *Cooper*, L. R. 5 Q. B. 457; 35 J. P. 37, the election was held to be incomplete in consequence of a failure to take the poll arising from a notice, made in mistake, that one of the candidates declined to stand.

(*c*) Before taking his seat, a waywarden must produce a certificate of having been duly elected, &c., signed by the chairman of vestry, &c., and he may sit for more places than one, but is only entitled to one vote (27 & 28 Vict. c. 101, s. 19). He is prohibited from contracting for the repair of roads, or for any other work to be executed within his own district (26 & 27 Vict. c. 61, s. 1); but may contract for the supply or cartage of materials, with the license of two justices (27 & 28 Vict. c. 101, s. 20), and with the consent of the inhabitants, in vestry, he may appoint a paid collector of highway rates (*Id.* s. 31). He continues in office till the 30th of April, in the year following that in which he was elected, and on that day his successor comes into office (41 & 42 Vict. c. 77, s. 11).

(*d*) These matters are provided for by 5 & 6 Will. 4, c. 50, ss. 6, 7, 11.

(*e*) By 27 & 28 Vict. c. 101, s. 10, where, previously to the passing of the provisional order forming a highway district, no surveyors or waywardens have been elected within any highway

parish in that district, and where the mode of electing a waywarden or waywardens in such parish is not provided for by this
Act, or the Highway Act, 1862, the justices shall by their provisional and final orders constituting the district, or by any subsequent provisional and final orders, make provisions for the annual
election of a waywarden or waywardens for such parish.

CONSEQUENCES OF FORMATION OF HIGHWAY DISTRICT (*f*).

11. At and after the first meeting in any highway Conse-quences of establish-ment of highway board.
district of the board of such district the following
consequences shall ensue :—

All such property, real and personal (*g*), including
all interests, easements, and rights in, to, and out
of property, real and personal, and including
things in action, as belong to or are vested in, or
would but for this Act have belonged to or been
vested in, any surveyor or surveyors of any
parish forming part of the district, shall pass to
and vest in the highway board of that district for
all the estate and interest of such surveyor or surveyors as aforesaid, but subject to all debts and
liabilities affecting the same :

All debts and liabilities incurred in respect of any
property transferred to the highway board may be
enforced against the board to the extent of the
property transferred :

All such powers (*h*), rights, duties, liabilities, capacities, and incapacities (*i*) (except the power of
making, assessing, and levying highway rates), as
are vested in or attached to, or would but for this
Act have become vested in or attached to, any
surveyor or surveyors of any parish forming part
of the district, shall vest in and attach to the
highway board (*k*) :

All property by this Act transferred to the board
shall be held by them upon trust for the several
parishes or places now maintaining their own
highways within their district to which such property belongs, or for the benefit of which it was
held previously to the formation of the district.

(*f*) As to the consequences of a rural sanitary authority exercising the powers of a highway board, see 41 & 42 Vict.
c. 77 s. 5.

(*g*) This includes all books, papers, writings and accounts,
materials, tools and implements, &c., mentioned in 5 & 6 Will. 4,
c. 50, ss. 41, 42.

(*h*) This section, combined with the 17th section, *infra*, enables a
highway board to license a gas company to open the highway and
lay down gas pipes; and to recover the sum agreed to be paid
for the grant of such license (*Edgeware Highway Board* v.
Harrow Gas Company, L. R. 10 Q. B. 92, 38 J. P. 806).

(*i*) By sect. 43 (3), *infra*, the board, for all the purposes of the
Principal Act, except that of levying highway rates, are deemed
to be the successor in office of the surveyor of every parish within
the district.   But by 27 & 28 Vict. c. 101 s. 20, the 46th section
of that Act, 5 & 6 Will. 4 c. 50 (as to contracts for purchasing,
getting, and carrying materials, &c.), is not to apply to the highway board of, or to any parish within, any highway district.

(*k*) But the outgoing surveyor's powers continue so far as
relates to the recovery of any outstanding rate (*R.* v. *Bluffield*, 29,
J. P. 245).   It may also be mentioned that any agreement or
contract made or entered into pursuant to the Highway Acts for
or relating to the making, maintaining, or repairing of highways
is subject to a 6*d.* stamp (33 & 34 Vict. c. 97 s. 3 and sched).

APPOINTMENT OF OFFICERS.

Power to
highway
board to
appoint
officers.

12. The highway board of a district shall, at their
first meeting or at some adjournment thereof, by
writing under their seal (*l*) appoint a treasurer, clerk,
and district surveyor (*m*); they may also at any meeting, if they think fit, appoint an assistant surveyor;
they may from time to time remove any of such
officers, and appoint others in the room of such as may

be so removed, or as may die or resign; they may also, Act '62, s. 12. out of any moneys in their hands, pay such salaries as they think reasonable to the clerk and district and assistant surveyor, and to the treasurer, if they think necessary : Provided that before the treasurer enter upon his office the board shall take sufficient security (*n*) from him for the due performance of the duties of his office; but no appointment, except the first, to any of the offices specified in this section, shall be made unless notice in writing has been sent to every member of the board (*o*).

(*l*) By 27 & 28 Vict. c. 101, s. 30, the appointment of any officer of the board may be made by a minute of the board, signed by the chairman and countersigned by the clerk of the board, and any appointment so made is as valid as if it were made under the seal of the board.

Nothing is said about stamp duty. But as the Stamp Act, 1870 (33 & 34 Vict. c. 97, s. 3 and sched), only imposes a duty on an "Admission and appointment or grant by *any writing*," it would seem that an appointment made merely by a minute of the board, and not by any separate written instrument delivered to the officer, is not subject to stamp duty at all. This does not, however, apply to the treasurer's security, which will be chargeable as a bond not specifically charged with any duty, or as a deed not described in the schedule, according to the nature of the security.

(*m*) Two or more boards may unite in appointing and paying the salary of a district surveyor (41 & 42 Vict. c. 77, s. 6).

(*n*) According to *R.* v. *Patterson*, 4 B. & Ad. 9, it seems that the taking security is not a condition precedent to the treasurer's enjoyment of the office, or to his liability to account for moneys received by virtue of his office, but that the appointment is complete without such security being given.

(*o*) If the board make default in appointing either a treasurer, clerk, or district surveyor, within three months after the day fixed for the first meeting, or after a vacancy, the quarter sessions may appoint, and fix the salary to be paid (27 & 28 Vict. c. 101, s. 45).

13. Not more than one office of treasurer, clerk, and Two Offices district or assistant surveyor of the same highway not to be held by the

Act '62, s. 13. board shall be held by the same person, or by persons
same   in partnership with each other, or by persons in the
person.   relation of employer and clerk, agent, or servant, one
of the other, or of the partner of either of them; and
if any person accepts or holds the office of treasurer,
clerk, or district or assistant surveyor, contrary to this
provision, he shall be liable to a penalty not exceeding £50 (*p*).

(*p*) There is a similar provision in 9 & 10 Vict. c. 95, s. 28,
against conjoining the offices of clerk, treasurer, and bailiff of a
county court, and the same penalty attached to the offence by
sect. 30. As to the general principle regulating the effect of
appointments to incompatible offices, see *R.* v. *Patterson,* 4 B. &
Ad. 9.

Duties of   **14.** The treasurer of each highway board shall
treasurer.   receive, and hold to the account of such board, all
moneys paid to or for the use of such board, and shall
make payments thereout under orders of such board,
and shall once in every three months, on or at such
days or times as the board may direct, or oftener if required by the board, make up an account of all moneys
received and paid by him, and deliver the same to the
clerk of the board.

Duties of   **15.** The clerk of every highway board shall in
clerk.   person, or by such deputy (*q*) as may be allowed by
such board, attend all meetings of the board, and shall
conduct the correspondence thereof, and enter and
keep in books to be provided for the purpose, notes,
minutes, or copies, as the case may require, of the
meetings, acts, orders, resolutions, proceedings, and
correspondence of such board, and shall keep all books,
papers, and documents committed to his charge, and
shall perform all such other duties as the board may
direct.

(*q*) This does not enable the board to appoint a deputy-clerk, but merely authorizes the clerk to attend and conduct correspondence, &c., by deputy, provided such deputy be allowed by the board.

In complaints for non-repair of highways the board may appear before the justices at petty sessions by their clerk (sect. 18, *infra*), and any summons, &c., required to be served upon the board, may be given personally to him (sect. 42 (6) *infra*).

16. The district surveyor shall act as the agent of the board in carrying into effect all the works and performing all the duties by this Act required to be carried into effect or to be performed by the board, and he shall in all respects conform to the orders of the board in the execution of his duties (*r*), and the assistant surveyor, if any, shall perform such duties as the board may require, under the direction of the district surveyor.

Duties of District Surveyor.

(*r*) The board may appear by their district surveyor before justices at petty sessions on complaints for non-repair of highways (sect. 18, *infra*), and any summons, &c., required to be served upon the board, may be given personally to him (sect. 42 (6), *infra*). He is exempt from turnpike tolls when executing or proceeding to execute his duties (sect. 37, *infra*), but is liable to action for an unlawful act, although done in obedience to the orders of the board (*Mill* v. *Hawker*, L. R. 9 Ex. 309 ; 10 Ex. (Ex. Ch.) 92, *supra*, p. 91, note (*y*).

WORKS AND DUTIES OF BOARD

17. The highway board shall maintain in good repair the highways (*s*) within their district, and shall, subject to the provisions of this Act, as respects the highways in each parish within their district, perform the same duties, have the same powers, and be liable to the same legal proceedings as the surveyor of such parish would have performed, had, and been liable to if this Act had not passed. It shall be the duty of the district surveyor to submit to the board at their first meeting in every year an estimate of the expenses likely to be incurred during the ensuing year for main-

Board to maintain highways.

Act '62, s. 17. taining and keeping in repair the highways in each parish within the district of the board, and to deliver a copy of such estimate as approved or modified by the board so far as the same relates to each parish to the waywarden of such parish.

(*s*) The board may repair any driftway or private carriage or occupation road which has been declared to be a public highway under sect. 36 (*infra*), and may contract to repair highways for the repair of which other parties are liable (27 & 28 Vict. c. 101, s. 22). This section, too, combined with the 11th (*supra*), enables the board to license a gas company to open the highway and lay down gas pipes; and to recover the sum agreed to be paid for the grant of such license. (*Edgeware Highway Board v. Harrow Gas Company*, L. R. 10 Q. B. 92, 38 J. P. 806).

The board are also liable to contribute to the repair of any turnpike road within their district under the same circumstances under which an order may be made on the parish surveyor in pursuance of 4 & 5 Vict. c. 59 (26 & 27 Vict. c. 94, s. 1). They are also liable to maintain so much as lies within their district of any highway which within seven years previous to 9th August, 1870, or since that date, has ceased to be a turnpike road (33 & 34 Vict. c. 73, s. 10). They may also, if they think fit, either repair or contribute to the repair of a turnpike road within their district, notwithstanding that no order of contribution may have been made upon them in pursuance of 26 & 27 Vict. c. 94, s. 1 (35 & 36 Vict. c. 85, s. 14). And, for the purpose of facilitating the abolition of tolls, they may agree with the trustees of any turnpike road within their district to take upon themselves the maintenance and repair of such road, or so much of it as is within their district (35 & 36 Vict. c. 85, s. 15). Moreover, where by any Annual Turnpike Acts Continuance Act it is or shall be provided that no money shall be expended in the repair of any turnpike road, such turnpike road shall be deemed to be a highway, and shall be repairable as such; and if it pass through any highway district, the cost of maintaining such highway shall be charged on the district fund (37 & 38 Vict. c. 95, s. 10.)

Proceedings where roads are out of repair.

18. Where complaint is made to any justice of the peace that any highway within the jurisdiction of the highway board is out of repair, the justice shall issue two summonses, the one addressed to the highway board and the other to the waywarden of the parish liable to the repair of such highway, requiring such board Act '62, s. 18. and waywarden to appear before the justices at some petty sessions, in the summons mentioned, to be held in the division where such highway is situate; and at such petty sessions, unless the board undertake to repair the road to the satisfaction of the justices, or unless the waywarden deny the liability (*t*) of the parish to repair, the justices shall direct the board to appear at some subsequent petty sessions to be then named, and shall either appoint some competent person to view the highway, and report to them on its state at such other petty sessions, or fix a day, previous to such petty sessions, at which two or more of such justices will themselves attend to view the highway.

At such last-mentioned petty sessions, if the justices are satisfied either by the report of the person so appointed, or by such view as aforesaid, that the highway complained of is not in a state of complete repair, it shall be their duty to make an order on the board limiting a time for the repair of the highway complained of; and if such highway is not put in complete and effectual repair by the time limited in the order, the justices in petty sessions shall appoint some person to put the highway into repair, and shall by order direct that the expenses of making such repairs, together with a reasonable remuneration to the person appointed for superintending such repairs, and amounting to a sum specified in the order, together with the costs of the proceedings, shall be paid by the board; and any order made for the payment of such costs and expenses may be removed into the Court of Queen's Bench, in the same manner as if it were an order of general or quarter sessions, and be enforced accordingly (*u*).

All expenses so directed to be paid by the board in
respect of the repairs of any highway shall be deemed
to be expenses incurred by the board in repairing such
highway, and shall be recovered accordingly (*w*).

The highway board may appear before the justices
at petty sessions by their district surveyor or clerk, or
any member of the board.

(*t*) If the waywarden appears and denies, *bonâ fide*, that the
road is a highway it seems from *Reg.* v. *Odell*, 34 J. P. 534, that
the justices ought not to proceed further in the matter.   In that
case the Court of Queen's Bench decided that if the waywarden
appears before the justices and denies that the road is a highway,
and that point is *bonâ fide* disputed, and the justices overrule the
objection to their jurisdiction, the court will review the finding.
of the justices, and if satisfied that their decision was wrong on
the question of highway or no highway, will quash any order
which they may have made upon the highway board directing
them to repair.

In the previous case of *Reg.* v. *Farrer*, L. R. 1 Q. B. 558, 30 J. P.
469, it had been decided that the jurisdiction of justices under
this and the following section is limited to admitted highways.
It appears, too, from *Milton* v. *Faversham*, 31 J. P. 341, that in
the event of the justices dismissing a complaint of this description a case may be stated for the opinion of the Court of Queen's
Bench under 20 & 21 Vict. c. 43.   In that case the justices were
of opinion that the obligation to repair certain roads, which were
admitted highways and out of repair, had not been established to
their satisfaction, because the roads in question formed part of the
town of Milton, and were repairable by the town commissioners
under a local Act, and consequently formed no part of the highway district of Faversham.   They, therefore, dismissed the complaint, but stated a case for the opinion of the Court of Queen's
Bench as to the correctness of their conclusions.   The court, after
laying down the principle on which the justices should proceed,
remitted the case back to them to be decided according to the
principle so laid down.

(*u*) The removal will be by order of the court or judge at.
chambers under 12 & 13 Vict. c. 45, s. 18, and 36 & 37 Vict.
c. 66, ss. 16, 34.   See *Foot's* Commentary on the Quarter Sessions Procedure Act, p. 67, where both the procedure and practice are explained at length.

(*w*) The words " and shall be recovered accordingly," appear to
be virtually repealed by 41 & 42 Vict. c. 77, s. 7, after the 25th
March, 1879, so far as relates to expenses to be paid by any
parish.   They refer to the 20th section (subsequently repealed.

and, substantially, re-enacted by 27 & 28 Vict. c. 101, s. 32), Act'62 s.18. under which the expense of repairing highways was to be "a separate charge on each parish." But by 41 & 42 Vict. c. 77, s. 7, the expense of repairing highways incurred by a highway board, on and after the 25th March, 1879, is to be "deemed to have been incurred for the common use and benefit of the several parishes within their district, and shall be charged on the district fund." Such expenses, therefore, after that date, can no longer be charged to the parish, and consequently cannot be "recovered" from it.

19. When on the hearing of any such summons When obligation to repair is disputed. respecting the repair of any highway, the liability (*x*) to repair is denied by the waywarden on behalf of his parish, or by any party charged therewith (*y*), the justices shall direct a bill of indictment to be preferred, and the necessary witnesses in support thereof to be subpœnaed, at the next assizes to be holden in and for the said county, or at the next general quarter sessions of the peace for the county, riding, division, or place wherein such highway is situate, against the inhabitants of the parish (*z*), or the party charged therewith (*y*), for suffering and permitting the said highway to be out of repair; and the costs (*a*) of such prosecution shall be paid by such party to the proceedings as the court before whom the case is tried shall direct, and if directed to be paid by the parish (*b*) shall be deemed to be expenses incurred by such parish in keeping its highways in repair, and shall be paid accordingly.

(*x*) This only applies when the fact of the road being a highway is admitted, and merely the liability to repair is denied. In *Reg.* v. *Farrer*, L. R. 1 Q. B. 558, 30 J. P. 469, it was held that if the fact of the road being a highway is denied, the justices have no power to order a bill of indictment to be filed at the assizes or sessions against the parish. But if the fact of highway is admitted, and the only question is whether the road is out of repair, or some other person is liable to the repairs, then the justices must make the order. And in *Reg.* v. *Odell*, 34 J. P. 534, the Court of Queen's Bench quashed an order of justices in

Act '62, s. 19. special sessions (ordering a highway board to repair) on the simple ground that the justices had wrongly decided that a road was a highway, and had overruled the waywarden's *bonâ fide* contention that the road was not a highway.

It seems very doubtful, however, whether this or the 18th section will be available after the 25th March, 1879, in any case where it is not sought to charge some other party than the parochial authority with the repairs. It is evident from the power given to the waywarden in the 18th section to " deny the liability of *the parish* to repair," and to the board to charge the expense of repairs *to the parish;* coupled with the provision in this (the 19th) section that if on the hearing of the summons " the liability to repair is denied by the waywarden *on behalf of his parish,*" the justices shall direct an indictment to be preferred, and that if the costs of the prosecution are directed " *to be paid by the parish,*" they shall be deemed to be expenses " *incurred by such parish in keeping its highways in repair,*" that the whole machinery provided by these sections proceeds upon the assumption that the parish is liable to maintain its own highways.

But after the 25th March, 1879, the expense of repairs will be no longer payable by the parish, but will be paid out of the district fund (41 & 42 Vict. c. 77, s. 7). Consequently the groundwork for the procedure fails, and the provisions of the sections will no longer be applicable when the highway board are the only parties chargeable with the repair of the highway in question. In that case, it would seem that recourse must be had to the new provisions in 41 & 42 Vict. c. 77, s. 10, as superseding those contained in the 18th and 19th sections of the Highway Act, 1862, in all cases where it is sought to make the highway board liable for repairs.

(*y*) The words " or by any person charged therewith " appear to have been inserted here by mistake, inasmuch as the words " *such* summons*"* to which the hearing applies, evidently refer to the summons mentioned in sect. 18, viz., a summons to the highway board or to the waywarden of the parish only. Similar words are found in 5 & 6 Will. 4 c. 50, s. 95; but, then, express provision is made in sect. 94 for summoning any other person than the surveyor, " chargeable with such repairs." No corresponding provision is made in sect. 18 of this Act, and therefore there is no " party charged therewith " to whom the 19th section can apply.

This view is confirmed by the fact that sect. 34, which provides for the recovery of expenses against such a party, as originally drawn, expressly required that the highway should be adjudged to be out of repair " in the manner provided *by the Principal Act.*" This was altered by 27 & 28 Vict. c. 101, s. 23, by substituting the words " in manner provided *by the Highway Act,* 1862," but no power was given to summon the party charged with the repair. Consequently, so far as *he* was concerned, the case remained the same as before, and it seems to·

follow that any proceedings against him must still be taken Act '62, s. 19.
under 5 & 6 Will. 4, c. 50, ss. 94, 95, and not under sects. 18 & 19
of this Act, unless the highway board, after an order for repair
under sect. 18, direct their surveyor to repair the highway, and
then summon the party under sect. 34, as amended by 27 & 28
Vict. c. 101, s. 23.

(z) In the case of an indictment preferred by the county
authority under 41 & 42 Vict. c. 77, s. 10, it will not be preferred
against " the inhabitants of the parish," but against " the defaulting authority," i.e., the highway board.

(a) The court has no power to order costs where the jury find
a verdict of not guilty on the ground that the road is not a highway (*Reg.* v. *Buckland*, 34 L. J. *m.* 178, 29 J. P. 526), nor where
the prosecutor fails to make out that the road is a highway of that
kind as to which the indictment was ordered (*Reg.* v. *Cleckheaton*,
29 J. P. 245 ; *Reg.* v. *Lee*, 45 L. J. *m.* 55, 40 J. P. 551).

(b) It would seem from 41 & 42 Vict. c. 77, s. 7 that after the
25th March, 1879, the court will no longer have power to direct
the costs to be paid by the parish (see notes (w) and (x) *supra*).

EXPENSES (c).

*   *   *   *   *   *   *

(c) Sects. 20 to 24, both inclusive, to which this heading applies,
were repealed by 27 & 28 Vict. c. 101, s. 32, and other provisions
made on the subject by that and the three following sections.

ACCOUNTS.

25. (d)   *   *   *   *   *   *

(d) This section was repealed by 27 & 28 Vict. c. 101, s. 36,
and other provisions made as to the making up of accounts.

26. (e)   *   *   *   *   *   *

(e) This section was repealed by 27 & 28 Vict. c. 101, s. 36,
and other provisions as to appeal against items of expense and
expenditure, &c., made by sect. 38.

27. (f) The clerk to every highway board shall, Clerk of
highway
within such thirty days after the said audit transmit such board to
transmit
statement to one of Her Majesty's principal Secretaries statement to
of State; and any such clerk who shall not within the Secretary of
State.
time aforesaid transmit the said statement to the said Penalty for
neglect.
Secretary of State shall for every such offence, upon a

Act '62, s. 27. summary conviction for the same before two justices of the peace, be liable to a penalty not exceeding £10.

Abstract of statements to be laid before Parliament.

28. (*f*) The Secretary of State shall cause the statements so transmitted to be abstracted, and the abstracts thereof to be laid before both House of Parliament, with the other statements in relation to highways required to be abstracted and laid before Parliament by the Act 12 & 13 Vict. c. 35.

(*f*) Sects. 27 and 28 appear to be virtually repealed by 27 & 28 Vict. c. 101, s. 36, and 41 & 42 Vict. c. 77, s. 9.

Secretary of State may cause form of statement to be prepared.

29. (*g*) It shall be lawful for one of Her Majesty's principal Secretaries of State to cause to be prepared such forms for such statement as he may from time to time deem suitable, and also from time to time alter the forms for the annual statement prescribed by the said Act 12 & 13 Vict. c. 35, but no statement shall be transmitted under that Act concerning parishes wholly within a highway district under this Act.

(*g*) Part of this section, viz., from "to cause" to "and also," both inclusive, appears to be virtually repealed by 27 & 28 Vict. c. 101, s. 36, and 41 & 42 Vict. c. 77, s. 9. A similar provision is made by the former of those sections, which is still in force, excepting that the powers conferred on the Secretary of State are transferred to the Local Government Board by 35 & 36 Vict. c. 79, s. 36.

30. (*h*) *   *   *   *   *   *

(*h*) This section, providing, for sending quarterly accounts to overseers, was repealed by 27 & 28 Vict. c. 101, s. 36.

Officers appointed by highway board to account to them when required.

31. All officers appointed by the highway board shall, as often as required by them, render to them or to such persons as they appoint a true, exact, and perfect account in writing under their respective hands, with the proper vouchers, of all moneys which they may respectively to the time of rendering such accounts have received and disbursed on account or by reason of their respective offices, and in case any money so Act '62, s. 31. received by any such officer remains in his hands, the same shall be paid to the board, or to such person or persons as they in writing under their hands empower to receive the same; and if any officer refuses or wilfully neglects to render and give such account, or to deliver up such vouchers, or for the space of fourteen days after being thereunto required by the board refuses or wilfully neglects to give up to them or to such person or persons as they appoint all books, papers, writings, tools, and things in his hands, custody, or power relating to the execution of his office, it shall be lawful for any justice of the peace for the county where the officer so making default is or resides, upon application made to him for that purpose by or on behalf of the board, to make inquiry of and concerning any such default as aforesaid in a summary way, as well by the confession of the party as by the testimony of any credible witness or witnesses upon oath, and by warrant under his hand and seal to cause such money as may appear to him to be due and unpaid to be levied by distress and sale of the goods and chattels of such officer, rendering to him the overplus (if any) on demand, after payment of the money remaining due and deducting the charges and expenses of making such distress and sale; and if sufficient distress cannot be found, or if it appears to any such justice in manner aforesaid that any such officer has refused or wilfully neglected to give such account, or to deliver up all books, papers, writings, tools, matters, and things in his custody or power relating to the execution of his office, the justice shall commit him to the house of correction or common gaol of the county where such offender is or resides, there to remain without bail until he gives a true and

Act '62, s. 31. perfect account and verifies the same in manner aforesaid, and produces and delivers up the vouchers relating thereto, and pays the money (if any) remaining in his hands as aforesaid according to the direction of the board, or has compounded with the board
for such money and paid such composition (which
composition the board are hereby empowered to make
and receive), or until he delivers up such books,
papers, and writings, tools, matters, and things as
aforesaid, or has given satisfaction to the board concerning the same; but no officer who may be committed on account of his not having sufficient goods
and chattels as aforesaid shall be detained in prison by
virtue of this Act for any longer time than six calendar
months.

SUPPLEMENTAL PROVISIONS.

Provision as
to extra-
parochial
places.

32. Where in pursuance of an Act, 20 Vict. c. 19,
*An Act for the Relief of the Poor in Extra-paro-
chial Places,* any place is declared to be a parish, or
where overseers of the poor are appointed for any
place, such place shall for the purposes of this Act be
deemed to be a parish separately maintaining its own
highways; and where in pursuance of the same Act
any place is annexed to any adjoining parish, or to
any district in which the relief of the poor is administered under a local Act, such place shall for the
purposes of this Act be deemed to be annexed to such
parish or district for the purposes of the maintenance
of the highways, as well as for the purposes in the
said Act mentioned (*i*).

(*i*) This section is confined to extra-parochial places included
in 20 Vict. c. 19, ss. 1, 4, 8. It does not apply to extra-parochial places incorporated with adjoining parishes by 31 & 32
Vict. c. 122, s. 27. But as the latter places are thereby

"annexed to and incorporated with" such parishes "*for all* Act '62, s. 22. *civil parochial purposes*," it seems that they are annexed to such parishes "for the purposes of the maintenance of the highways" just as much as they would have been if they had been included in this section.

The section, however, does not subject extra-parochial places to the common law liability of indictment for non-repair of highways. It only subjects them to the operation of 25 & 26 Vict. c. 61, as highway parishes liable to be put into a highway district, but does not render the inhabitants of such places liable to be separately indicted for the non-repair of any highways within it (*Reg* v. *Central Wingland*, 2 Q. B. D. 849, 41 J. P. 711).

By 27 & 28 Vict. c. 101, s. 9, justices in petty sessions are enabled to appoint overseers, and otherwise deal with any extra-parochial place with a view to constituting it a highway parish or part of a highway parish in the same manner as they may deal with it under 20 Vict. c. 19, for the purpose of constituting it a place or part of a place maintaining its own poor.

33. Where part of a parish is not contiguous to the parish of which it is a part, such outlying part may at the discretion of the justices be annexed (*k*) to a district, and, when so annexed, it shall for all the purposes of the Highway Acts be deemed to be a parish separately maintaining its own highways.

Provision for outlying part of parishes.

(*k*) This provision appears to have been suggested by 20 Vict. c. 19, s. 4, as to annexing extra-parochial places. But it is difficult to see how it can be carried out. The 39th section gives power to alter any district "by the addition of any parishes." But that seems to be confined to *entire* parishes, and not to apply to the annexing of a part. Beyond this there is no provision at all applicable to the case, and certainly none which applies to "annexing" part of a parish.

34. Where any highway which any body politic or corporate or person is liable to repair by reason of tenure of any land, or otherwise howsoever, shall be adjudged in the manner provided by the Principal Act (*l*) to be out of repair, the highway board of the district in which such highway is situate may, if they see fit, direct their surveyor to repair the same, and the

Expenses of repair of highways may be recovered from party liable to repair ratione tenure.

Act '62, s. 34. expenses to be incurred in such repair shall be paid by the party liable to repair as aforesaid; and it shall be lawful for any justice, upon the application of any person authorized in this behalf by the highway board, to summon the party liable to pay such expenses to appear before two justices at a time and place to be named in such summons, and upon the appearance of the parties, or in the absence of either of them, it shall be lawful for such justices to hear and determine the matter, and make such order (*m*), as well as to costs or otherwise, as to them may seem just.

(*l*) By 27 & 28 Vict. c. 101, s. 23, the words "the Highway Act, 1862," are substituted for "the Principal Act." Consequently before any expenses can be recovered under this section an order for repair must have been made on the highway board under sect. 18. As already explained (*supra*, note (*y*), p. 102) no power is given to summon the party charged with the repairs when the order is made upon the board. He will, therefore, have had no means of showing cause against its being made, and the only opportunity of disputing his liability will occur when he is summoned to pay the expenses. Even then he has no right of appeal, so that he will in this respect be worse off than if proceedings had been taken against him under 5 & 6 Will. 4, c. 50, ss. 94, 95; for it can hardly be contended that the requirement of adjudication of the highway being out of repair "*in the manner provided by* the Highway Act, 1862," gives power to summon him under sect. 18 of that Act, so as to give a right to dispute his liability under sect. 19. It will be observed that the board have complete discretion as to whether they will or will not direct their surveyor to repair the road. If they decline to repair they must then proceed against the party liable to repair for the penalty and order under 5 & 6 Will. 4, c. 50, s. 94.

(*m*) There is no appeal against the order. An appeal is given by sect. 47 where any sum adjudged to be paid in respect of penalties or moneys recoverable as penalties exceeds £5. But that clearly does not apply to the present case. The appeal given by 27 & 28 Vict. c. 101, is only given to ratepayers against rates under sect. 37, or to waywardens or ratepayers against items of expense and expenditure of the board under sect. 38. An order under this section evidently does not fall within either of those categories.

35. Where any person or corporation is liable, by Act '62, s. 35. reason of tenure of lands or otherwise, to repair any Highways repairable ratione tenure may be made repairable by the parish. highway situate in a highway district, the person or corporation so liable may apply to any justice of the peace for the purpose of making such highway a highway to be repaired and maintained by the parish in which the same is situate; and such justice shall thereupon issue summonses requiring the waywarden of such parish, the district surveyor, and the party so liable to repair such highway as aforesaid to appear before two or more justices in petty sessions assembled, and the justices at such petty sessions shall proceed to examine and determine the matter, and shall, if they think fit, make an order under their hands that such highway shall thereafter be a highway to be thereafter repaired and maintained by the parish, and shall in such order fix a certain sum to be paid by such person or corporation to the highway board of the district in full discharge of all claims thereafter in respect of the repair and maintenance of such highway (*n*); and in default of payment of such sum the board may proceed for the recovery thereof in the same manner as for the recovery of penalties or forfeitures recoverable under this Act (*o*): Provided always that when the sum so fixed to be paid in full discharge of all claims thereafter in respect of the repair and maintenance of such highway exceeds £50, the same, when received, shall be invested in the name of the highway board of the district in some public government securities, and the interest and dividends arising therefrom shall be applied by such board towards the repair and maintenance of the highways within the parish in which such highway is situate (*p*); but when such sum does not exceed £50 the same or any part thereof, at the discretion of such

Act '62, s. 35. highway board, shall from time to time be applied by such board towards the repair and maintenance of the highways within such parish (*p*): Provided that any person (*q*) aggrieved by any order of justices made in pursuance of this section may appeal to a court of general or quarter sessions holden within four months from the date of such order; but no such appeal shall be entertained unless the appellant has given to the other party to the case a notice in writing of such appeal, and of the matter thereof, within fourteen days after such order, and seven clear days at the least before such sessions, and has entered into a recognizance, with two sufficient sureties, before a justice of the peace conditioned to appear at the said sessions and to try such appeal, and to abide the judgment of the court thereupon, and to pay such costs as may be by the court awarded; and upon such notice being given, and such recognizance being entered into, the court at such sessions shall hear and determine the matter of the appeal, and shall make such order thereon, with or without costs to either party, as to the court may seem meet.

From and after the making of such order by the justices, or by the court on appeal, as the case may require, such highway shall be repaired in like manner and at the like expense as highways which a parish is liable to repair (*r*).

(*n*) Nothing is said about costs, but it is presumed that justices in their discretion may order them to be paid by the party liable to repair, under 11 & 12 Vict. c. 43, s. 18.

(*o*) Penalties and moneys recoverable as penalties are recoverable summarily before two or more justices under 11 & 12 Vict. c. 43. (See sect. 47, *post.*)

(*p*) It would seem that the parish will still be entitled to the benefit of such interest and dividends, &c., notwithstanding the fact that after the 25th March, 1879, the expense of maintaining highways is to be charged on the district fund under 41 &

42 Vict. c. 77, s. 7, instead of being a separate charge on each **Act '62, s. 35.** parish under 27 & 28 Vict. c. 101, s. 32. It is presumed that the case would fall within the last paragraph of the 33rd section of 27 & 28 Vict. c. 101, which enacts that all sums of money payable in pursuance of the precept of a highway board (including contribution to the district fund), shall be subject to all charges to which ordinary highway rates are subject by law.

(q) The right of appeal is confined to any "person" aggrieved, whereas the right of application for the order is given to any "person or corporation." It would seem, therefore, that a corporation has no power to appeal, and consequently that no appeal can be maintained by the highway board, although probably the waywarden may do so. In proceedings under 41 & 42 Vict. c. 77, the word "person" includes "a body of persons corporate or unincorporate" (sect. 38). But as there is no provision requiring the two Acts to be construed together it seems very doubtful whether the later Act obviates the difficulty.

(r) By 27 & 28 Vict. c. 101, s. 24, the highway board are enabled to apply for an order under this section in the same manner as the person or corporation liable to repair.

36. Where the inhabitants of any parish are de- **Provision as** sirous of undertaking the repair and maintenance of **out.** any driftway or any private carriage or occupation road, within their parish, in return for the use thereof, the district surveyor may, at the request of the inhabitants of such parish assembled in a vestry duly convened for the purpose, and with the consent in writing of the owner and the occupier of every part thereof, apply to the justices in petty sessions to declare such driftway or road to be a public highway to be repaired at the expense of the parish; and upon such application being made it shall be lawful for the justices to declare the same to be a public carriage road to be repaired at the expense of the parish.

37. No toll shall be demanded by virtue of any Act **Surveyor of** of parliament on any turnpike road from the surveyor **board ex-** of a highway board when executing or proceeding to **empted** execute his duties as such surveyor, and all provisions **pike to** 1 applicable to the exemptions in the Act 8 Geo. 4, c. 126,

Act '62, s. 37. shall apply to the case of the exemptions conferred by this enactment.

Limiting
jurisdiction
of justices.

38. No justice of the peace shall act as such in any matter in which he has already acted as a member of the highway board, and in which the decision of such board is appealed against (*s*),

(*s*) This section is virtually repealed by 27 & 28 Vict. c. 101, s. 46, so far as relates to any justice who is merely an *ex officio* member of a highway board, and acting as a justice at any petty or special or general quarter sessions.

Power to
alter high-
way dis-
tricts.

39. Any highway district formed under this Act may from time to time be altered by the addition of any parishes (*t*) in the same or in any adjoining county, or the subtraction (*u*) therefrom of any parishes (*w*), and new highway districts may be formed by the union of any existing highway districts, in the same or in any adjoining county, or any parishes forming part of any existing highway districts, or any highway district may be dissolved; but any such alteration of existing districts, or formation of new districts, or dissolution of any district, shall be made by provisional and final orders of the justices; and all the provisions of this Act with respect to the formation of highway districts and provisional and final orders of justices, and the notices to be given of and previously to the making of such orders, and all other proceedings relating to the formation of highway districts, shall, in so far as the same are applicable, extend to such alteration of existing or formation of new districts, or dissolution of districts, as is mentioned in this section; and in addition thereto provision shall be made, if necessary, in any orders of justices made under this section for the adjustment of any matters of account arising between parishes or parts of districts ın consequence of the exercise of the powers given by this section. Where any parish is added to or any district united with any district in another county, the final order of the justices of the county in which such parish or district is situate shall not be confirmed by them until they shall have received the approval (*x*) of their provisional order for such addition or union from the justices of the county in which the district is situate to or with which such addition or union is to be made. Where any highway district is dissolved, or where any parish is excluded from any highway district, the highways in such district or parish shall be maintained, and the provisions of the Principal Act in relation to the election of surveyors and to all other matters shall apply to the said highways, in the same manner as if such highways had never been included within the limits of a highway district (*y*).

Act '09, s. 39.

(*t*) *Quære* whether this section applies to "annexing" the outlying part of a parish under sect. 33, *ante*. It would seem not, as the word "parishes," it is presumed, is confined to entire parishes, and does not include part of a parish.

(*u*) See *Reg.* v. *JJ. of Cumberland*, 42 J. P. 361, as to the part which an *ex-officio* member of a highway board may take in opposing an order for separation.

(*w*) By 27 & 28 Vict. c. 101, s. 14, this section is extended to the "separation" of any townships, &c., separately maintaining their own highways, and consolidated by any previous order of justices, and to an alteration in the number of waywardens of any parish. Parishes, therefore, are to be " subtracted," and consolidated townships, &c., "separated," from the district. As to the costs of parishes applying to be removed, see 27 & 28 Vict. c. 101, s. 15.

(*x*) This approval must be testified by provisional and final orders of the justices. See 27 & 28 Vict. c. 101, s. 14.

(*y*) Where an alteration is made in part only of a highway district, the residue of the district is not affected thereby, but continues subject to the Highway Acts in the same manner as if no such alteration had been made (27 & 28 Vict. c. 101, s. 17).

ɪ

Act'62, s. 40.
Provision
in case of
failure of
board to
hold first
meeting.

40. If any highway board make default in holding its first meeting in pursuance of this Act (z), such board shall not thereupon become disqualified from acting, but the justices in general or quarter sessions shall, on the application of any persons liable to pay highway rates within the district, make such order as they think fit, for the holding of such board at some other time, and any order so made shall be deemed to be an order capable of being removed into the Court of Queen's Bench, in pursuance of the Act 12 & 13 Vict. c. 45, and may be enforced accordingly (a), and the costs of any application to the court of quarter sessions in pursuance of this section shall be defrayed out of the district fund of the board.

(z) This refers to sect. 6 (5), repealed by 27 & 28 Vict. c. 101, s. 10, which makes other provisions in lieu of that sub-section. As the latter Act is to be construed as one with the former (27 & 28 Vict. c. 101, s. 2), this provision applies to the failure to hold the first meeting under the latter Act, in the same manner as before such repeal it applied to the failure to hold the meeting pursuant to the former Act.

(a) The removal will be by order of the court or judge at chambers, under 12 & 13 Vict. c. 45, s. 18, and 36 & 37 Vict. c. 66, ss. 16, 34. See *Foot's* Commentary on the Quarter Sessions Procedure Act, p. 67, where both the procedure and practice are explained.

41. (b) Any parish or part of a parish included in a highway district may adopt the Local Government Act in the same manner and under the same circumstances in and under which it might have adopted the same if it had not been included in such district; and upon such adoption being made such parish or part of a parish shall cease to form part of such district, subject nevertheless to the payment of any contribution that may at the time of such adoption be due from such parish or part of a parish to the highway board.

(*b*) This section is virtually repealed by the repeal of 21 & 22 Act'62, s. 41. Vict. c. 98, by 38 & 39 Vict. c. 55, s. 343, and the consequent abolition of the power of adopting the Local Government Act (see also 38 & 39 Vict. c. 55, s. 5). In *Denver* v. *Kingston Highway Board*, 35 J. P. 696, the board were held liable for the cost of repairs executed during the period between the passing of the resolution to adopt the Local Government Act, and the date of its taking effect under 21 & 22 Vict. c. 98, s. 20.

APPLICATION OF PRINCIPAL ACT.

42. The following regulations shall be observed with respect to the construction of the Principal Act and this Act:— *Constructio of Principal Act and this Act.*

1. This Act shall be construed as one with the Principal Act so far as is consistent with the provisions of this Act (*c*):

2. The 9th section of the Principal Act, whereby it is enacted that a surveyor may be appointed by the inhabitants of a parish with a salary, shall not apply to any parish within any district formed under this Act:

3. The 10th section of the Principal Act, whereby it is enacted that the surveyor or surveyors at the time of passing his or their accounts as therein mentioned shall deliver to the justices a statement in writing of the name and residence of the person or persons appointed to succeed him or them as a surveyor or surveyors, shall not apply to any parish within any district formed under this Act:

4. The 13th, 14th, 5th, 16th and 17th sections of the Principal Act, providing for the formation of parishes into districts, and the 18th and 19th sections of the Principal Act, providing for the appointment of a board in large parishes, shall

not apply to any parish within any district
formed under this Act :

5. The penalty imposed by sect. 20 of the Principal
Act on the surveyor for neglect of duty shall
not apply to a highway board constituted under
this Act :

6. Any summons or notice, or any writ or any proceeding, at law or in equity, requiring to be
served upon (c) the board, may be served by
the same being left at or transmitted through
the post in a pre-paid letter directed to the
office of the board, or being given personally to the district surveyor or clerk of the
board :

7. The 35th section of the Principal Act, whereby
it is provided that the ratepayers of any parish
may divide amongst themselves the carriage
of materials in manner therein mentioned, shall
not apply to any parish within any district
formed under this Act :

8. The 39th, 40th, 43rd, 44th and 45th sections of
the Principal Act relating to the accounts of
surveyors, shall not apply to the highway
board of any district formed under this
Act.

(c) Consequently property which was exempt from the payment of highway rates under 5 & 6 Will. 4, c. 50, s. 33, still
continues exempt when the parish is included in a highway district (see *Reg.* v. *Heath,* L. R. 1 Q. B. 218, 30 J. P. 82, and
Carter v. *Wareham,* 30 J. P. 341).

(d) As to service of notices, &c., issued *by* the board, see 27 &
28 Vict. c. 101, s. 26.

43. On the formation of a highway district the following regulations shall be enacted with respect to the
surveyors and the highway board :—

1. No surveyor shall be appointed under the Prin-

cipal Act for any parish within such district:

2. The outgoing surveyor of every parish within the district shall continue in office until seven days after the appointment of the district surveyor by the highway board of the district of such outgoing surveyor (*e*), and no longer; and he may recover any highway rate made and then remaining unpaid, in the same manner as if this Act not been passed, and the money so recovered shall be applied, in the first place, in reimbursing any expenses incurred by him as such surveyor, and in discharging any debts legally owing by him on account of the highways within his jurisdiction, and the surplus (if any) shall be paid by him to the treasurer of the highway board; and he shall be entitled to receive from the highway board any sum (*f*) . . . which on the allowance of his account shall be found to be due to him as such surveyor after the collection and expenditure of the whole of the highway rate made in such parish during the last year:

3. The highway board shall, for all the purposes of the Principal Act except that of levying highway rates, be deemed to be the successor in office of the surveyor of every parish within the district.

(*e*) But the powers of the outgoing surveyor as to collecting rates continue until any outstanding rate is collected, and are not determined by the expiration of the seven day: *Reg.* v. *Bluffield*, 29 J. P. 245.

(*f*) The words "not exceeding £5," which were originally in the section, were virtually repealed by 27 & 28 Vict. c. 101, s. 28, and were afterwards actually repealed by the Statute Law Revision Act, 1875.

Provisions of Principal Act to be applicable to highways under local or personal Acts.

44. All the provisions of the Principal Act for widening, diverting, and stopping up (g) highways shall be applicable to all highways which now are or may hereafter be paved, repaired, or cleansed under or by virtue of any local or personal Act or Acts of Parliament, or which may be situate within the limits of any such Act or Acts, except highways which any railway company, or the owners, conservators, commissioners, trustees, or undertakers of any canal, river, or inland navigation, are liable by virtue of any Act of Parliament relating to such railway, canal, river, or inland navigation to make, maintain, repair, or cleanse.

(g) The provisions referred to are sects. 82 to 93, both inclusive.

Enabling councils of certain boroughs to adopt parish roads and highways and to apply rates for their repair.

45. Whereas there are in certain boroughs in *England* and *Wales* roads and highways that are now and have heretofore been repaired by the inhabitants of the several parishes or townships within which such roads and highways are situated, and who also contribute and pay to the general rates levied for the repair of the public streets, roads and highways maintained and kept in repair by the council of such boroughs, by reason whereof a great burthen is imposed upon the ratepayers of the said parishes and townships; and it being doubtful whether the council of such boroughs have the power to adopt such parish roads and highways, or to apply the rates collected in such boroughs in repairing the same: Be it enacted that it shall and may be lawful for the council of every such borough (h) in *England* and *Wales*, upon the petition of the majority of the ratepayers of such parishes or townships present at a public meeting duly convened, to adopt all or any of such parish roads and highways as the council shall in its discretion consider advisable, and to apply the rates levied and collected by the said council for the repair of the public streets, roads and highways within such borough in repairing and maintaining such parish roads and highways : Provided always, that it shall be competent for such council, previous to adopting such parish roads and highways, to require the provisions contained in any local Act applying to the public streets, roads, and highways of such borough to be complied with.

(*h*) The boroughs here referred to are such as are defined by 5 & 6 Will. 4, c. 76, or any places to which the provisions of that Act are extended (sect. 2, *ante*).

46. No person through whose land a highway passes, which is to be repaired by the parish, shall become liable for the repair of such highway by erecting fences between such highway and the adjoining land, if such fences are erected with the consent in writing of the highway board of the district within which such highway is situate in the case of a place within the jurisdiction of a highway board, and in the case of any other place with the consent (*i*) of the surveyor or other authority having jurisdiction over the highway.

(*i*) In the case of a highway board the consent must be "in writing ;" but in any other case than that of a highway district it seems that a parol consent is sufficient.

47. All penalties under this Act, and all moneys recoverable as penalties (*k*), may be recovered summarily before any two or more justices in the manner directed by the Act 11 & 12 Vict, c. 43, and any Act amending the same ; but where any sum adjudged to be paid under this Act in respect of such penalties or moneys exceeds £5, an appeal may be had by any person aggrieved to a court of general or quarter sessions in manner provided by the Act 24 & 25 Vict.

Act '62. s. 45.

District highway boards may permit landowners to erect fences without incurring liability to repair highways.

Recovery of penalties.

Act 24 & 25. c. 96, s. 110, *An Act to consolidate and amend the Statute Law of England and Ireland relating to larceny and other similar Offences.*

(k) This only applies to the recovery of penalties and of moneys recoverable as penalties. It does not extend to orders excepting in so far as is otherwise expressly provided.

SCHEDULE.

PROCEEDINGS OF HIGHWAY BOARDS (*l*).

*   ❖   *   ❖   *

FORM (A.)

NOTICE is hereby given, that at the Court of *General* or *Quarter* Sessions to be held on the   Day of   a Proposal will be made *to divide the County of Lincoln into Highway Districts* [or *to divide the Parts of Holland, in the County of Lincoln, into Highway Districts, or to constitute the County of Rutland a Highway District, or to constitute the Parishes of Alford, Castle Carey, and Lovington, in the County of Somerset, a Highway District*].

FORM (B.)

WHEREAS at a Court of *General* or *Quarter* Sessions, held on the   Day of   last, a Provisional Order was made in the Words following; that is to say, [*here set out the Provisional Order*].

Notice is hereby given, that the Confirmation of the said Provisional Order by a Final Order will be taken into consideration by the Justices at the Court of *General* or *Quarter Sessions* to be held on the Day of   next.

(*l*) These proceedings were repealed by 27 & 28 Vict. c. 101, s. 27, and other regulations contained in the 1st schedule to that Act were substituted for them.

HIGHWAY ACT, 1864.

27 & 28 VICT. c. 101.

An Act to amend the Act for the better Management of Highways in England.

[20th July, 1864.]

WHEREAS it is expedient to amend an Act, 25 & 26 Vict. c. 61, intituled An Act for the better Management of Highways in England: be it enacted by the Queen's most Excellent Majesty, by and with the advice and consent of the Lords spiritual and temporal, and Commons, in this present Parliament assembled, and by the authority of the same, as follows:— *25 & 26 Vict. c. 61.*

PRELIMINARY.

1. The Acts hereinafter mentioned may be cited for all purposes by the short titles following ; that is to say,— *Short titles of Highway Acts.*

The Act 5 & 6 Will. 4, c. 50, An Act to consolidate and amend the Laws relating to Highways in that part of Great Britain called England, by the short title of the Highway Act, 1835:

The said Act, 25 & 26 Vict. c. 61, by the short title of the Highway Act, 1862:

This Act by the short title of the Highway Act 1864.

All the above-mentioned Acts, and any Acts passed or to be passed amending the same, shall be included under the short title of the Highway Acts.

Act '64, s. 2.

This Act shall be construed with 25 & 26 Vict. c. 61.

2. This Act, so far as is consistent with the tenor thereof, shall be construed as one with the Highway Act, 1862.

Definition of " Poor Law Parish," " Highway Parish," " Highway Rate," and " County."

3. " Poor law parish " shall mean a place that separately maintains its own poor :

" Highway parish " shall mean a place that after the constitution of a highway district separately maintains its own highways, and is entitled to return a waywarden or waywardens to the highway board of the district :

" Highway rate " shall include any rate, whether poor rate or not, out of the produce of which moneys are payable in satisfaction of precepts of a highway board :

" County " shall include any division of a county that has a separate county treasurer.

AMENDMENTS AS TO ORDERS OF JUSTICES.

Amendment of sect. 6 of Highway Act of 1862.

4. Where more highway districts than one are comprised in any order of justices, whether provisional or final, and whether made before or after the passing of this Act, the formation of each of such districts is to be deemed independent of the formation of any other district, and the order shall for all purposes be construed and take effect as if a separate order had been made in respect of each district; and any variation in a provisional order altering the parishes in any one or more districts comprised in that order shall make that order provisional only as to the particular district or districts in which the alterations are made, and not as to any other district or districts included in the same order.

Certain places to be deemed

5. Any parish, township, tithing, hamlet, or other place having a known legal boundary in which there are no highways repairable at the expense of the place, or in which the highways are repaired at the expense of any person, body politic or corporate, by reason of any grant, tenure, limitation, or appointment of any charitable gift, or otherwise howsoever than out of a highway rate or other general rate, shall, for the purposes of the Highway Acts, be deemed to be a place separately maintaining its own highways (*m*). Act '64, s. 5. places separately maintaining their own highways.

Where part of a parish is, in pursuance of the Local Government Act, 1858, Amendment Act, 1861 (*n*), sect. 9, treated as forming part of a district constituted under the Local Government Act, 1858, for all purposes connected with the repair of highways and the payment of highway rates, but for no other purpose, such part shall, for the purposes of the Highway Act, 1862, and this Act, be deemed to be a place separately maintaining its own highways, and capable of being included in a highway district, without requiring the consent of the local board to be given.

Where the highways of one part of a parish are, in pursuance of a private Act of Parliament, repairable out of a different rate from that out of which the highways of the other part are repairable, each of such parts shall, for the purposes of the Highway Acts, be deemed to be a place separately maintaining its own highways.

(*m*) See *Reg.* v. *Gascoign*, 29 J. P. 389, where the district was formed before the passing of 27 & 28 Vict. c. 101, s. 6, and it was held that in a parish which included a town maintaining its own highways, but not co-extensive with the parish, the suburban part was a place separately maintaining its own highways, and that the waywarden ought to be appointed only by the inhabitants of that part, and not by the inhabitants of the whole parish. (See also 25 & 26 Vict. c. 61, ss. 32, 33.)

(*n*) This Act is now repealed by 38 & 39 Vict. c. 55, s. 343, subject, however, to the proviso that the repeal shall not affect (*inter alia*) "anything duly done or suffered," or "any right or liability acquired, accrued, or incurred" under the repealed enactment. It may also be noticed that the section in question only applied to "part of a *township or place,*" and not to "part of a *parish,*" as is mentioned above.

6. (*o*) * * * When it is proposed that only part of a county is to be constituted a highway district, not less than two out of the five justices making such proposal shall be resident in the said district, or acting in the petty sessional division in which such district or some part thereof is situate.

(*o*) The part omitted, repealing the proviso to 25 & 26 Vict. c. 61, s. 5, and making other provisions in lieu of it, is repealed by the Statute Law Revision Act, 1875, as spent.

7. The power given by section 7 of the Highway Act, 1862, of combining townships, tithings, hamlets, or places separately maintaining their own highways, and situate in a poor law parish, shall extend to combining any two or more of such townships, tithings, hamlets, or places, and any combination so formed shall for all the purposes of the Highway Acts be deemed to be a highway parish.

Where a township, tithing, hamlet, or other place separately maintaining its own highways is situate in two or more poor law parishes, each part of such township, tithing, hamlet, or other place may be combined with the parish in which that part is situate.

The justices may, by their provisional and final order, declare that any poor law parish within their jurisdiction, or residue of a poor law parish, after excluding such part, if any, as is prohibited by the Highway Act, 1862, either wholly or without the consent of the governing body, from being included in the highway district (*p*), shall henceforward become a highway parish; and upon such declaration being made such poor law parish, or residue of a poor law parish, shall thereafter be a highway parish entitled to return a waywarden or waywardens to the highway board of the district in which it is included; and no rate shall be separately levied for the maintenance of the highways, and no separate waywardens be elected in any township, tithing, hamlet, or other subdivision of such poor law parish or residue of a poor law parish.

Where, previously to the passing of the provisional order forming a highway district, no surveyors or waywardens have been elected within any highway parish in that district, and where the mode of electing a waywarden or waywardens in such parish is not provided by this Act or the Highway Act, 1862, the justices shall, by their provisional and final orders constituting the district, or by any subsequent provisional and final orders, make provisions for the annual election of a waywarden or waywardens for such parish (*q*).

(*p*) This refers to 25 & 26 Vict. c. 61, s. 7, and provides for the difficulty which appears to have been felt in *Reg.* v. *Gascoign*, 29 J. P. 389, *supra.*

(*q*) This appears to be an amendment of the 3rd regulation in 25 & 26 Vict. c. 61, s. 10, and in fact supersedes it.

8. Where a parish or place separately maintaining Provision for places its own highways is situate partly within and partly partly without the limits of a borough, the justices may by partly without their provisional and final orders include in a highway borough. district the outlying part of such parish or place; and where the outlying part of a parish or place situate as aforesaid has been, previously to the passing of this Act, or may be hereafter, included in a highway district, each part of such parish or place shall for all the purposes of the Highway Acts be deemed to be a

Act '64, s. 8. place separately maintaining its own highways; and a waywarden or waywardens shall be elected by the ratepayers in each such part at such time and in such manner as may be provided by the said justices (r).

(r) This appears to be a kind of supplement to the 2nd restriction in 25 & 26 Vict. c. 61, s. 7.

Power of justices as to extra-parochial places.

9. The justices in petty sessions may appoint overseers or otherwise deal with any extra-parochial place with a view to constituting it a highway parish or part of a highway parish in the same manner as the justices may deal with such place for the purpose of constituting it a place or part of a place maintaining its own poor, in pursuance of the powers for that purpose given by the Act 20 Vict. c. 19 (s).

(s) The object of this section appears to be to bring such places within the operation of sect. 33, *infra*, so as to enable the board to issue their precepts for contribution from those places.

Part of s. 6 of Highway Act of 1862 as to meetings of board repealed, and other provisions enacted.

10. (t) * * * The first meeting of the highway board (u) after the formation of a district shall be held at such time (w) as may be appointed by the provisional or final order of the justices, so that the time appointed be not more than seven days after the expiration of the time limited by law for the election of waywardens, or, in the case of a special day being appointed for such election as hereinafter mentioned, be not more than twenty-one days after that day.

The day appointed for the first meeting of the board shall for all the purposes of the Highway Acts be deemed to be the day of the formation of the district (x); and the surveyor for the time being of every parish within the district shall continue in office until

seven days after the appointment of the district sur- Act '64, s. 10.
veyor, and no longer (*y*).

(*t*) The part omitted, repealing the 5th paragraph in 25 & 26
Vict. c. 61, s. 6, and making other provisions in lieu of it, is
repealed by the Statute Law Revision Act, 1875, as spent.

(*u*) In *Reg.* v. *JJ. of Lindsey*, L. R. 1 Q. B. 648, 30 J. P.
86, the justices in their final order fixed the first meeting of the
highway board for the first Thursday after the 25th March, and
no day was specially fixed for the election of waywardens.
According to the custom of the parishes it had been usual to
elect highway surveyors on the 25th March, or within two or
three days thereafter. And it was *held* that the order was not
bad, though it did not provide for 14 days elapsing after the
25th March, but provided only for 5 clear days, though it would
have been better to have given more time.

(*v*) Nothing is said about the place of meeting, although that
was provided for by the repealed paragraph of 25 & 26 Vict. c.
61, s. 6, and is assumed in the proceedings of highway boards,
1. *a* (*post* p. 161) to be provided for by the justices' order.

(*x*) The board do not become disqualified from acting by
making default in holding the first meeting; but the justices in
quarter sessions, on the application of a ratepayer, may make
such order as they think fit for the holding of the board at some
other time (25 & 26 Vict. c. 61, s. 40).

(*y*) But he continues in office after the expiration of the 7
days for the purpose of recovering any outstanding rate (*Reg.* v.
Bluffield, 29 J. P. 245).

11. In forming a highway district under the High- Power to justices to bring Highway Act into operation on a particular day.
way Act, 1862, the justices may, for the purpose of
avoiding delay in bringing the Act into operation,
appoint by their final order a day (*z*) on which the
first election of waywardens as members of the highway board is to take place in the district.

On the day appointed for the election waywardens
shall be elected in every parish in the district entitled
to elect such officers by the same persons and in the
same manner by and in which waywardens are elected
under the Highway Act, 1862 (*a*), and all the provisions of the Highway Acts relating to the qualifications of surveyors or waywardens, and to the appoint-

ment of surveyors and waywardens by justices in the event of no election taking place, shall apply accordingly (*b*) ; but the waywardens elected under this section shall continue in office only (*c*) until the time at which the next annual election of surveyors would have taken place in the several parishes of the district if the same had not been constituted a highway district, and at that time new waywardens shall be elected in manner provided by the Highway Acts.

(*z*) It appears to be quite in the justices' discretion as to what day they will fix, the only limitation being that the first meeting of the board must be held not more than 21 days afterwards (see sect. 10).

(*a*) That is to say, by the persons and in the manner mentioned in 25 & 26 Vict. c. 61, s. 10.

(*b*) These matters are provided for by 5 & 6 Will. 4, c. 50, ss. 6, 7, 11, and 25 & 26 Vict. c. 61, s. 10.

(*c*) But now, by 41 & 42 Vict. c. 77, s. 11, they continue in office till the 30th April in the year following that in which they were elected, and on that day their successors come into office.

Publication of orders in Gazette made permissive. 12. No order of the justices forming a highway district shall be invalidated by reason of its not being published in the *London Gazette* (*d*) ; and where any reference is made in any section (*e*) of the Highway Act, 1862, to the date of the publication in the Gazette of the order, such section shall be construed as if the date of the making of the final order under which the district is formed were substituted for " the date of the publication in the Gazette of the order under which the district is formed ;" and any copy of the provisional or final order of the justices forming a highway district, certified under the hand of the clerk of the peace to be a true copy (*f*), shall be receivable in all courts of justice and in all legal proceedings as evidence of the formation of the district and of the matters in the said order mentioned.

(*d*) Publication in the *London Gazette* is required by 25 & 26
Vict. c. 61, s. 6 (6), but is made discretionary by this section.
  (*e*) This refers to 24 & 25 Vict. c. 61. s. 8.
  (*f*) This is an additional mode of proof to that provided by
25 & 26 Vict. c. 61, s. 8, which required the production of a copy
of the *London Gazette*.

13. Contiguous places situate in different counties ^{As to union of parishes in different counties.}
and places situate partly in one county and partly in
another county or counties (*g*) shall, for the purpose of
being united in one highway district, be deemed to be
subject to the jurisdiction of the justices of any county,
who may make a provisional and final order constituting them an highway district, in the same manner
as if all such places or parts of places were situate in
such last-mentioned county; subject to this proviso,
that the provisional and final orders of the justices of
the said county shall be of no validity unless provisional and final orders to the same effect are passed
either concurrently with or subsequently to the first-
mentioned provisional and final orders by the justices
of every other county in which any of the said places
or parts of places are situate.

(*g*) But by the third restriction in 25 & 26 Vict. c. 61, s. 7,
where a parish is situate in more than one county the whole of
such parish is to be deemed to be within the county within which
the church of such parish, or (if there be no church) the greater
part of such parish is situate.

14. The approval of the justices of any county to ^{Amendment of s. 39 of Highway Act, 1862.}
any provisional order made by the justices of another
county affecting any place in such first-mentioned
county, in pursuance of section 39 of the Highway
Act, 1862, shall be testified by provisional and final
orders of the justices of the said first-mentioned
county (*h*).
The powers conferred on justices by section 39 of the
Highway Act, 1862, shall be deemed to extend to the

Act 64, s. 14. separation of any townships, tithings, hamlets, or places separately maintaining their own highways which may have been consolidated by any previous order of the justices, and to an alteration in the number of way-wardens of any parish (*i*).

(*h*) This refers to that part of 25 & 26 Vict. c. 61, s. 39, which relates to the addition of any parish to, or the union of any district with, a district in another county; and requires the "approval" of the justices of the county in which the district is situate to or with which such addition or union is to be made, before the final order of the justices of the county in which such parish or district is situate is confirmed.

(*i*) The power of subtraction under 25 & 26 Vict. c. 61, s. 39, only applied to "parishes," including places maintaining their own highways (*Id.* s. 3). This section extends its operation to the "separation of any townships," &c., which had been consolidated by previous order under the 7th section of that Act, and had, therefore, ceased to maintain their own highways; and also enables the justices to alter the number of waywardens of a parish, a matter which had not been provided for by sect. 39.

As to the costs of parishes applying to be removed from one district to another.

15. Where, after the formation of an highway district, an application is made by any parish in that district to any court of general or quarter sessions, praying that the said parish may be removed from that district, all costs incidental to or consequential on such application and the removal of the said parish shall, unless the court otherwise directs, be paid by the parish that has made the application in such manner as the said court may direct. The amount of such costs shall be raised in the same manner as if they were expenses incurred in maintaining and keeping in repair the highways of that parish (*k*).

(*k*) If the application is granted, and the parish removed from the district, these costs will be payable out of the highway rate under 5 & 6 Will. 4, c. 50, s. 27 (25 & 26 Vict. c. 61, s. 39, last par.). But if the application is refused, the costs will be payable by the parish under sects. 32, 33, *infra*, until the 25th March, 1879. After that date the costs, on refusal of the application, will be charged on the district fund under 41 & 42 Vict. c. 77, s. 7.

16. No order of the justices forming a highway Act '64, s. 16. district, whether made before or after the passing of As to validity of order of justices. this Act, shall be void by reason that it includes in such district a place which the justices are not entitled to include under the provisions of this Act or the Highways Act, 1862, or one of such Acts; and any order containing such prohibited place shall be construed and take effect as if that place had not been mentioned therein.

All expenses properly incurred by the justices of any county in maintaining the validity of any provisional or final order made by them shall be payable out of the county rate of that county.

17. All powers and jurisdictions vested in justices Extent of powers of justices. by the Highway Act, 1862, and this Act, or either of such Acts, may from time to time be exercised in relation to highway districts, highway boards, and highway parishes already formed, as well as upon the occasion of forming new highway districts, boards, or parishes; and where an alteration is made in part only of a highway district the residue of that district shall not be affected thereby, but shall continue subject to the Highway Acts in the same manner as if no such alteration had been made (*l*).

(*l*) As to the effect of such alteration upon any parish excluded from a district, see 25 & 26 Vict. c. 61, s. 39, last par. And as to the effect of an alteration of boundaries of a district, see 41 & 42 Vict. c. 77, s. 5 (2).

18. The expression "provisional and final order," as Definition of "provisional and final orders." used in this Act, shall mean a provisional and final order passed and published in manner provided by this Act and the Highway Act, 1862, with the necessary variations as to notices and otherwise (*m*).

(*m*) See 25 & 26 Vict. c. 61, ss. 5, 6, 8; and 27 & 28 Vict. c. 101, s. 12, *ante*.

MISCELLANEOUS AMENDMENTS.

Appoint-
ment and
vote of
waywardens.

19. Every waywarden, before taking his seat as a·
member of a highway board, shall produce a certificate
of his having been duly elected or appointed a waywarden, and such certificate shall, in the case of an
elected waywarden, be signed by the chairman of the
vestry or other meeting at which he was elected; and
in the case of a waywarden appointed by justices, be
signed by the justices making the appointment (*n*).

A waywarden may sit as such for more places than
one, but he shall be entitled to one vote only as waywarden.

(*n*) As to the regulations respecting the election of waywardens, see 25 & 26 Vict. c. 61, s. 10.

Power to
waywardens
to contract
for supply or
cartage of
materials.

20. Whereas doubts are entertained whether section
46 of the Highway Act of 1835 (*o*) applies to a highway
district: Be it enacted, that that section shall not
apply to the highway board of any highway district or
to any parish within any highway district.

Notwithstanding anything contained in the Act
26 & 27 Vict. c. 61 (*p*), or in any other Act, any waywarden may contract for the supply or cartage of
materials within the parish for which he is waywarden,
with the license of two justices assembled at petty sessions; such license to be granted on the application of
the clerk of the highway board, who must be authorized to make such application by a resolution of his
board assembled at a meeting of which notice has been
given.

(*o*) This section enacts that the surveyor, with the consent of
the inhabitants in vestry, may contract for purchasing, getting,
and carrying the materials for the repair of the highway; and

that if he has any part, share, or interest, directly or indirectly, in any contract or bargain for work or materials to be made, done, or provided, &c., &c., or upon his own account, directly or indirectly, uses or lets to hire any team, or uses or sells, or disposes of any materials, &c., &c. (unless a written license from two justices for the sale of such materials, or letting to hire such team, be first obtained), he shall forfeit, on conviction, £10, &c., &c.

In *Wakefield* v. *Senechall*, 29 J. P. 375, it was held that a surveyor of highways who does repairs to the roads without the consent of the vestry, doing the work himself without a certificate from two justices, is not entitled to be repaid the cost of the materials supplied, or labour employed in doing such repairs.

(*p*) This Act, after reciting that it is expedient that waywardens appointed under 25 & 26 Vict. c. 61, should be prevented from contracting for any works to be executed under the said Act within their own districts, enacts:—

1. No such waywarden shall, directly or indirectly, in his own name or in the name of any other person or persons, contract for the repair of any road, or for any other work to be executed under the provisions of the said recited Act within the parish for which he is elected waywarden, or within any other parish in the same district, under the pain of forfeiting the sum of £10, with full costs of such suit, to any person or persons who shall sue for the same by action for debt in any county court within the jurisdiction of which the parish in which the roads to be repaired, or the work so contracted for, is situate.

2. It shall not be lawful for any highway board to pay knowingly for any repair or work so contracted for; and any money paid by any board under any such contract shall be recoverable by them, with full costs, from the person or persons to whom the same shall have been paid, by action of debt in any of Her Majesty's Courts of Record at Westminster, if the same shall amount to above £50, or in any county court as aforesaid if below that amount; and the balance so recovered, after paying all expenses, shall be placed to the credit of the district fund.

3. This Act shall be construed with and held to be part of the said recited Act for the better management of highways in England.

21. (*q*) When any highway board consider any highway unnecessary for public use, they may direct the district surveyor to apply to two justices to view the same, and thereupon the like (*r*) proceedings shall be had as where application is made under the Highway Act, 1835, to procure the stopping up any highway, save

Provisions for discontinuance of maintenance of unnecessary highways.

Act '64, s. 21. only that the order to be made thereupon, instead of directing the highway to be stopped up, shall direct that the same shall cease to be a highway which the parish is liable to repair, and the liability of the parish shall cease accordingly; and for the purpose of such proceedings under this enactment, such variation shall be made in any notice, certificate, or other matter preliminary to the making of such order as the nature of the case may require: Provided that if at any time thereafter, upon application of any person interested in the maintenance of such highway, after one month's previous notice in writing thereof to the clerk of the highway board for the district in which such highway is situated, it appear to any court of general or quarter sessions of the peace that from any change of circumstances since the time of the making of any such order as aforesaid under which the liability of the parish to repair such highway has ceased the same has become of public use, and ought to be kept in repair by the parish, they may direct that the liability of the parish to repair the same shall revive from and after such day as they may name in their order, and such liability shall revive accordingly as if the first-mentioned order had not been made; and the said court may by their order direct the expenses of and incident to such application to be paid as they may see fit.

(q) But now, see 41 & 42 Vict. c. 77, s. 24, which appears to virtually repeal this section by the introduction of a new mode of procedure inconsistent with its provisions. (See *Ex parte Baker*, 26 L. J. m. 164, 21 J. P. 486; *Whiteley* v. *Heaton*, 27 L. J. m. 217, 22 J. P. 161; *Michell* v. *Brown*, 28 L. J. m. 55, 23 J. P. 548.)

(r) This includes the right of appeal under 5 & 6 Will. 4, c. 50, s. 88 (*Reg.* v. *JJ. of Surrey*, L. R. 5 Q. B. 87, 34 J. P. 199); and the affixing of proper notices under sect. 85 of the same Act (*Reg.* v. *JJ. of Surrey*, L. R. 5 Q. B. 466, 34 J. P. 614.)

In the latter case it was also decided that a party aggrieved by an order of justices at quarter sessions under sect. 91 of the same Act, is entitled, *en debito justiciæ*, to apply for a *certiorari* to quash the order.

22. The highway board of any district may from time to time contract for any time not exceeding three years with any person or body of persons, corporate or unincorporate, to repair any highways, turnpike roads, or roads over county or other bridges, or any part thereof, for the repairing of which such persons or body of persons are liable; and any persons or body of persons liable to repair any roads may contract with the highway board for the repairing any highways, inclusive as aforesaid (*s*), or any part thereof, which the highway board is liable to make or repair; and the money payable under any contract made in pursuance of this section shall be raised in the same manner and be paid out of the same rates (*t*) as would have been applicable to defray the expenses of the repair of such highways if no contract had been made in respect thereto.

Highway board may contract to repair highways for the repair of which other parties are liable.

(*s*) These words seem to refer to "turnpike roads or roads over county or other bridges." The board may also, by sect. 52, contract, for not exceeding three years, for purchasing, getting, and carrying materials for repairing, and also for maintaining and keeping in repair any highways within their district. The contract requires a 6*d.* stamp. (See 33 & 34 Vict. c. 97, s. 3, and sched., tit. "Agreement or Contract"). The board may also recover in a summary manner for extraordinary weight or traffic under 41 & 42 Vict. c. 77, s. 23.

(*t*) See sect. 33.

23. Section 34 of the Highway Act, 1862, shall be construed as if, instead of the words "shall be adjudged in the manner provided by the Principal Act to be out of repair," the words were substituted, "shall be adjudged in manner provided by the Highway Act, 1862, to be out of repair" (*u*).

Amendment of s. 34 of Highway Act, 1862.

(*u*) The mode of proceeding, therefore, will be under 25 & 26

Vict. c. 61, s. 18, instead of under 5 & 6 Will. 4, c. 50, ss. 94, 95. As explained, *ante*, p. 108, note (*l*), it seems that there is no power to summon the party liable to repair; but the summons must be issued against the highway board, and when they have done the repairs they may recover the expense from the party liable to repair, under 25 & 26 Vict. c. 61, s. 34.

Amendment of s. 35 of Highway Act of 1862. **24.** The highway board may apply, under section 35 of the Highway Act of 1862, for the purpose of making any highway to which that section refers a highway to be repaired and maintained by the parish in which the same is situate, and upon such application being made the same proceedings may be had as upon the application of the person or corporation liable to repair the same (*w*).

(*w*) Therefore, the justice to whom application is made must issue summonses requiring the waywarden of the parish, the district surveyor, and the party liable to repair, to appear before two or more justices in petty sessions, who will proceed to examine and determine the matter. As nothing is said about costs, it is presumed that the party liable to repair may be ordered to pay them under 11 & 12 Vict. c. 43 s. 18, if the justices think fit.

Sect. 74 of 5 & 6 Will. 4 c. 50, repealed, and other provisions made as to cattle found straying, &c., on highways. **25.** Section 74 of the Highway Act, 1835, shall be repealed, and instead thereof be it enacted, If any horse, mare, gelding, bull, ox, cow, heifer, steer, calf, mule, ass, sheep, lamb, goat, kid, or swine is at any time found straying (*x*) on or lying about any highway, or across any part thereof, or by the sides thereof (except on such parts of any highway as pass over any common or waste or uninclosed (*y*) ground), the owner or owners thereof shall, for every animal so found straying or lying, be liable to a penalty not exceeding 5*s*., to be recovered in a summary manner, together with the reasonable expense of removing such animal from the highway where it is found to the fields or stable of the owner or owners, or to the common pound (if any) of the parish where the same shall be found, or to such

other place as may have been provided for the purpose:
Provided always, that no owner of any such animal
shall in any case pay more than the sum of 30s., to be
recovered as aforesaid, over and above such reasonable
expenses as aforesaid, including the usual fees and
charges of the authorized keeper of the pound: Provided also, that nothing in this Act shall be deemed to
extend to take away any right of pasturage (z) which
may exist on the sides of any highway.

(x) In *Morris* v. *Jeffries*, L. R. 1 Q. B. 261, 30 J. P. 198, it
was held that horses under the control of a keeper cannot be
said to be "straying" within the meaning of the Turnpike Act,
4 Geo. 4, c. 95 s. 75. But in *Lawrence* v. *King*, L. R. 3 Q.B. 345,
32 J. P. 310, it was held that where cattle are found straying on
or lying about a highway, the offence is complete under this section, whether they are found with or without a keeper.

In the case of *Horwood* v. *Goodall*, and of *Horwood* v. *Hill*,
36 J. P. 486, a shepherd was driving 100 sheep from one farm to
another along the highway. One day he was seen to rest for a
quarter of an hour, when the sheep began to eat the grass and
hedges, and some to stand on the highway. On another day the
sheep had got half a mile ahead of him, and were eating the
grass and standing on the highway when he came up to them.
And it was *held* that the justices could only lawfully convict the
owner for his sheep being found straying on the highway if
they were satisfied that the shepherd was not *bonâ fide* driving
the sheep all the while, for that resting occasionally during the
progress was not inconsistent with driving.

(y) A highway had wide strips of grass on each side and then
fences, the strips belonging to F., and the land beyond the fences
to different owners. F. was rated separately to the poor-rate for
these strips, and there were gates at each end of them across the
highway. One day he sent out eight horses and a cow to pasture
on these strips, and a man with a whip was lying on the grass
thirty yards from the cattle, which wandered over the road. On an
information against F. for suffering and allowing the horses and
cow to stray upon the highway, it was *held* that the strips were
not uninclosed land within the meaning of this section, and that
no question of title arose in the case; that F. was liable in the
same way as a stranger would be if he allowed his cattle to lie or
stray on the highway, and that he was rightly convicted.—
Freestone v. *Caswell*, L. R. 4 Q. B. 516, 33 J. P. 581.

In *Bothamley* v. *Danby*, 36 J. P. 135, certain local trustees
were authorized to let the herbage of a bank made to protect

drainage districts, and on the top of the bank was a highway. B. rented the herbage and depastured his sheep there, but they strayed on the highway. And it was *held* that he was rightly convicted under this section, and that the highway did not pass through uninclosed ground within the meaning of the exception.

(z) The owner of a farm adjoining a highway, to whom the pasturage on the sides of the highway belonged, sent out 25 bullocks to graze thereon, under charge of a boy who was at a distance driving back some of them out of a field, the rest straying over the metalled part of the highway, and obstructing the passage. On an information against the owner under this section it was held that there was evidence justifying a conviction for allowing the cattle to stray, and that the right of pasturage made no difference as regarded the defendant's liability.— *Golding* v. *Stocking*, L. R. 4 Q. B. 516, 33 J. P. 566.

As to service of notices issued by highway board.

26. Any notice in respect of which no other mode of service is provided by the highway board in pursuance of powers in that behalf conferred on them (a), and any precept, summons, or order issued by (b) the highway board, may be served—

By delivery of the same personally on the party required to be served; or

By leaving the same at the usual or last known place of abode of such party as aforesaid; or

By forwarding the same by post as a prepaid letter addressed to the usual or last known place of abode of such party.

In proving service of a document by post it shall be sufficient to prove that the document was properly directed, and that it was put as a prepaid letter into the post-office; and in serving notices on the overseers or the waywardens (if more than one) of any parish it shall be sufficient to serve the same on any one of such officers in a parish.

(a) There does not appear to be any express provision on the subject.

(b) As to the service of notices, &c., required to be served *upon* the board, see 25 & 26 Vict. c. 61 s. 42 (b).

27. (c) * * * The proceedings of highway
boards shall, after the passing of this Act, be subject
to the regulations contained in the first schedule to
this Act annexed.

(c) The omitted part repealed the schedule annexed to the
Highway Act, 1862, so far as relates to the proceedings of high-
way boards, and was itself repealed by the Statute Law Revision
Act 1875, as spent.

28. (d) * ·* * * *

(d) This section which amended 25 & 26 Vict. c. 61, s. 43, sub-
sect. 2, by requiring that the words "not exceeding five pounds"
should be omitted, is itself repealed by the Statute Law Revision
Act, 1875, as spent.

29. (e) A justice of the peace acting for the county
in which a highway district is situate, if he is resident
in any place which is prohibited either altogether or
without the consent of the local authority from being included in a highway district by section 7 of the Highway Act of 1862, and which is surrounded by or
adjoins in any part such highway district, shall, by
virtue of his office, be a member of the highway board
of such district, subject to this qualification, that if in
pursuance of this section any justice of the peace
would be entitled to be a member of two or more highway boards in the same county, he shall, by letter
under his hand, addressed to the clerk of the highway
board for which he elects to act, and by him to be
transmitted to the clerk of the peace of the county,
declare of which of the said highway boards he elects
to be a member, and having made that election he
shall be bound thereby, and shall not be entitled by
virtue of his office of justice to be a member of any
other of the said boards.

(e) By 25 & 26 Vict. c. 61 s. 9 the justices acting for the county
and residing within the highway district are *ex officio* members of

the highway board. By sect. 7 of that Act certain places are prohibited from being included in the district. This section puts a county justice residing in any such excluded place on the same footing as a county justice residing within the district, provided the excluded place is surrounded by the district, or adjoins it in any part. He cannot, however, be an *ex officio* member of more than one highway board in pursuance of this section, and if so entitled to be a member of two or more boards, must elect for which he will act.

Appointment of officers of board.

30. The appointment of any officer of a highway board may be made by a minute of the board, signed by the chairman and countersigned by the clerk of the board, and any appointment so made shall be as valid as if it were made under the seal of the board (*f*).

(*f*) By 25 & 26 Vict. c. 61 s. 12 the board are required to appoint officers " by writing under their seal." This section enables them to make such appointments by a minute of the board, and by that means, as it seems, to avoid the necessity of paying stamp duty (see note (*l*) *ante*, p. 95). The minute of the board, signed, &c., is receivable in evidence under 25 & 26 Vict. c. 61, s. 9, sub-sect. 5, without further proof.

Power to appoint paid collectors of highway rates.

31. The power of appointing paid collectors of highway rates with the consent of the inhabitants in vestry assembled, which is vested in a surveyor by the Highway Act, 1835, and all the provisions of that Act relating to such appointment, shall be vested in and extend to any waywarden required to levy rates in pursuance of the Highway Act, 1862, and this Act, or either of such Acts; and for the purposes of this Act any meeting of ratepayers entitled to elect a waywarden or waywardens shall be deemed to be included under the expression " Inhabitants in vestry assembled," as used in this section, and the Highway Acts (*g*).

(*g*) Under this section waywardens may appoint paid collectors of highway rates provided they obtain the consent of the meeting of ratepayers entitled to elect waywardens under 25 & 26 Vict.

c. 61, s. 10. In all other respects waywardens, as regards this ^{Act '64, s. 31.} matter, are placed in the same position as highway surveyors under 5 & 6 Will. 4, c. 50 s. 36.

32. (h)   *   *   *   *   *

The salaries of the officers appointed for each dis- Expenses how to be charged. trict, and any other expenses incurred by any highway board for the common use or benefit of the several parishes within such district, shall be annually charged to a district fund (i) to be contributed by and charged upon the several highway parishes within such district in proportion to the rateable value of the property in each parish, but the expenses of maintaining and keeping in repair the highways of each highway parish within the district, and all other expenses legally payable by the highway board in relation to such parish, including any sums of money that would have been payable out of the highway rates of such parish if the same had not become part of a highway district, except such expenses as are in this Act authorized to be charged to the district fund, shall be a separate charge on each parish (k).

The rateable value of the property in each parish shall be ascertained according to the valuation list or other estimate for the time being in force in such parish for the purposes of the poor rate, or if no such valuation list or estimate be in force, then in such manner as may be determined by the justices in petty sessions, subject to an appeal (l) by any person aggrieved to the next general or quarter sessions.

(h) The first paragraph of this section, repealing 25 & 26 Vict. c. 61, ss. 20-24, both inclusive, is itself repealed by the Statute Law Revision Act, 1875, as spent.

(i) The following expenses are also chargeable upon the district fund, viz., contributions to the repair of turnpike roads, under 26 & 27 Vict. c. 94, s. 1, and 34 & 35 Vict. c. 115, s. 15 ; maintenance of highways within the district which within

Act '64, s. 32. seven years previous to the 9th August, 1870, or since that date,
have ceased to be turnpike roads (33 & 34 Vict. c. 73, s. 10); repairs,
or contributions to repairs of, turnpike roads within the district,
without any order of contribution under 26 & 27 Vict. c. 94, s. 1
(35 & 36 Vict. c. 85, s. 14); the cost of maintaining turnpike
roads as to which any Annual Turnpike Act Continuance Act
has provided that no money shall be expended in their repair (37
& 38 Vict. c. 95, s. 10). See also 35 & 36 Vict. c. 85, s. 15, and
36 & 37 Vict. c. 90, s. 15, as to the liability of parishes to contribute to the expense of paying off debts of turnpike trusts, in the
same proportion as they contribute to the district fund.

And by 41 & 42 Vict. c. 77, s. 7, all expenses incurred by any
highway board in maintaining and keeping in repair the highways of each parish within their district, and all other expenses
legally incurred by such board, shall, on and after the 25th
March, 1879, be deemed to have been incurred for the common
use or benefit of the several parishes within their district, and
shall be charged on the district fund ; with a proviso as to highway boards dividing their respective districts into two or more
parts under exceptional circumstances. Moreover by 41 & 42
Vict c. 77, s. 8, all moneys borrowed by a highway board after the
25th March, 1879, under the Highway Acts will be charged on
the district fund.

(*k*) The costs incurred by the board in prosecuting an indictment for an obstruction in a parish within the district, is properly chargeable to the parish as an expense which is necessary
to keep and maintain the highway in repair (*Reg.* v. *Heath*, 29
J. P. 452). The board, however, have no right to charge the
parishes with their share of the expense of opposing a turnpike
bill in Parliament where the turnpike road only lies in some of
the parishes of the district, and does not affect the liability of the
others, even though the opposition to the bill is successful (*Reg.*
v. *Kingsbridge*, 32 J. P. 502). But after the 25th March, 1879,
such questions will become unimportant, as from that date this
part of the section will be virtually repealed by 41 & 42 Vict.
c. 77, s. 7.

(*l*) Nothing is said about the conditions of appeal. But if the
determination by justices in petty sessions be by order, the appeal
will probably be subject to the conditions prescribed by sect. 39,
infra. Looking, however, to the fact that sect. 42 only enables
the court to confirm, &c., "any order of the *highway board*,"
and is silent as to orders of justices, it is by no means clear that
either sect. 39 or sect. 42 applies to appeals against orders of
justices.

Mode of
defraying
expenses of
the highway
board.

33. For the purpose of obtaining payment from the
several highway parishes within their district of the
sums to be contributed by them, the highway board
shall order precepts to be issued to the waywardens or

overseers of the said parishes according to the provi- _{Act '64, s.33.}
sions hereinafter contained, stating the sum to be con-
tributed by each parish, and requiring the officer to
whom the precept is addressed, within a time to be
limited by the precept, to pay the sum therein mentioned to the treasurer of the board.

Where a highway parish is not a parish separately
maintaining its own poor, or where in any highway
parish it has, for a period of not less than seven years
immediately preceding the passing of the Highway Act,
1862, been the custom of the surveyor of highways
for such parish to levy a highway rate in respect of
property not subject by law to be assessed to poor
rates, the precept of the highway board shall be
addressed to the waywarden of the parish, and in all
other cases it shall be addressed to the overseers (m).

Where the precept is addressed to a waywarden he
shall pay the sum thereby required out of a separate
rate, and such separate rate shall, in the case of a
parish in which for such period aforesaid it has been
the custom of the surveyor of highways to levy a highway rate in respect of property not subject by law to
be assessed to poor rate, be assessed on and levied
from the persons and in respect of the property on,
from, and in respect of which the same has been
assessed and levied during such period as aforesaid,
and in all other cases such rate shall be assessed on and
levied from the persons and in respect of the property
on, from, and in respect of which a poor rate would be
assessable and leviable if the parish of which he is
waywarden were a place separately maintaining its
own poor.

No rate leviable by a waywarden under this Act
shall be payable until the same has been published in
manner in which rates for the relief of the poor are by
law required to be published.

A waywarden shall account to the highway board for the amount of all rates levied by him, and at the expiration of his term of office shall pay any surplus in his hands arising from any rate so levied, above the amount for which the rate was made, to the treasurer of the highway board, to the credit of the parish within which such rate was made, and such surplus shall go in reduction of the next highway rate that may be leviable in such parish.

Where the precept is addressed to the overseers they shall pay the sum thereby required out of a poor rate (*n*) to be levied by them, or out of any moneys in their hands applicable to the relief of the poor.

No contribution required to be paid by any parish at any one time in respect of highway rates shall exceed the sum of tenpence in the pound, and the aggregate of contributions required to be paid by any parish in any one year in respect of highway rates shall not exceed the sum of two shillings and sixpence in the pound, except with the consent of four-fifths of the ratepayers of the parish in which such excess may be levied, present at a meeting specially called for the purpose, of which ten days' previous notice has been given by the waywarden of such parish, and then only to such extent as may be determined by such meeting (*o*).

All sums of money payable in pursuance of the precepts of a highway board shall, whether they are or not payable by the overseers of the poor, be subject to all charges to which ordinary highway rates are subject by law (*p*).

(*m*) The fact that a highway parish includes property which is exempt from highway rate, under 5 & 6 Will. 4 c. 50, s. 33, does not justify the precept being addressed to the waywarden. It must still be addressed to the overseers, who must make a reduction in the amount of the poor-rate to which the occupier would otherwise be liable, commensurate with the amount of the exemption (*Carter* v. *Wareham*, 30 J. P. 341; and see *Reg.* v. *Heath*, L. R. 1 Q. B. 218, 30 J. P. 182).

(*n*) But where the parish includes property which is exempt from highway rate under 5 & 6 Will. 4 c. 50, s. 33, the occupier is still entitled to the benefit of the exemption, and ought not to be rated for such property so far as the repair of highways is concerned (*Reg.* v. *Heath*, L. R. 1 Q. B. 218, 30 J. P. 182). In such a case the amount assessed for the highways should appear on the face of the rate, so that the ratepayers may see how much is for the maintenance of the poor, and how much for highways, and why one occupier who is liable to both is charged with the aggregate, and another who is liable to one only, with that one *Id.*, and see *Carter* v. *Wareham*, 30 J. P. 341).

(*o*) This is similar to 5 & 6 Will. 4 c. 50, s. 29. But *quære* whether this limitation will be of any effect after the 25th March, 1879, when by 41 & 42 Vict. c, 77, s. 7, the expenses incurred by any highway board in maintaining and keeping in repair the highways of each parish within their district, and all other expenses legally incurred by the board, are to be deemed to have been incurred for the common use or benefit of the several parishes within their district, and to be charged on the district fund.

(*p*) This probably includes exemption from highway rates under 5 & 6 Will. 4, c. 50, s. 33, as in *Reg.* v. *Heath*, and *Carter* v. *Wareham*, *supra*, and the benefit of interest and dividends, or principal (as the case may be) of sums paid under 25 & 26 Vict. c. 61, s. 35, in respect of highways repairable *ratione tenuræ*.

34. All waywardens and overseers to whom precepts of a highway board are hereby directed or authorized to be issued shall within their respective parishes have the same powers, remedies, and privileges, for and in respect of assessing and levying any rates required to be levied for making payments to a highway board, in the case of overseers, as they have in assessing and levying ordinary rates for the relief of the poor, and in the case of waywardens as they would have if the parish of which they are waywardens were a place separately maintaining its own poor, and they were overseers thereof, and the rate to be levied by them were a duly authorized poor rate (*q*).

L

Act'64, s.34.

(q) They have no power to include in the rate property which is exempt from liability to be rated to the highway rate under 5 & 6 Will. 4, c. 50, s. 33 (*Reg.* v. *Heath* and *Carter* v. *Wareham, supra*). But it would seem that they may still include "such woods, mines, and quarries of stone, or other hereditaments" as are mentioned in 5 & 6 Will. 4, c. 50, s. 27, and had usually been rated to the highways before the passing of that Act. See also 37 & 38 Vict. c. 54, s. 1, as to the rating of woods, mines, &c., to the poor rate.

Mode of enforcing payments to highway boards.

35. If any payment required to be made by the overseers or waywardens of any parish of moneys due to a highway board is in arrear, it shall be lawful for any justice, on application under the hand of the chairman for the time being or by the clerk of such board to summon the said overseers or waywardens to show cause at petty sessions why such payment has not been made; and the justices at such petty sessions (r), after hearing the complaint preferred on behalf of the board, may, if they think fit, cause the amount of payment in arrear, together with the costs occasioned by such arrear, to be levied and recovered from the said overseers or waywardens, or any of them, in like manner as moneys assessed for the relief of the poor may be levied and recovered, and the amount of such arrear, together with the costs aforesaid, when levied and recovered, to be paid to the said board.

(r) In *Giles* v. *Glubb*, 30 J. P. 38, it was held that L., an ancient borough, separately maintaining its own poor and highways, which had charters with non-intromittant clauses, and was entirely surrounded by the county of C., was properly included by the justices of the county within a highway district under 25 & 26 Vict. c. 61, s. 5, notwithstanding the non-intromittant clause; and consequently that the justices of the county of C. at petty sessions had jurisdiction to enforce payment of a contribution under a precept from the highway board addressed to the appellants as overseers of the poor law parish, highway parish, or place of L. in the county of C.

ACCOUNTS OF BOARD.

36. (*s*)   *   *   *   Within thirty days after the signature of the accounts by the chairman the board shall cause a statement (*t*) showing the receipt and expenditure in respect of each parish, and the apportioned part of expenditure chargeable thereto in respect of the district fund, and such other particulars and in such form as the Secretary of State (*u*) may direct, to be printed, and sent by post or otherwise to each member of the board, and to the overseers of every parish within the district having overseers; and the clerk of the board shall furnish a copy of such statement to any ratepayer or owner of property situate within the district, on his application, and on the payment of a sum not exceeding one penny.

The books of account of the board shall at all seasonable times be open to the inspection of any ratepayer of any highway parish within the district of the board.

(*s*) The first paragraph of this section repealed sects. 25, 26, 30 of 25 & 26 Vict. c. 61, and is itself repealed by the Statute Law Revision Act, 1875, as spent. The next three paragraphs, relating respectively to the making up, examination, and auditing of accounts, are repealed by 41 & 42 Vict. c. 77, s. 9, which makes other provisions on the subject.

(*t*) By 41 & 42 Vict. c. 77, s. 9, this statement is now to be furnished within 30 days after the completion of the audit under that section, instead of within 30 days after the signature of the accounts by the chairman.

(*u*) The powers conferred by this section on the Secretary of State are transferred to the Local Government Board by 35 & 36 Vict. c. 79, s. 36.

37. If any person feels aggrieved by any rate levied on him for the purpose of raising moneys payable under a precept of a highway board, on the ground of incorrectness in the valuation of any property included in such rate, or of any person being put on or left out of such rate, or of the inequality or unfairness of the sum charged on any person or persons therein, he may appeal to the justices in special sessions in manner provided by the Act 6 & 7 Will. 4, c. 96, sections 6 and 7, and all the provisions of the said sections shall be applicable to such appeal (*v*).

(*v*) This is the only provision made for appealing against rates, and is confined to appeals to special sessions on the ground of incorrectness in valuation, omission of parties, or the inequality or unfairness of the sum charged. An appeal to quarter sessions (except by way of appeal from the justices' decision under this section) can only be had in respect of the matters mentioned in the next section, which does not apply to rates. Consequently no other objection can be taken by appeal against a rate than such as is mentioned in this section.

Power to appeal to quarter sessions against items of expense and expenditure, &c.

38. Where any waywarden of a highway parish of a district, or any ratepayer of such parish, feels aggrieved in respect of the matters following :—

(1.) In respect of any order of the highway board for the repair of any highway in his parish on the ground that such highway is not legally repairable by the parish, or in respect of any other order of the board on the ground that the matter to which such order relates is one in regard to which the board have no jurisdiction to make an order;

(2.) In respect of any item of expense charged to the separate account of his parish on the ground that such item of expense has not in fact been incurred, or has been incurred in respect of a matter upon which the board have no authority by law to make any expenditure whatever;

(3.) In respect of any item of expenditure charged to the district fund on the ground that such item of expense has not in fact been incurred, or has been incurred in respect of a matter Act '64, s. 88.

    upon which the board has no authority by
    law to make any expenditure whatever;

  (4.) In respect of the contribution required to be
      made by each parish to the district fund on
      the ground that such amount, when com-
      pared with the contribution of other parishes
      in the district, is not according to the pro-
      portion required by this Act;

he may, upon complying with the conditions hereinafter mentioned, appeal to the court of general or
quarter sessions having jurisdiction in the district; but
no appeal shall be had in respect of any exercise of
the discretion of the board in matters within their discretion; and no (*w*) appeal shall be had except in
respect of the matters and upon the grounds hereinbefore mentioned.

    (*w*) This presumably must be restricted to appeals in respect
of matters mentioned in this section. An appeal is expressly
given by sect. 32 against the determination of justices in petty
sessions respecting the rateable value of property.

   39. No appeal shall be entertained by any court of Conditions
general or quarter sessions in pursuance of this Act, of appeal to general or
unless the following conditions have been complied quarter sessions.
with :—

  (1.) Notice of the intention of appeal must be
      served by the appellant on the clerk of the
      highway board in the case of an appeal
      against an order (*x*) within two months after
      the order, and in the case of an appeal in
      respect of any item of expense or contribu-
      tionwithin one month after the statement of
      the account of the board has been sent to
      each member of the board as hereinbefore
      mentioned :

(2.) The notice must state the matter appealed
against, and the ground of the appeal:

On the receipt of the notice the board may serve a
counter notice on the appellant, requiring him to
appear in person or by his agent at the next meeting
of the board, and support his appeal.   On hearing
the appellant the board may rectify the matter complained of, and if they do so to a reasonable extent,
and tender to the appellant a reasonable sum for the
costs of his attendance, it shall not be lawful for the
appellant to proceed with his appeal.   In any (*y*)
other case the appellant may proceed with his appeal,
and the reasonable costs of his attendance on the
board shall be deemed part of the costs of the appeal.

(*x*) *Quære* whether this applies to an appeal against the
determination of justices in petty sessions under sect. 32 ?
Judging from the context, and the last paragraph of sect. 42, it
would seem to be confined to an order of the highway board.
But the declaration in the first paragraph of this section that
no appeal shall be entertained, &c., "in pursuance of this Act,"
unless, &c., may possibly extend it to an order of justices.

(*y*) This seems to include the case of the appellant's omitting
or declining to appear before the board in obedience to the
counter notice.   The board can only rectify the matter complained of "on hearing the appellant," and there is no power
to compel his appearance, although the section speaks of "requiring " him to appear before them.

Power to
refer case to
arbitration.   **40.** If at any time after notice of appeal has been
given it appears to the court of general or quarter
sessions, on the application of either party in the
presence of or after notice has been given to the other
party, that the matter in question in such appeal consists wholly or in part of matters of mere account
which cannot be satisfactorily tried by the court, it
shall be lawful for such court to order that such
matters, either wholly or in part, be referred to the
arbitration of one or more persons, to be appointed by

the parties, or, in case of disagreement, by the court; Act '64, s. 40. and the award made on such arbitration shall be enforceable by the same process as the order of the court of quarter sessions.

41. The provisions of the Common Law Procedure Provisions Act, 1854, relating to compulsory references, shall be of 17 & 18 Vict. c. 125. deemed to extend to arbitrations directed by the court incorporated. of quarter sessions; and the word "court" in the said Act shall be deemed to include the court of quarter sessions.

42. If upon the hearing of the appeal it appears to Proceedings on appeal. the court that the question in dispute involves an inquiry as to whether a road is or is not a highway repairable by the public, or an inquiry as to any other important matter of fact, the court may either themselves decide such question, or may empanel a jury of twelve disinterested men out of the persons returned to serve as jurymen at such quarter sessions, and submit to such jury such questions in relation to the matters of fact in dispute as the court think fit; and the verdict of such jury, after hearing the evidence adduced, shall be conclusive as to the questions submitted to them.

The questions so submitted shall be in the form and shall be tried as nearly as may be in the manner in which feigned issues are ordinarily tried, and the court shall decide the parties to be plaintiffs and defendants in such trials.

Subject as aforesaid, the court may, upon the hearing of any appeal under this Act, confirm, reverse, or modify any order of the highway board (z), or rectify any account appealed against.

Act '64, s. 42.   (z) But nothing is said about an order of justices determining
— —   the rateable value of property under sect. 33.

Costs of   **43.** If the appellant is successful, the costs shall,
appeal.   unless the court otherwise orders, be paid by the board,
and shall be charged to the parishes within the jurisdiction of the board other than the parish to which
the appellant belongs in the same proportions in which
such parishes contribute to the common fund of the
board.

If the appellant is unsuccessful, the board, if the
waywarden be the appellant, may charge the costs of
the appeal to the parish to which the appellant
belongs in the same manner as if they were expenses
incurred in repairing the roads in such parish (*a*),
and may levy the sum accordingly, and may carry the
sum so levied to the account of the several parishes
within the jurisdiction of the board, other than the
parish to which the appellant waywarden belongs, in
the same manner as if they were expenses contributed
by such parishes to the common fund of the board;
but if some ratepayer other than the waywarden is
the appellant, the court may order the costs of the
appeal to be paid by such appellant; and such costs
shall be recoverable in the same manner as a penalty
is recovered under the Highway Act, 1862.

(*a*) But after 25th March, 1879, there will be no means of
charging the expenses of repairing roads to any parish (see 41
& 42 Vict. c. 77, s. 7), and consequently no means of charging it
with the costs of the appeal.

Jurisdiction   **44.** Places situate in different counties, and places
as to districts   situate partly in one county and partly in another
in different
counties.   county, when united in one highway district, shall,
for all matters connected with the provisions of this
Act relating to appeals to quarter sessions against

accounts, be deemed to be subject to the jurisdiction Act '64, s. 44.
of the justices of the county in which the district is
situate to which such places shall have been united by
any provisional and final order or orders, or to which
after the passing of this Act any such district shall be
declared to be subject by the orders constituting the
same, in the same manner as if all such places or parts
of places were situate in such county.

SUPPLEMENTAL PROVISIONS.

45. If the highway board of a district make default in
appointing a treasurer, clerk, and district surveyor (*b*),
or any of such officers, in pursuance of the Highway
Act, 1862, within three months after the day fixed by
the justices for the holding of the first meeting of the
board, or within three months after a vacancy occurring
in any of the said offices, the justices in general or
quarter sessions assembled may, if they think fit, appoint a person to any of the said offices in respect of
which the default has been made, and may fix the
salary to be paid to the officer appointed; and any
such appointment shall take effect and salary be recoverable in the same manner as if the officer appointed by the justices had been appointed by the
highway board of the district; and it shall not be
lawful for such board, without the consent of the
said justices, to remove any officer appointed by them
under this section, or to lessen his salary within one
year from the date of his appointment.

*In case of de-
fault of high-
way board
appointing
officers.*

(*b*) By 25 & 26 Vict. c. 61, s. 12, the board are required to
appoint these officers at their first meeting, or at some adjournment thereof, and are authorized to remove any of them, and to
appoint others in their stead or in the room of such as may die
or resign.

46. The justices assembled in petty sessions at their usual place of meeting may exercise any jurisdiction which they are authorized under the Highway Acts or any of them to exercise in special sessions (*c*); and no justice of the peace shall be disabled from acting as such at any petty or special or general quarter sessions in any matter merely on the ground that he is by virtue of his office a member of any highway board complaining, interested, or concerned in such matter, or has acted as such at any meeting of such Board (*d*).

(*c*) Hence justices in petty sessions, at their usual place of meeting, may now appoint a surveyor under 5 & 6 Will. 4, c, 50, ss. 11, 12, excuse persons from payment of highway rate, *Id.* s. 32; and perform other acts required by that Act to be done by justices in special sessions.

(*d*) But a justice who, on an application to subtract certain townships from a highway district, appears by counsel and gives evidence to oppose the subtraction, makes himself a party to the proceedings, and notwithstanding this section, is not entitled to vote upon them at quarter sessions (*Reg.* v. *JJ. of Cumberland,* 42 J. P. 361). Such proceedings are judicial and not administrative (*Id.*) But *quære* whether the mere giving of evidence in such a matter by a justice would disentitle him to vote (*Id.*)

Power of
highway
board to
make im-
provements
and borrow
money for
the same. but
previously to
cause an
estimate to
be made.
47. A highway board may make such improvements as are hereinafter mentioned in the highways within their jurisdiction, and may, with the approval of the justices in general or quarter sessions assembled, borrow money for the purpose of defraying the expenses of such improvements (*e*):

Previously to applying for the approval of the justices the highway board shall cause an estimate of the expense of the improvements to be made, and two months at the least before making their application shall give notice of their intention so to do.

The notice shall state the following particulars :—

(1.) The nature of the work, the estimated amount of expense to be incurred, and the sum proposed to be borrowed :

(2.) The parish or parishes within the district by which the sum borrowed and the interest thereon is to be paid, and in case of more parishes than one being made liable to pay the principal and interest the annual amounts to be contributed by each parish towards the payment thereof :

(3.) The number of years within which the principal moneys borrowed are to be paid off, not exceeding twenty years, and the amount to be set apart in each year for paying off the same :

(4.) The sessions at which the application is to be made.

Notice shall be given as follows :—

(1.) By transmitting a copy to the clerk of the peace for the county or division :

(2.) By placing a copy of such notice for three successive *Sundays* on the church (*f*) door of every church of the parish or parishes on behalf of which such works are to be done, or in the case of any place not having a church, in some conspicuous position in such place.

Upon the hearing of the application any person or persons may oppose the approval of the justices being given, and it shall be lawful for the justices to give or withhold their approval, with or without modification, as they think just.

All moneys borrowed in pursuance of this Act, to-

Act '64, s. 47. gether with the interest thereon, shall be a first charge on the highway rates of each parish liable to contribute to the payment thereof, after paying the sums due to the highway board on account of the district fund, in the same manner, so far as the creditor is concerned, as if the money had been borrowed on account of each parish alone; and the sums necessary to repay the said borrowed moneys, with interest, shall in each such parish be recoverable in the same manner as if they were expenses incurred by the board in keeping in repair the highways of that parish (g).

But it shall be the duty of the highway board, in case of any one parish paying more than its share of such borrowed money, or of the interest thereon, to make good to that parish the excess so paid out of the rates of the other parishes liable to contribute thereto.

The justices may from time to time make general orders in relation to the mode in which applications are to be made to them for their consent under this Act to the borrowing of any moneys.

(e) By 35 & 36 Vict. c. 85, s. 15, the abolition of tolls on any turnpike road within or passing through a highway district, by voluntary agreement, is deemed to be an improvement of highways within the meaning of this section and sects. 48, 50 (*infra*), and for such purpose the highway board may borrow money in accordance with the provisions of those sections, subject to the following provisions, viz. :—

That the improvement shall be deemed to be on behalf of all the parishes within the district, and each parish shall contribute thereto in the same proportion as it contributes to the district fund.

And by 36 & 37 Vict. c. 90, s. 16, the abolition of tolls on a turnpike road in consequence of an order of the Local Government Board under sect. 15 of that Act is, in the case of a highway district, to be deemed to be an improvement of highways within the meaning of the same sections, 47, 48, 50, and for such purpose the highway board may borrow money in the same manner and subject to the same provisions as are contained in 35 & 36 Vict. c. 85, s. 15.

(*f*) The copy need not be placed on chapel doors as under

7. Will. 4 and 1 Vict. c. 45, and most other recent Acts providing for the publication of notices.

(g) That is to say, by precept, &c., as in sect. 33, *ante.*

48. The following works shall be deemed to be improvements of highways (h) :—

(1.) The conversion of any road that has not been stoned into a stoned road :

(2.) The widening of any road, the cutting off the corners in any road where land is required to be purchased for that purpose, the levelling roads, the making any new road, and the building or enlarging bridges :

(3.) The doing of any other work in respect of highways beyond ordinary repairs essential to placing any existing highway in a proper state of repair.

(h) To this may now be added the abolition of tolls on turnpike roads by voluntary agreement under 35 & 36 Vict. c. 85, s. 15, and by order of the Local Government Board under 36 & 37 Vict. c. 90, ss. 15, 16.

49. Any parish may, with the consent of its waywarden, contribute to any improvements made in another parish, whether situate or not in the same district, if such first-mentioned parish (i) consider such improvements to be for its benefit; and any highway board may contribute to any improvements made in another district if such improvements are, in the opinion of the highway board of the first-mentioned district, for the benefit of their district. The contribution to be made by one parish to another shall be payable in the same manner as if such contributions were moneys due from the contributing parish in respect of expenses incurred in keeping in repair the highways of that parish, and moneys contributed by one district to

Act '64, s. 49. another district shall be payable out of the common fund of the contributing district.

(i) No provision is made for showing how the "first-mentioned parish consider such improvements to be for its benefit." Perhaps it may be by meeting in vestry, or possibly by the " consent of its waywarden " alone.

Certain clauses of 10 & 11 Vict. c. 16, incorporated. **50.** The clauses of The Commissioners Clauses Act, 1847, with respect to mortgages to be created (*j*) by the commissioners, shall form part of and be incorporated with this Act, and any mortgagee or assignee may enforce payment of his principal and interest by appointment of a receiver.

In the construction of the said clauses "the Commissioners" shall mean the "Highway Board."

Mortgages and transfers of mortgages shall be valid if made in the forms prescribed (*k*) by the last-mentioned Act, or in the forms appearing in the second schedule annexed to this Act, or as near thereto as circumstances admit.

(*j*) The clauses intended to be incorporated, no doubt, are sects. 75 to 88 of 10 & 11 Vict. c. 16. But it may be mentioned that the heading of those clauses is " with respect to the mortgages to be *executed* by the commissioners," not "*created*" by the commissioners, as mentioned in the section.

(*k*) The forms referred to are those contained in Schedules (B.) and (C.) to 10 & 11 Vict. c. 16. It may, however, be observed that sect. 75 of that Act merely says that the mortgage, " *may* be according to the form in Schedule (B.)," and sect. 77 that the transfer "*may* be according to the form in Schedule (C.)," and therefore does not "*prescribe*" the form, but merely authorizes its use.

As to encroachment on highways. **51.** From and after the passing of this Act if any person shall encroach (*l*) by making or causing to be made any building, or pit, or hedge, ditch, or other fence, or by placing any dung, compost, or other materials for dressing land or any rubbish, on the side or sides of any carriageway or cartway within fifteen feet of the centre thereof, or by removing any soil or turf from the side or sides of any carriageway or cartway, except for the purpose of improving the road, and by order of the highway board, or, where there is no highway board, of the surveyor, he shall be subject on conviction for every such offence to any sum not exceeding forty shillings, notwithstanding that the whole space of fifteen feet from the centre of such carriageway or cartway has not been maintained with stones or other materials used in forming highways; and it shall be lawful for the justices assembled at petty sessions, upon proof to them made upon oath, to levy the expenses of taking down such building, hedge, or fence, or filling up such ditch or pit, and removing such dung, compost, materials, or rubbish as aforesaid, or restoring the injury caused by the removal of such soil or turf, upon the person offending : Provided always, that where any carriageway or cartway is fenced on both sides no encroachment as aforesaid shall be allowed whereby such carriageway or cartway shall be reduced in width to less than thirty feet between the fences on each side.

(*l*) In *Thorne* v. *Field*, 33 J. P. 727, the owner of land adjoining a highway, and of a ditch by the side of the highway, built a fence on the site of the ditch. On information under this section for unlawfully encroaching on the highway it was proved that the fence was within seven feet of the centre of the highway. And it was held that the owner could not be convicted, for he put the fence only on his own land, the ditch being no part of the highway. And in *Easton* v. *Richmond Highway Board*, L. R. 7 Q. B. 69, 36 J. P. 485, it was held that "the sides of any carriageway or cartway" in this section, mean any land forming part of the highway, though not part of the metalled road ; but do not extend to land which, though by the side of the road, has not been dedicated as highway to the use of the public.

In *Ranking* v. *Forbes*, 34 J. P. 486, it was held that if an encroachment be made upon a highway by erecting a fence within fifteen feet from the centre of the road, proceedings must be taken under this section within six months after the

Act '64, s. 51. erection of the fence, and that the encroachment is not a continuing offence. The same point was decided in *Coggins* v. *Bennett*, 2 C. P. D. 568, where it was held that the encroachment is not a continuing offence, and that the six months' limitation created by 11 & 12 Vict. c. 43, s. 11, commences from the time when the party encroaches by making the fence.

Power to contract for materials for repairing highways.

52. The highway board may and is hereby authorized to contract for purchasing, getting, and carrying the materials required for the repair of the highways, and for maintaining and keeping in repair all or any part of the highways of any parish within their highway district, for any period not exceeding three years (*m*).

(*m*) By sect. 22 the board may also contract for three years to repair highways, for the repair of which other parties are liable (See *ante*, p. 135, note (*s*).)

8 & 9 Vict. c. 18, and 23 & 24 Vict. c. 106, incorporated.

53. A highway board for the purpose of improving the highways within their district may purchase such lands or easements relating to lands as they may require; and The Lands Clauses Consolidation Act, 1845, and the Act amending the same, 23 & 24 Vict. c. 106, shall be incorporated with this Act, with the exception of the clauses relating to the purchase of land otherwise than by agreement.

In the construction of this Act and the said incorporated Acts this Act shall be deemed to be the special Act, and the board shall be deemed to be the promoters of the undertaking, and the word "land" or "lands" shall include any easement in or out of lands (*n*).

(*n*) By 25 & 26 Vict. c. 61, s. 9 (2), the board are a body corporate with power to acquire and hold lands for the purposes of the Highway Acts, without any license in mortmain.

FIRST SCHEDULE.

PROCEEDINGS OF HIGHWAY BOARDS.

(1.) The board shall meet for the despatch of
business, and shall from time to time make
such regulations with respect to the summoning, notice, place (*m*), management, and
adjournment of such meetings, and generally
with respect to the transaction and management of business, including the quorum at
meetings of the board, as they think fit,
subject to following conditions :—

    (*a.*) The first meeting (*n*) after the formation
of the district shall be held at the time
and place fixed by the order of the
justice* in that behalf;   • *Sic.*

    (*b.*) One ordinary meeting shall be held in
each period of four months, and of
such meetings one shall be held on
some day between the seventh and
fourteenth days of April ;

    (*c.*) An extraordinary meeting may be sum-
moned at any time on the requisition
of three members of the board addressed to the clerk of the board ;

    (*d.*) The quorum to be fixed by the board
shall consist of not less than three
members ;

    (*e.*) Every question shall be decided by a
majority of votes of the members voting
on that question ;

    (*f.*) The names of the members present at a
meeting shall be recorded.

M

(2.) The board shall at the first meeting, and afterwards from time to time at their first meeting after each annual appointment of members of the board as hereafter mentioned (*o*), appoint one of their members to be chairman and one other of their members to be a vice-chairman for the year following such choice.

(3.) If any casual vacancy occur in the office of chairman or vice-chairman, the board shall, as soon as they conveniently can after the occurrence of such a vacancy, choose some member of their number to fill such vacancy; and every such chairman or vice-chairman so elected as last aforesaid shall continue in office so long only as the person in whose place he may be so elected would have been entitled to continue if such vacancy had not happened.

(4.) If at any meeting the chairman is not present at the time appointed for holding the same, the vice-chairman shall be the chairman of the meeting; and if neither the chairman nor vice-chairman shall be present, then the members present shall choose some one of their number to be a chairman of such meeting.

(5.) In case of an equality of votes at any meeting the chairman for the time being of such meeting shall have a second or casting vote.

(6.) All orders of the board for payment of money, and all precepts issued by the board, shall be deemed to be duly executed if signed by two or more members of the board authorized to sign them by a resolution of the board, and countersigned by the clerk; but it shall not be necessary in any legal proceeding to prove

that the members signing any such order or
precept were authorized to sign them, and
such authority shall be presumed until the
contrary is proved.

(*m*) Where any local government district or any other place
is surrounded by or adjoins a highway district constituted under
the Highway Acts, the first-mentioned district or other place,
for the purpose of any meeting of the highway board, is deemed
to be within the highway district (26 & 27 Vict. c. 17, s. 6).

(*n*) The time for holding the first meeting of the board is
fixed by the provisional or final order of the justices under sect.
10, *ante.* But nothing is said about the place of meeting.

(*o*) No other mention is made in the proceedings of the
"annual appointment of members of the board."

SECOND SCHEDULE. 2nd Sched.

Forms.

Form of Mortgage.

The Highway Board of the   District, in NOTE.—See Section 50 of Act.
consideration of   Pounds paid to the Treasurer
of the said Board by *A.B.* of   , assigns unto
the said *A.B.*, his Executors, Administrators, and NOTE.—Highway Rate includes Poor Rate, when the Highways are maintained out of Poor Rate. See Sect. 33 of Act.
Assigns, such proportion of the Highway Rates leviable
in the Highway Parish or Parishes of [*name the*
Parishes] as the said sum of   Pounds bears
to the whole Sum borrowed on the Credit of the said
Rates, to hold to the said *A.B.*, his Executors, Administrators, and Assigns, until the said Sum of
Pounds, with Interest at the Rate of   Pounds NOTE.—Highway Parish means every Parish that separately returns a
per Centum per Annum, is paid.

The Interest on this Mortgage will be paid at
on the   Day and   Days of
in every year.

M 2

Act '64.
2nd Sched.
Waywarden
or Way-
wardens to
the Highway
Board. See
Sect. 3 of
Act. The Principal will be paid at on the Day of .

Given under our Corporate Seal this Day of 18 .

Note—*The Mortgage must be under the Corporate Seal of the Board, and duly stamped. See Commissioners Clauses Act,* 10 *Vict. c.* 16, *s.* 75.

Transfer of Mortgage by Indorsement.

The within-named *A.B.*, in consideration of the Sum Pounds paid to him by *C.D.* of ,
hereby transfers to the said *C.D.*, his Executors, Administrators, and Assigns, all his Interest in the Moneys secured by the within-written Mortgage and and in the within-named Rates.

In witness whereof the said *A.B.* has hereunto set his Hand and Seal this Day of 18 .

Note—*The Transfer must be under Seal and duly stamped. See Sect.* 77 *of Commissioners. Clauses Act,* 10 *Vict. c.* 16.

HIGHWAYS AND LOCOMOTIVES, (AMENDMENT) ACT, 1878.

41 & 42 Vict. Cap. 77.

An Act to amend the Law relating to Highways in England and the Acts relating to Locomotives on Roads; and for other purposes.

[16th August, 1878.]

WHEREAS it is expedient to amend the law relating to highways in England, and to amend the Locomotive Acts, 1861 and 1865: 24 & 25 Vict. c. 70. 28 & 29 Vict. c. 83.

Be it enacted by the Queen's most excellent Majesty by and with the advice and consent of the Lords spiritual and temporal, and Commons in this present Parliament assembled, and by the authority of the same, as follows:—

PRELIMINARY.

1. This Act may be cited as the Highways and Locomotives (Amendment) Act, 1878. Short title.

2. This Act shall not apply to Scotland or Ireland (a); and, save as is by this Act expressly provided (b), Part I. of this Act shall not apply to the Isle of Wight; nor to any part of the metropolis; nor to any part of a county to which the Act 23 & 24 Vict. c. 68, "An Act for the better management and control of the highways in South Wales," extends. Application of Act.

(a) The same limitation is prescribed by 25 & 26 Vict. c. 61, s. 1.

(b) The only part of the Act to which this applies is sect. 27, in

Act '78, s. 2. which the saving as to minerals is expressly extended to the Isle
of Wight, and to South Wales. Both of those places, as well as
the metropolis, were prohibited from being included in a highway district by 25 & 26 Vict. c. 61, s. 7. The interpretation of
the word "metropolis," in this Act (see sect. 38) is however, much
more extensive than the restriction under that section, and consequently the non-application of Part I. extends to places which
were not included in the original prohibition.

PART I.

AMENDMENT OF HIGHWAY LAW.

HIGHWAY DISTRICTS.

Highway
districts to
be made so
far as pos-
sible coinci-
dent with
rural sani-
tary dis-
tricts.

3. In forming any highway districts, or in altering
the boundaries of any highway districts, the county
authority shall have regard to the boundaries of the
rural sanitary districts in their county, and shall, so
far as may be found practicable, form highway districts
so as to be coincident in area with rural sanitary districts, or wholly contained within rural sanitary
districts (c).

(c) Rural sanitary districts are interpreted by sect. 38 to mean
the districts declared to be rural sanitary districts by the
Public Health Act, 1875 (38 & 39 Vict. c. 55). And such a district is by sect. 9 of the latter Act defined as "the area of any
union" (defined by sect. 4 of that Act), "which is not coincident
in area with an urban district, nor wholly included in an urban
district, with the exception of those portions (if any) of the area
which are included in any urban district."

According to the marginal note it seems that the object of this
section is to make highway districts, so far as possible, coincident with rural sanitary districts. That intention, however,
does not appear to have been carried out, for the body of the section
only applies to cases where new highway districts are formed, or
the boundaries of old ones altered, but does not make it compulsory on the county authority, or any one else, to alter existing
boundaries.

In substance it only provides that *if* new highway districts are
formed, or the boundaries of old ones altered, the county authority shall have regard to the boundaries of rural sanitary districts, and so far as practicable, form highway districts coinci-

dent in area with them, &c. But before any alteration can be made there must be a notice from five or more justices, and other proceedings taken under 25 & 26 Vict. c. 61, ss. 5, 39, which leaves the whole matter entirely to the discretion of the justices as to whether they will or will not get the boundaries altered, or leave them as they are.

By sect. 38 "county authority" means the justices of a county in general or quarter sessions assembled.

4. Where a highway district, whether formed before or after the passing of this Act, is or becomes coincident in area with a rural sanitary district, the rural sanitary authority (*d*) of such district may apply (*e*) to the county authority, stating that they are desirous to exercise the powers of a highway board under the Highway Acts within their district (*f*).

On such application the county authority may, if they see fit, by order (*g*) declare that from and after a day to be named in the order (in this Act called the commencement of the order) such rural sanitary authority shall exercise all the powers of a highway board under the Highway Acts (*h*); and as from the commencement of the order the existing highway board (if any) for the district shall be dissolved (*i*), and waywardens or surveyors shall not hold office or be elected for any parish in the district.

An order made under this section may be amended, altered, or rescinded by a subsequent order of the county authority.

Where a highway district, being coincident in area with a rural sanitary district, is situate in more than one county, an order under this section may be made by the county authority of any county in which any part of such district is situate, but such order, and any order amending, altering, or rescinding the same, shall not be of any force or effect until it has been approved (*k*) by the county authority or authorities of

Act, '78, s. 3.

Power for rural sanitary authority of district coincident with highway district to become highway board.

Act '78. s. 4. the other county or counties in which any part of such district is situate.

(*d*) A rural sanitary authority, is interpreted by sect. 38, to mean the authority declared to be a rural sanitary authority by the Public Health Act, 1875 (38 & 39 Vict. c. 55). And such an authority is defined by sect. 9 of the latter Act, as the guardians of any union (defined by sect. 4 of that Act), which is not coincident in area with an urban district, nor wholly included in an urban district, with the exception of those portions (if any) of the area which are included in any urban district. They are, in fact, the same body as the guardians of the union or parish for or within which they act. (*Id.*)

(*e*) No restriction is placed upon the guardians either as to time or the manner in which they may apply to the county authority. No previous notice of intention to bring the matter before the board of guardians appears to be necessary, and the application, it seems, may be made on the resolution of a simple majority of those who are present when the matter happens to be brought forward by any guardian who may think fit to do so. It does not appear how the application is to be made, whether by motion in open court, by memorial, petition, or how otherwise.

(*f*) The application must state that the highway district in question is coincident in area with the rural sanitary district, and that the rural sanitary authority (or in other words, the board of guardians), are "desirous to exercise the powers of a highway board under the Highway Acts, within their district." It must not state, as the marginal note implies may be done, that the sanitary authority are desirous "*to become a highway board,*" but merely that they are desirous "to exercise the powers" of such a board. The county authority has no power to order that the rural sanitary authority shall *become* a highway board, but merely that they "shall *exercise all the powers,*" of such a board.

(*g*) The making of the order is entirely in the discretion of the county authority, and, it is presumed, can only take place in open court. There does not appear to be any power, on the part of ratepayers or others, to oppose the making of the order, though the court would, probably, not refuse to listen to any *bond fide* objections, if such should be raised, although they would only be available for the purpose of assisting the court in coming to a right conclusion.

(*h*) The Highway Acts are 5 & 6 Will. 4, c. 50, 25 & 26 Vict. c. 61, and 27 & 28 Vict. c. 101, and any Acts passed or to be passed amending the same (27 & 28 Vict. c. 101, s. 1.)

(*i*) The consequences arising from the dissolution are provided for by sect. 5 (*infra*).

(*k*) Nothing is said about the mode of approval. A similar

5. (1.) From and after the commencement of the order declaring a rural sanitary authority entitled to exercise the powers of a highway board within their district (*l*), the following consequences shall ensue (*m*) :

All such property, real or personal, including all interests, easements and rights in to and out of property real and personal and including things in action, as belongs to or is vested in or would but for such order have belonged to or been vested in the highway board, or any surveyor or surveyors of any parish forming part of the district, shall pass to and vest in the rural sanitary authority for all the estate and interest of the highway board, or of such surveyor or surveyors, but subject to all debts and liabilities affecting the same :

All debts and liabilities incurred in respect of any property transferred to the rural sanitary authority may be enforced against that authority to the extent of the property transferred :

All such powers rights duties liabilities capacities and incapacities (except the power of obtaining payment of their expenses by the issue of precepts in manner provided by the Highway Acts (*n*), or the power of making, assessing, and levying highway rates) as are vested in or attached to or would but for such order have become vested in or attached to the highway board, or any surveyor or surveyors of any parish forming part of the district, shall vest in and attach to the rural sanitary authority :

All property by this Act transferred to the rural sanitary authority shall be held by them on trust

Consequences of rural sanitary authority becoming highway board.

for the several parishes for the benefit of which it was held previously to such transfer.

(2.) If at any time after a rural sanitary authority has become invested with the powers of a highway board in pursuance of this Act, the boundaries of the district of such authority are altered, the powers and jurisdiction of such authority in their capacity of highway board shall be exercised within such altered district (*o*); and on the application of any authority or person interested the Local Government Board may by order provide for the adjustment of any accounts, or the settlement of any doubt or difference so far as relates to highways consequent on the alteration of the boundaries of such rural sanitary district.

(3.) All expenses incurred by a rural sanitary authority in the performance of their duties as a highway board shall be deemed to be general expenses of such authority within the meaning of the Public Health Act, 1875 (*p*).

36 & 39 Vict. c. 55.

(*l*) The marginal note, as in sect. 4, speaks of the consequences of a rural sanitary authority *becoming* a highway board, though the body of the section only applies to an order declaring that they are "*entitled to exercise the powers of a highway board*," and exempts from their powers "the power of obtaining payment of their expenses by the issue of precepts in manner provided by the Highway Acts," &c., one of the essential characteristics of a highway board.

The provision in sub-sect. (2) as to the powers of the rural sanitary authority *in their capacity of highway board*, and in sub-sect. (3), for expenses incurred by a rural sanitary authority, in the performance of their duties "*as a highway board*," evidently means "whilst exercising the powers of a highway board," and not that the rural sanitary authority are a highway board.

(*m*) The consequences set forth in sub-sect. (1), with the necessary variations, are very similar to those contained in 25 & 26 Vict. c. 61, s. 11, as to the consequences of the formation of highway districts. It may, however, be observed that neither a highway board under 25 & 26 Vict. c. 61, s. 11, nor a rural sanitary authority under this section, can exercise the powers of the inhabitants in vestry, although they may be exercised by an *urban* sanitary authority under 38 & 39 Vict. c. 55, s. 144.

(*n*) This refers to 27 & 28 Vict. c. 101. s. 33.

(*o*) A somewhat similar provision is made in 27 & 28 Vict. c. 101, s. 17, as to an alteration in part of a district. The remainder of the sub-section, as to the adjustment of accounts, &c., is new.

(*p*) The expenses incurred by a highway board for the common use or benefit of the several parishes within their district, including the repair of highways after the 25th March, 1879, are chargeable to the district fund under 27 & 28 Vict. c. 101, s. 32, and sect. 7 of this Act. But the corresponding expenses incurred by a rural sanitary authority will be payable as general expenses under 88 & 39 Vict. c. 55, ss. 229, 230.

6. Any two or more highway boards may unite in appointing and paying the salary of a district surveyor, who shall in relation to the district of each of the boards by whom he is appointed have all the powers and duties of a district surveyor under the Highway Acts (*q*).

Highway boards may combine to appoint a district surveyor.

(*q*) Although "the Highway Acts" include 5 & 6 Will. 4, c. 50 (see 27 & 28 Vict. c. 101, s. 1), this does not apply to the powers, &c., of a district surveyor under sect. 16 of that Act, as 25 & 26 Vict. c. 61, s. 42, sub-sect. 4, expressly declares that that section shall not apply to any parish within any district formed under that Act. The powers and duties in question are those which are specified in sect. 16 of the latter Act.

7. All expenses incurred by any highway board in maintaining and keeping in repair the highways of each parish within their district, and all other expenses legally incurred by such board, shall, notwithstanding anything contained in the Highway Acts, on and after the 25th March, 1879, be deemed to have been incurred for the common use or benefit of the several parishes within their district, and shall be charged on the district fund (*r*): Provided, that if a highway board think it just (*s*), by reason of natural differences of soil or locality, or other exceptional circumstances, that any parish or parishes within their district should bear the expenses of maintaining its or their own highways, they may (with the approval of the county authority or

Expenses of highway boards to be paid out of district fund.

authorities of the county or counties within which their
district, or any part thereof, is situate) divide their
district (t) into two or more parts, and charge exclusively on each of such parts the expenses payable by
such highway board in respect of maintaining and
keeping in repair the highways situate in each such
part; so, nevertheless, that each such part shall consist
of one or more highway parish or highway parishes.

(r) At present these expenses are a separate charge on each
parish within the highway district under 27 & 28 Vict. c. 101,
s. 32; but after the 25th March, 1879, they will be charged on
the district fund as expenses deemed to have been incurred for
the common use or benefit of the several parishes within the district. In order to obtain payment of such expenses, precepts are
now issued under sect. 33, stating the sum to be contributed by
each parish, subject to the proviso that no contribution required to be paid at one time in respect of highway rates shall
exceed 10d. in the pound, and that the aggregate of such contributions shall not exceed 2s. 6d. in the pound, except with the
consent of four-fifths of the ratepayers, &c.

According to this section "all" expenses incurred after the
25th March, 1879, are to be charged to the district fund, and no
"highway rates" will be levied at all. Consequently it seems
that this limitation, (which corresponds with the restriction imposed by 5 & 6 Will. 4, c. 50, s. 29), will be abolished after that
date, so far as highway districts are concerned, and that there
will be no limitation as to the amount to which highway parishes
will be liable for the repair of roads, any more than for the salaries
of officers and other expenses chargeable on the district fund
under 27 & 28 Vict. c. 101, s. 32.

(s) The initiative rests with the highway board, and the parishes
affected by their decision appear to have no voice in the matter,
excepting in so far as the opposition of their waywardens is concerned. If the board think it just, for reasons mentioned in the
section, that certain parishes should maintain their own highways,
they may, with the approval of the county authority, &c., divide
their district into two or more parts. But how or when the approval is to take place, whether before or after the division is
made, or whether by provisional and final orders, or how otherwise, is not stated.

(t) It is presumed that what is called "dividing the district,"
in point of fact, will only amount to combining certain parishes
within it for chargeability for the maintenance of highways independently of the other parishes, and that, so far as other matters

are concerned, there will be no actual division of the district requiring a provisional and final order of justices to make it valid.

8. All moneys borrowed by a highway board after the 25th March, 1879, under the Highway Acts, shall be charged on the district fund (*u*), but nothing in this Act shall affect the security, chargeability, or repayment of any moneys borrowed before the 25th March, 1879.

(*u*) By 27 & 28 Vict. c. 101, s. 47 highway boards are authorized, with the approval of the justices in quarter sessions, to borrow money for defraying the expense of improvements. But the moneys so borrowed are to be "a first charge on the highway rates of each parish liable to contribute to the payment thereof, after paying the sums due to the highway board on account of the district fund, in the same manner so far as the creditor is concerned,' as if the money had been borrowed on account of each parish alone." That liability will remain unaltered as regards moneys borrowed previously to the 25th March, 1879. But all moneys borrowed after that date will be charged on the district fund, and not on the parish or parishes in which they are expended, as is the case at present.

9. The accounts of the highway authority of every highway district and highway parish shall be made up in such form as the Local Government Board shall from time to time prescribe (*v*), and shall be balanced to the 25th March (*w*) in each year, and as soon as conveniently may be after such day the said accounts shall be audited and examined by the auditor of accounts relating to the relief of the poor for the audit district in which the highway district or highway parish, or the greater part thereof in rateable value, is situate (*x*).

Every such auditor shall (as nearly as may be) have, in relation to the accounts of the highway authority of a highway district or highway parish, and of their officers, the same powers and duties as he has in the case of accounts relating to the relief of the poor; and any person aggrieved by the decision of the auditor

Act '78, s. 2. shall have the same rights and remedies as in the case of such last-mentioned audit (y).

The auditor shall receive such remuneration as the Local Government Board direct; and such remuneration, together with the expenses incident to the audit, shall be paid by the highway authority of the highway district or highway parish out of the fund or rate applicable to the repair of highways within such district or parish; and such remuneration and expenses may, in default of payment, be recovered in a summary (z) manner.

5 & 6 Will 4, c. 50. 27 & 28 Vict. c. 101. Section 44 of the Highway Act, 1835, is hereby repealed, and section 36 of the Highway Act, 1864, is hereby repealed down to the words " to be paid out of the district fund," and the statement of receipt and expenditure by the said section directed to be furnished by every highway board within thirty days after the signature of the accounts by the chairman shall be furnished within thirty days after the completion of the audit under this section.

Nothing in this section shall affect any proceeding commenced before the passing of this Act.

(v) This is a new provision, and applies to all highway districts, and to all highway parishes, whether included in a highway district or not. Until the passing of this Act there was no prescribed form for making up the accounts, nor any other audit than by the board of a highway district, or by a person appointed by the board, or by the justices in special sessions under 5 & 6 Will. 4, c. 50, s. 45 as regards parishes not included in a highway district.

(w) By 27 & 28 Vict. c. 101, s. 36 the accounts of every highway board were required to be made up and balanced to the 31st December in every year. That part of the section is now repealed, and for the future the accounts must be made up and balanced to the 25th March in each year. There will consequently be no audit of accounts during this year and the next statement of accounts will include the period between the 31st December, 1877, and the 25th March, 1879, so far as highway boards are concerned, and between the date of the last account and the 25th March, 1879, as regards parishes not included in a highway district.

Act 78, s. 9.

(*x*) Until now the accounts of a highway board have been examined by the board ,or audited by a person appointed by the board under 27 & 28 Vict. c. 101, s. 36, and those of a highway parish by the justices at special sessions under 5 & 6 Will. 4, c. 50, s. 45. For the future they will be audited by the poor law auditor of the district in which the highway district or highway parish, &c., is situate.

The accounts of the rural sanitary authority will also be audited by the poor law auditor (see 38 & 39 Vict. c. 55, s. 248, and order for accounts 14th January, 1867, Art. 38).

(*y*) The auditor's powers and duties, &c., &c., are regulated by 7 & 8 Vict. c. 101, ss. 32, 33, 35, 36. And see order for accounts, 14th January, 1867, and Arch. Poor Law, by Glen, pp. 22–46, 13th ed.

(*z*) Recovery "in a summary manner," it is presumed means recovery "before a court of summary jurisdiction," under sect. 36 *infra*.

10. Where complaint is made to the county authority (*a*) that the highway authority (*b*) of any highway area within their jurisdiction has made default in maintaining or repairing all or any of the highways within their jurisdiction, the county authority, if satisfied after due inquiry and report (*c*) by their surveyor that the authority has been guilty of the alleged default, shall make an order (*d*) limiting a time for the performance of the duty of the highway authority in the matter of such complaint.

If such duty is not performed by the time limited in the order, and the highway authority fail to show to the county authority sufficient cause (*e*) why the order has not been complied with, the county authority may appoint some person to perform such duty, and shall by order direct that the expenses of performing the same, together with the reasonable remuneration of the person appointed for superintending such performance, shall be paid by the authority in default, and any order made for payment of such expenses and costs may be removed (*f*) into the High Court of

Justice, and be enforced in the same manner as if the
same were an order of such court.

Any person appointed under this section to perform
the duty of a defaulting highway authority shall, in
the performance and for the purpose of such duty, be
invested with all the powers of such authority other
than the powers of making rates or levying contributions by precept, and the county authority may
from time to time by order change any person so
appointed (*g*).

Where an order has been made by a county authority for the repair of a highway on a highway authority alleged to be in default, if such authority, within
ten days after service on them of the order of the
county authority, give notice to the clerk of the peace
that they decline to comply with the requisitions of
such order until their liability to repair the highway
(*h*) in respect to which they are alleged to have made
default has been determined by a jury, it shall be the
duty of the county authority either to satisfy the
defaulting authority by cancelling or modifying (*i*) in
such manner as the authority may desire the order of
the county authority, or else to submit to a jury the
question of the liability of the defaulting authority to
repair the highway (*k*).

If the county authority decide to submit the question to a jury they shall direct a bill of indictment to
be preferred to the next practicable assizes (*l*) to be
holden in and for their county, with a view to try the
liability of the defaulting authority to repair the highway. Until the trial of the indictment is concluded
the order of the county authority shall be suspended.
On the conclusion of the trial, if the jury find the
defendants guilty, the order of the county authority
shall forthwith be deemed to come into force; but if

the jury acquit the defendants the order of the county authority shall forthwith become void.

The costs of the indictment, and of the proceedings consequent thereon, shall be paid by such parties to the proceedings as the court before whom the case is tried may direct (m). Any costs directed to be paid by the county authority shall be deemed to be expenses properly incurred by such authority, and shall be paid accordingly out of the county rate; and any costs directed to be paid by the highway authority shall be deemed to be expenses properly incurred by such authority in maintenance of the roads within their jurisdiction, and shall be paid out of the funds applicable to the maintenance of such roads (n).

(a) The complaint may be made by any body, but can only be made at general or quarter sessions. (See interpretation of "county authority," sect. 38, *infra*).

(b) This means as respects an urban sanitary district the urban sanitary authority, and as respects a highway district the highway board, and as respects a highway parish the surveyor or surveyors or other officers performing similar duties (see sect. 38, *infra*). It does not include a rural sanitary authority exercising the powers of a highway board under sect. 4, *ante*, unless indeed such an authority can be treated as a highway board, which, as already mentioned, *ante*, pp. 168, 170, does not seem to be the case.

The omission appears the more remarkable as urban sanitary authorities are expressly included, although they are liable to other proceedings under 38 & 39 Vict. c. 55, s. 144.

(c) The report it is presumed will, in the ordinary course of things, be made after the complaint is made to sessions and the matter referred to the county surveyor, a course which will evidently occasion considerable delay, as the report in that case will probably not be presented before the following sessions. There does not, however, appear to be any objection to the sessions acting on the general report of their surveyor, although presented before the complaint is made, provided it satisfies them that the highway in question is really out of repair.

(d) The order it seems will be made by the court of quarter sessions simply on the complaint (of any one who thinks fit to make it) that the highway authority has made default in maintaining or repairing a certain highway within its jurisdiction, and after being satisfied by due inquiry of the complainant or otherwise, and by the report of their surveyor that the highway authority has been guilty of the alleged default. The highway

N

Act. '78, s. 10. authority appears to have no opportunity of being heard in
opposition to the complaint as it formerly had under 5 & 6 Will.
4, c. 50, ss. 94, 95, and 25 & 26 Vict. c. 61, ss. 18, 19. The
order will be made in its absence, and will limit a time within
which the highway in question must be put in repair by such
authority, leaving it to contest its liability at a future stage of
the proceedings.

(*e*) Cause can only be shown to the justices in general or
quarter sessions; and the appointment of the person to perform
the duty specified in the order, and of the person appointed to
superintend its performance must also be made by them. The
notice given by the highway authority to the clerk of the peace as
hereinafter mentioned, will, it is presumed, be "sufficient cause,"
and prevent the appointment of any one to perform the duty
neglected by the highway authority. A *bonâ fide* dispute as to
the road in question being a highway would also appear to be
" sufficient cause."

(*f*) The order, it is presumed, will be removed by order of the
court or a judge of the Queen's Bench Division of the High
Court of Justice, under 12 & 13 Vict. c. 45, s. 18, and 36 & 37
Vict. c. 66, ss. 16, 34. See Foot's Commentary on the Quarter
Sessions Procedure Act, p. 67, where the procedure and practice
are described at length.

(*g*) This provision was not contained in 24 & 25 Vict. c. 61,
s. 18, the section on which this section is modeled.

(*h*) The "liability to repair " is still the question for determination under this Act, as well as under 5 & 6 Will. 4 c. 50, s. 95,
and 24 & 25 Vict. c. 61, s. 19. In the present instance, however,
the difficulty about the road not being an admitted highway,
upon which *Reg.* v. *Farrer*, L. R. 1 Q. B. 558, 30 J. P. 469, and
other similar cases turned, is obviated by making the question
not a matter of jurisdiction of the justices making the order, but
a matter of defence by the highway authority who decline to
comply with the requisitions of the order.

(*i*) There appears to be no means of either cancelling or
modifying the order excepting at quarter sessions, although the
notice to the clerk of the peace may be given at any time within
ten days after service of the order on the highway authority, and
therefore long before the day for holding sessions. In 27 & 28
Vict. c. 101, s. 39, there is a somewhat similar power conferred
on the highway board enabling it to serve a counter-notice on
the appellant in the case of an appeal against orders for the
repair of highways, &c.

(*k*) Under this question, it is presumed, the question of " highway or no highway " may be raised.

(*l*) Under this section the indictment can only be preferred to
the assizes; whereas under 5 & 6 Will. 4 c. 50, s. 95, and 25 & 26
Vict. c. 61, s. 19, the justices have the option of directing it

'to be preferred either to the assizes or the general quarter sessions, as they think fit.

(*m*) Under 5 & 6 Will. 4, c. 50, s. 95, the costs must in all cases be paid out of the highway rate, whereas under this section they will be payable by such parties to the proceedings as the court may direct. In proceedings under 25 & 26 Vict. c. 61, s. 19, the costs may be ordered to be paid as under this section.

(*n*) At present "the funds applicable to the maintenance of roads" in the case of parishes in a highway district, as well as in ordinary highway parishes, are the highway rates of the parish (27 & 28 Vict. c. 101, s. 32, 5 & 6 Will 4, c. 50, s. 27). But after the 25th March, 1879, the fund applicable to the maintenance of roads in a highway district will be the district fund instead of the highway rate (see sect. 7, *supra*), and these expenses will consequently be payable out of that fund like any other expenses incurred for the common use or benefit of the parishes within the district.

It seems that this section virtually repeals 25 & 26 Vict. c. 61, ss. 18 & 19 (see *ante* p. 102, note (*x*) ; and looking to the difference between the mode of procedure under it, and that under 5 & 6 Will. 4, c. 50, ss. 94, 95, it will probably be held to repeal those sections also.

11. Notwithstanding anything in the Highway Acts, waywardens shall continue in office till the 30th April in the year following the year in which they were elected (*o*), and on that day their successors shall come into office. Duration of office of waywarden

(*o*) By 25 & 26 Vict. c. 61, s. 10, a waywarden is to be elected every year for the year next ensuing, and to continue to act until his successor is appointed. And by 27 & 28 Vict. c. 101, s. 11, a waywarden elected on the day fixed for the election of waywardens by the final order of justices forming the highway district, is to continue in office only until the time at which the next annual election of surveyors would have taken place in the several parishes of the district if they had not been constituted a highway district. He will now continue to act until the 30th of April in every year, and his successor will come into office on, but not before, that day, although the election may have taken place weeks before.

12. So much of section 7 of the Highway Act, 1862, as prohibits the inclusion in a highway district of any parish or place the highways of which were at the Repeal of part of s. 7 of 25 & 26 Vict. c. 6

Act '78. s. 12. time of the passing of that Act, or within six months afterwards, under the superintendence of a board established in pursuance of section 18 of the Principal Act, unless with the consent of such board, is hereby repealed (*p*).

(*p*) The repealed section had long ceased to be operative, by lapse of time.

MAIN ROADS.

Disturn-piked roads to become main roads, and half the expense or maintenance to be contributed out of county rate.

13. For the purposes of this Act, and subject to its provisions, any road which has, within the period between the 31st December, 1870, and the date of the passing of this Act, ceased to be a turnpike road, and any road which, being at the time of the passing of this Act a turnpike road, may afterwards cease to be such, shall be deemed to be a main road (*q*); and one-half of the expenses (*r*) incurred from and after the 29th September, 1878, by the highway authority (*s*) in the maintenance of such road shall, as to every part thereof which is within the limits of any highway area (*t*), be paid to the highway authority of such area by the county authority of the county in which such road is situate out of the county rate, on the certificate of the surveyor of the county authority, or of such other person or persons as the county authority may appoint, to the effect that such main road has been maintained to his or their satisfaction (*u*).

Provided that no part of such expenses shall be included in—

(1.) Any precept or warrant for the levying or collection of county rate within the metropolis (*v*), subject and without prejudice to any provision to be hereafter made;

(2.) Any order made on the council of any borough having a separate court of quarter sessions

under section 117 (*w*) of the Municipal Corporation Act, 1835.

The term "expenses" in this section shall mean the
cost of repairs defrayed out of current rates (*x*), and
shall not include any repayment of principal moneys
borrowed, or of interest payable thereon.

(*q*) By 33 & 34 Vict. c. 73, s. 10, it is enacted that with regard
to any highway which seven years previous to the passing of that
Act (9th August, 1870) had ceased, or which thereafter might
cease to be a turnpike road, the cost of maintaining so much
thereof as passes through any highway district constituted under
the Highway Acts, 1862 and 1864, should after 31st December,
1870, &c., be a charge on the common fund of such district under
sect. 32 of the Highway Act, 1864.

The present section introduces a considerable alteration in this
respect with regard to any highway which has ceased to be a
turnpike road between the 31st December, 1870, and the 16th
August, 1878, and any turnpike road which may hereafter
cease to be such. These roads are declared to be "main roads."
Their maintenance will still continue to be chargeable in the first
instance to the district fund as provided by 33 & 34 Vict. c. 73,
s. 10, so far as regards highways within a highway district, and
will be payable out of the current rates, in the case of highways
within an urban sanitary district or a highway parish not included
in either of such districts. But one-half of the expenses incurred
after the 29th September, 1878, in such maintenance within any
urban sanitary district, or highway district or highway parish not
included within either of such districts, will be payable to the
highway authority of such area by the county authority out of
the county rate on the certificate of the county surveyor, &c.,
that the road has been maintained to his satisfaction.

This does not apply to any highway which has ceased to be a
turnpike road before the 31st December, 1870, and its maintenance will consequently still continue to be a charge upon the
district fund or current rates, as the case may be, but without
any contribution by the county authority out of the county rate
or otherwise.

It may also be mentioned that boroughs having a separate
court of quarter sessions are excluded from the definition of an
"urban sanitary district" in sect. 38, and are, therefore, not entitled to contribution from the county rate under this section.

(*r*) "Expenses" are confined to the cost of repairs defrayed
out of current rates.

(*s*) A rural sanitary authority exercising the powers of a highway board under sect. 4 is not mentioned in the interpretation of
"highway authority" in sect. 38.

(*t*) Highway areas are defined by sect. 14, *infra*.

(*u*) Therefore, unless the road has been maintained to the county surveyor's, &c., satisfaction, the highway authority will have no right to contribution from the county authority. It would seem, too, that " has been maintained " means has been maintained during the time covered by the certificate, and not merely that the road is maintained to the surveyor's satisfaction at the date of the certificate.

(*v*) The effect of this proviso is to exempt the Metropolis from contributing towards the payment of any part of the expenses incurred in the maintenance of roads passing through highway. areas, which have been disturnpiked since the 31st December,. 1870, or which may hereafter be disturnpiked, beyond what it was liable to at the date of the passing of this Act.

(*w*) By this section the county treasurer is required to keep an account " of the sum of money expended out of the county rate for other purposes than the costs arising out of the prosecution,. maintenance, and punishment, conveyance and transport of offenders committed for trial in such county, and in the case of boroughs having a separate court of quarter sessions of the peace,. other than out of coroners' inquests ; " and to send a copy of the account to the council of every borough situate within the county having a separate court of quarter sessions, and before the passing of 2 & 3 Will. 4, c. 64, liable to contribute to the county rate, and to make an order on the council for the payment of such portion of the sum as would have been chargeable after deducting all sums of money received in aid of the county rate, &c., &c.

As the contribution towards the expense of maintaining disturnpiked roads will form an item in the sum expended out of the county rate for purposes other than those directed to be excluded from county treasurer's account, it is clear that such boroughs would have had to pay their proportion of the amount if provision had not been made to the contrary.

(*x*) This expression does not seem to be very happily chosen. It would suit the case of an urban sanitary authority, or of an ordinary highway parish, rightly enough : but can scarcely be considered applicable to parishes included in a highway district. after the 25th March, 1879, when the cost of repairs will be defrayed out of the district fund, and not out of highway. rates, and, therefore, not " out of current rates ; " or to the cost of repairs of disturnpiked roads within highway districts, which by 33 & 34 Vict. c. 75, s. 10 is also a charge on the district fund.

Another question which will probably arise will be as to what shall be considered the " cost " of repairs. Does it mean simply the cost of labour and materials, or does it include establishment. expenses under 27 & 28 Vict. c. 101, s. 32 ? The only items specifically excluded are the "repayment of principal moneys borrowed" and " interest payable thereon."

14. The following areas shall be deemed to be high-way areas for the purposes of this Act; (that is to say),

    (1.) Urban sanitary districts (*y*):

    (2.) Highway districts:

    (3.) Highway parishes not included within any highway district or any urban sanitary district.

(*y*) See the definition of "urban sanitary districts," &c., sect. 38, *infra*.

15. Where it appears to any highway authority (*z*) that any highway within their district ought to become a main road by reason of its being a medium of communication between great towns, or a thoroughfare to a railway station, or otherwise, such highway authority may apply to the county authority for an order declaring such road, as to such parts as aforesaid, to be a main road; and the county authority, if of opinion that there is probable cause for the application, shall cause the road to be inspected, and, if satisfied that it ought to be a main road, shall make an order accordingly.

A copy of the order so made shall be forthwith deposited at the office of the clerk of the peace of the county, and shall be open to the inspection of persons interested (*a*) at all reasonable hours; and the order so made shall not be of any validity unless and until it is confirmed by a further order of the county authority made within a period of not more than six months after the making of the first-mentioned order (*b*).

(*z*) It seems very doubtful whether the power conferred by this section can be acted upon by a rural sanitary authority exercising the powers of a highway board under sect. 4. They are

not expressly included in the definition of a "highway authority" in sect. 38; and it seems that they are not a highway
board (although they exercise the powers of such a board), and
consequently are not impliedly included in the definition in sect.
38, that a highway authority means "as respects a highway district, the highway board."

The initiative must be taken by the highway authority (meaning "as respects a highway parish the surveyor or surveyors or
other officers performing similar duties," sect. 38), who must
apply to the justices in general or quarter sessions for an order
declaring that certain specified parts of the highway in question
may be declared o be a main road by reason of its being a
medium of communication between certain great towns there
specified, or a thoroughfare to a certain railway station there
mentioned or otherwise. It is not at all clear what the words
" as to such parts as aforesaid" really mean. But it is presumed
they mean " as to such parts as are a medium of communication,"
&c., &c.

The application must be supported by sufficient evidence to
satisfy the justices that there is probable cause for it. If they
should be of that opinion they will then " cause the road to be
inspected," but whether by a delegation from their own body,
or by the county surveyor, or how otherwise, is not stated. If
satisfied from this inspection that the road ought to be a main
road, they will make an order declaring it to be a main road.

(a) A copy of the order must forthwith be deposited at the
office of the clerk of the peace and will be open to the inspection
of persons "interested" at all reasonable hours. What the nature
of the interest is to be, whether pecuniary or speculative, or otherwise, does not appear. The order need not be advertised, but it
will not be of any validity unless it is confirmed by a further
order of justices made within six months after it was made. It
seems that the order cannot be altered or varied, but must be
confirmed in its entirety or else be abortive.

(b) What the effect of the order will be when made is not
quite clear. The order, it is presumed, will simply declare that
the road in question shall be a "main road." But what the consequences of its becoming a main road will be, nowhere appears.
In the case of a disturnpiked road, which has become a main
road, one-half of the expenses of maintenance will be contributed
out of the county rate under sect. 13. But that is only a special
provision, applicable to disturnpiked roads. There is no corresponding provision applicable to main roads generally, or to ordinary highways becoming main roads; and this section merely
provides for the making of the order declaring the roads to be
main roads, but says nothing as to the consequences which are
to follow from their becoming main roads. Under sect. 18, if
the highway authority makes default in complying with the
provisions of that section, &c., &c., the county authority may

withhold "the contribution *payable by them under this Act* towards the expenses of the maintenance of main roads by such highway authority for the year in which such default appears." But no contribution is payable by them under this section, and, therefore, no such contribution can be withheld, although it seems that the county authority may still require the highway authority to keep the account there mentioned.

16. If it appears to a county authority that any road within their county which, within the period between the 31st December, 1870, and the date of the passing of this Act, ceased to be a turnpike road, ought not to become a main road in pursuance of this Act, such authority shall, before the 1st February, 1879, make an application to the Local Government Board for a provisional order declaring that such road ought not to become a main road (*c*).

Subject as aforesaid, where it appears to a county authority that any road within their county which has become a main road in pursuance of this Act ought to cease to be a main road and become an ordinary highway, such authority may apply to the Local Government Board for a provisional order declaring that such road has ceased to be a main road and become an ordinary highway (*d*).

The Local Government Board, if of opinion that there is probable cause for an application under this section, shall cause the road to be inspected, and if satisfied that it ought not to become or ought to cease to be a main road and become an ordinary highway shall make a provisional order accordingly, to be confirmed as hereinafter mentioned (*e*).

All expenses incurred in or incidental to the making or confirmation of any order under this section shall be defrayed by the county authority applying for such order (*f*).

(*c*) The object of this part of the section is to enable the

Act '78, s. 16. county authority to obtain the opinion of the Local Government
Board as to whether certain roads which have been disturnpiked
between the 31st December, 1870, and the 16th August, 1878,
should be partly maintained out of the county rate under sect.
13, or should continue to be wholly maintained by the highway
authority under 33 & 34 Vict. c. 73, s. 10. The application to
the Local Government Board must be made before the 1st
February, 1879, or they cannot entertain it. As the Local
Government Board have to consider whether there is or is not
probable cause for the application before they cause the road to
be inspected, it would seem that the grounds on which it appears
to the county authority that the road in question ought not to
become a main road under sect. 13, must be stated in their
application, and these grounds must also have been agreed to in
general or quarter sessions.

(*d*) This application may be made at any time, but, as in the
former case, must contain the grounds on which it appears to
the county authority that the main road in question ought to
cease to be a main road and become an ordinary highway, and
these grounds must also have been agreed to in general or quarter
sessions.

(*e*) The order is only provisional and will be of no validity
until it is confirmed by Parliament under sect. 34.

(*f*) It is not stated out of what fund these expenses are to be
defrayed. The contribution under sect. 13 is to be paid "out of
the county rate." And as that is the only fund at the disposal
of the county authority, it seems, although not so expressed,
that these expenses must also be payable out of the county
rate.

Turnpike
road in
several
counties.

17. Where a turnpike road subject to one trust
extends into divers counties, such road, for the purposes of this Act, shall be treated as a separate turnpike road in each county through which it passes (*g*).

(*g*) And, therefore, each county will have to pay a contribution under sect. 13 proportioned to the length of the road within
that county. It is presumed that the section does not mean that
the *whole* road shall be treated as a separate turnpike road in
each county, but that the portion of the road in each county
shall be treated as a separate turnpike road in that county.

Accounts of
expenses of
maintenance
of main
roads.

18. Every highway authority shall keep, in such
form as may be directed by the county authority, a
separate account of the expenses of the maintenance of
the main (*h*) roads within their jurisdiction, and shall

forward copies thereof to the county authority at such
time or times in every year as may be required by the
county authority, and the accounts so kept shall, where
the accounts of the highway authority are audited
under this Act (*i*) or under sect. 247 (*j*) of the Public
Health Act, 1875, be audited in the same manner as
the other accounts of such authority, and where the
accounts of the highway authority are not so audited
shall be subject to such audit as the county authority
may direct.

If any highway authority makes default in complying with the provisions of this section, or with any
directions given in pursuance thereof by the county
authority, the county authority may withhold all or
any part of the contribution payable by them under
this Act towards the expenses of the maintenance of
main roads by such highway authority for the year in
which such default occurs.

(*h*) These accounts only apply to the maintenance of "main
roads." Other accounts are by sect. 9 required to be "made up"
in such form (which it is presumed is the same thing as "keeping" under this section), as the Local Government Board prescribe.
But whether or not the keeping of these accounts in the form
directed by the county authority will exonerate the highway
authority from the necessity for making up accounts respecting
main roads in the form prescribed by the Local Government
Board under sect. 9 is left in doubt.

(*i*) See sect. 9, *ante.*

(*j*) This section only applies to an urban sanitary authority
who are not the council of a borough. The audit of accounts of
a rural sanitary authority is regulated by sect. 248 of the same
Act, and not "under this Act." Hence, it would appear that if
a rural sanitary authority is entitled to contribution out of the
county rate under sect. 13, its accounts, so far as the maintenance
of main roads is concerned, are "subject to such audit as the
county authority may direct." The accounts of the town council
of a borough, as regards the maintenance of main roads, will also
be subject to a similar audit.

19. Where a highway district is situate in more
than one county, the provisions of this Act, with

respect to the expenses of the maintenance of main roads, shall apply as if the portion of such district situate in each county were a separate highway district in that county (*k*).

(*k*) The effect of this will be that each county will only contribute to the maintenance of such portions of the main roads as lie within its own boundaries.

20. Notwithstanding the provisions of this Act, in the case of any county in which certain of the bridges within the county are repairable by the county at large, and others are repairable by the several hundreds within the county in which they are situate, it shall be lawful for the county authority from time to time, by order, to declare any main road or part of a main road within their county (*l*) to be repairable (*m*) to the extent only and in manner provided by section 13 of this Act, either by the county or by the hundred in which such main road or part is situate, as they think fit; and where a main road or part thereof is declared to be repairable by a hundred, the expense of repairing the same shall, to the extent to which but for this section the expense or any contribution towards the expense of repairing the same would be repayable (*n*) out of the county rate, be repayable out of a separate rate which shall be raised and charged in the like manner as the expenses of repairing the hundred bridges in the same hundred would have been raised and charged (*o*).

(*l*) The expression " any main road . . . within their county," it is presumed, must mean any main road within their county, " leading to and passing over any such bridge." It cannot mean any main road whatever within their county.

(*m*) There is nothing in sect. 13 which says that main roads shall be " repairable " by the county; but only that one-half of the expenses incurred in their maintenance shall be paid to the highway authority out of the county rate. But assuming that

an order may be made declaring that any such main road shall Act '78, s. 20.
be repairable either by the county or hundred, as the county
authority think fit, the order must direct that one-half of the
expenses of maintenance shall be repaid to the highway authority
by the county or hundred, as the case may be; and must also
declare that the main road in question is repairable to the extent
of one-half of the expenses incurred in its maintenance, by the
county or hundred, as the case may be.

There must have been an order under sect. 15 declaring the
road in question a "main road," before this part of the section
can be brought into operation.

In connection with this matter it may be mentioned that by
33 & 34 Vict. c. 73, s. 12, where a turnpike road becomes an
ordinary highway, all bridges which were previously repaired by
the trustees of the road become county bridges, and are repairable accordingly; subject to the proviso that for the purposes of
that Act such bridges shall be treated as if they were built subsequently to the passing of 5 & 6 Will. 4, c. 50. And by 5 & 6
Will. 4, c. 50, s. 21, if any bridge shall hereafter be built which
shall be liable by law to be repaired by and at the expense of
any county or part of a county, then and in such case all highways leading to, passing over and next adjoining to such bridge,
shall be from time to time repaired by the parish, person or body
politic or corporate, or trustees of a turnpike road, who were by
law before the erection of the said bridge bound to repair the said
highways. With a proviso saving the liability of the county to
repair the walls, &c., &c., of the bridge.

(*n*) The object of the section is to shift the liability to contribute to the maintenance of such roads from the county to the
hundred, and to place the hundred in the position of the county,
so far as relates to the liability arising from the order declaring
any such road a main road. It will be observed that the matter
is left entirely to the county authority, and that neither the hundred, nor any one representing it, has any power whatever to
oppose the making of the order. The order must be made at
general or quarter sessions.

(*o*) The rate will be raised and charged under 22 Hen. 8, c. 5,
and 1 Anne, c. 12 (Rev. Ed.), c. 18 (Ruff.).

BRIDGES.

21. Any bridge erected before the passing of this Certain existing
Act in any county without such superintendence as is bridges may be accepted
provided in 43 Geo. 3, c. 59, s. 5, and which is cer- by county authority.
tified by the county surveyor or other person appointed
in that behalf by the county authority to be in good
repair and condition (*p*), shall, if the county authority

see fit so to order, become and be deemed to be a bridge which the inhabitants of the county shall be liable to maintain and repair.

(*p*) The 43 Geo. 3, c. 59, s. 5, requires that the bridge "shall be erected in a substantial and commodious manner." But under this section the county surveyor is only required to certify that it is "in good repair and condition," without saying anything about its having been "erected in a substantial and commodious manner."

Contribution out of country rates towards erecting bridges.

22. The county authority may make such contribution as it sees fit out of the county rates towards the cost of any bridge to be hereafter erected, after the same has been certified in accordance with the provisions of 43 Geo. 3, c. 59, s. 5 (*q*), as a proper bridge to be maintained by the inhabitants of the county ; so always that such contribution shall not exceed one-half the cost of erecting such bridge.

(*q*) No certificate is required under 43 Geo. 3, c. 59, s. 5. That section merely declares that no bridge, &c., " shall be deemed or taken to be a county bridge, or a bridge which the inhabitants of any county shall be compellable or liable to maintain or repair, unless such bridge shall be erected in a substantial and commodious manner under the direction or to the satisfaction of the county surveyor," &c.

Probably, what is meant by this section is that the county authority may contribute towards the cost of any bridge after it has been certified as a proper bridge to be maintained by the inhabitants of the county in accordance with the provisions of 43 Geo. 3, c. 59, s. 5.

EXTRAORDINARY TRAFFIC.

Power of road authority to recover expenses of extraordinary traffic.

23. Where by a certificate of their surveyor it appears to the authority which is liable or has undertaken (*r*) to repair any highway, whether a main road or not, that, having regard to the average expenses of repairing highways in the neighbourhood, extraordinary expenses have been incurred by such authority in repairing such highway by reason of the damage.

caused by excessive weight passing along the same, or extraordinary traffic thereon, such authority may recover in a summary manner (*s*) from any person by whose order such weight or traffic has been conducted the amount of such expenses as may be proved to the satisfaction of the court having cognizance of the case to have been incurred by such authority by reason of the damage arising from such weight or traffic as aforesaid.

Provided that any person against whom expenses are or may be recoverable under this section may enter into an agreement with such authority as is mentioned in this section for the payment to them of a composition (*t*) in respect of such weight or traffic, and thereupon the persons so paying the same shall not be subject to any proceedings under this section.

(*r*) This includes cases under 25 & 26 Vict. c. 61, s. 36. It is doubtful, however, whether it applies to highways contracted to be repaired under 27 & 28 Vict. c. 101, s. 22.

(*s*) It is presumed that this means "before a court of summary jurisdiction" under sect. 36. But before proceedings can be taken it will be necessary for the highway authority to be furnished with a certificate from their surveyor that, in comparison with the average expense of repairing highways in the neighbourhood, extraordinary expenses have been incurred by them in repairing the highway in question by reason of the damage caused by excessive weight passing along it, or extraordinary traffic thereon. Having received that certificate, they must find out the person or persons by whose order such weight or traffic has been conducted, and then summon such parties to show cause why an order should not be made upon them under sect. 36, requiring them to pay to the highway authority so much of such expenses as may be proved to the satisfaction of the justices to have been incurred by reason of the damage arising from so much of such weight or traffic as may be proved to have been ordered by such parties respectively.

There will be some difficulty in apportioning the share of liability to which each of several parties using the highway may be liable; and also in determining what portion of the weight may be fairly used, and what portion of it must be considered as "excessive," and to be paid for by the party using it. Moreover, it will not be quite easy to determine what is ordinary, and what "extraordinary" traffic, so far as particular parties are concerned. There is nothing which fixes the precise number of carriages or carts which a man may use upon a highway, and consequently nothing by which it can be determined what portion of the traffic which he occasions can be considered ordinary and what "extraordinary" so as to make him liable to pay for the extra damage arising from it.

Another difficulty will be experienced in determining the person "by whose *order* such weight or traffic has been conducted." In many cases the question will be simple enough. But in the case, for instance, of a contract for building, and in other cases where there may be contractors and sub-contractors, considerable difficulty will be experienced in deciding who is the party that actually "*ordered*" the excessive weight or extraordinary traffic. But, nevertheless, it seems that the justices can make no order on any one else.

(*t*) It is not stated upon what scale the composition is to be made. The composition, therefore, may be comparatively nominal or substantial, as the parties may agree, according to the circumstances of each particular case.

DISCONTINUANCE OF UNNECESSARY HIGHWAYS.

Unnecessary highways may be declared not repairable at the public expense.

24. If any authority (*u*) liable to keep any highway in repair is of opinion that so much of such highway as lies within any parish situate in a petty sessional division (*v*) is unnecessary for public use, and therefore ought not to be maintained at the public (*w*) expense, such authority (in this section referred to "as the applicant authority") may apply to the court of summary jurisdiction (*x*) of such petty sessional division to view by two or more justices, being members of the court, the highway to which such application relates, and on such view being had, if the court of summary jurisdiction is of opinion that the application ought to be proceeded with, it shall by notice (*y*) in writing to the owners or reputed owners and occupiers of all lands abutting upon such highway, and by public notice (*z*), appoint a time and place, not earlier than one month from the date of such notice, at which it will be prepared to hear all persons objecting to such highway being declared unnecessary for public use, and not _{Act '78, s. 24.} repairable at the expense of the public (*w*).

On the day and at the place appointed, the court shall hear any persons objecting to an order being made by the court that such highway is unnecessary for public use and ought not to be repairable at the public (*w*) expense, and shall make an order either dismissing the application or declaring such highway unnecessary for public use, and that it ought not to be repaired at the public (*w*) expense.

If the court make such last-mentioned order as aforesaid, the expenses of repairing such highway shall cease to be defrayed out of any public rate (*a*).

Public notice of the time and place appointed for hearing a case under this section shall be given by the applicant authority as follows (*b*); that is to say,—

(1.) By advertising a notice of the time and place appointed for the hearing and the object of the hearing, with a description of the highway to which it refers in some local newspaper circulating in the district in which such highway is situate once at least in each of the four weeks preceding the hearing; and

(2.) By causing a copy of such notice to be affixed, at least fourteen days before the hearing, to the principal doors of every church and chapel in the parish in which such highway is situate, or in some conspicuous position near such highway.

And the application shall not be entertained by the court until the fact of such public notice having been given is proved to its satisfaction (*c*).

If at any time after an order has been made by a court of summary jurisdiction under this section, upon

o

Act '78, s. 24. application of any person interested in the maintenance
of the highway in respect of which such order has been
made, after one month's previous notice in writing
thereof to the applicant authority, it appears to the
court of quarter sessions that from any change of circumstances since the time of the making of any such
order as aforesaid such highway has become of public
use, and ought to be maintained at the public (*w*)
expense, the court of quarter sessions may direct that
the liability of such highway to be maintained at the
public (*w*) expense shall revive from and after such day
as they may name in their order, and such highway
shall thenceforth be maintained out of the rate (*d*)
applicable to payment of the expenses of repairing
other highways repairable by the applicant authority;
and the said court of quarter sessions may by their
order direct the expenses of and incident to such application to be paid as they may see fit.

Any order of a court of summary jurisdiction under
this section shall be deemed to be an order from which
an appeal lies to a court of quarter sessions (*e*).

(*u*) This includes a "highway authority" as defined by sect.
38, and any other authority not comprised in that definition, but
liable to keep the highway in question in repair.

(*v*) There are provisions having the same object as the present in 5 & 6 Will. 4, c. 50, ss. 84, 85, and 27 & 28 Vict. c. 101,
s. 21, but not confined to a parish "situate in a petty sessional
division." So far as relates to parishes which are so situate, this
section appears to operate as a virtual repeal of those contained
in the former Acts, by reason of the introduction of a new mode
of procedure which is inconsistent with that contained in those
Acts (see *Whiteley* v. *Heaton*, 27 L. J. m. 217, 22 J. P. 161;
Ex parte Baker, Per Bramwell, B., 26 L. J. m. 164, 21 J. P.
486; *Michell* v. *Brown*, 28 L. J. m. 55, 23 J. P. 548). As
regards any parish which may not be situate in a petty sessional
division those sections, of course, still remain in force. And the
provisions of 5 & 6 Will. 4, c. 50, ss. 84, 85, so far as relates to
stopping up, diverting, and turning highways so as to make them
nearer or more commodious to the public, are also unaffected by
the present.

(*w*) The expression "public expense" seems to be misapplied, Act '78, a. 24. inasmuch as it means an expense which is charged upon the consolidated fund or is defrayed out of moneys which are voted by Parliament, whereas the maintenance of highways is a charge upon local funds or rates.

(*x*) The expression "court of summary jurisdiction" is defined by sect. 36. It will be observed that the procedure under this section differs materially from that prescribed by 5 & 6 Will. 4, c. 50, ss. 84, 85, and 27 & 28 Vict. c. 101, s. 21.

(*y*) Notice to the owners and occupiers is entirely new, as well as the hearing of objections and the making of the order by the justices in petty sessions and the finality of an order so made, if not appealed against under sect. 37.

(*z*) See as to the manner of giving public notice, *infra*.

(*a*) There is no rate out of which the expenses of repairing highways are defrayed which can properly be called a "*public rate.*" Neither the highway rate under 5 & 6 Will. 4, c. 50, s. 29, nor the district fund under 27 & 28 Vict. c. 101, s. 32, nor any rate levied under sect. 33 of the latter Act is, either theoretically or practically, a "public rate," which means, as the name evidently implies, a rate made for "public," and not for "local" purposes.

An appeal lies against the making of the order under sect. 37; and the order itself must be lodged with the clerk of the peace of the county under 11 & 12 Vict. c. 43, s. 14. There does not appear to be any means of obtaining the costs of the order. The section makes no provision for them, and the case does not seem to fall within the operation of 11 & 12 Vict. c. 43, s. 18. In this respect, therefore, the matter remains the same as under 5 & 6 Will. 4, c. 50, ss. 84, 85, and 27 & 28 Vict. c. 101, s. 21. But express provision is made for the payment of the expenses of an application to revive the liability of highways to be maintained out of rates applicable to the payment of expenses of repairing highways. (See *infra*.)

(*b*) This notice is somewhat similar to that required to be given under 5 & 6 Will. 4, c. 50, s. 85, but differs from it in many important particulars.

(*c*) This is similar to the second proviso to 5 & 6 Will. 4, c. 50, s. 88.

(*d*) The word "rate" seems hardly comprehensive enough for the purpose to which it is applied. In the case of highway districts the expense of repairing highways, after the 25th March, 1879, will be a charge upon the district fund (see sect. 7, *ante*), and consequently "other highways repairable by the applicant authority" will not be maintainable out of any such "rate" as is mentioned in the section. In the corresponding provision in 27 & 28 Vict. c. 101, s. 21, the declaration as to the future maintenance of the highway is omitted, and simply the liability of the *parish* to repair is revived.

o 2

Act '78, s. 94.   (*c*) The appeal is subject to the conditions and regulations
———   contained in sect. 37, *infra.*

APPOINTMENT OF SURVEYORS IN CERTAIN PARISHES.

Removal of
doubt as to
appointment
of surveyors
in certain
parishes.
5 & 6 Will. 4,
c. 50.

25. Whereas doubts have arisen whether a surveyor of highways can be appointed, in pursuance of the Highway Act, 1835, for a parish which does not maintain any highway : Be it therefore enacted, that it shall be lawful for the inhabitants in vestry assembled of any parish or place having a known legal boundary (notwithstanding the inhabitants at large are not for the time being liable to maintain any highway or to contribute to any rate applicable to the maintenance of highways), or, on the neglect or refusal of such inhabitants, for the justices at a special sessions for the highways or in petty sessions assembled, at any time to exercise all the powers of the Highway Acts with respect to the election or appointment of a surveyor of highways with or without a salary for such parish or place ; and any surveyor so elected or appointed shall have all the powers and duties (including the power of making, assessing, and levying of highway rates) of a surveyor under the Highway Acts (*f*).

(*f*) The election of surveyors is provided for by 5 & 6 Will. 4, c. 50, s. 6, which enacts that "the inhabitants of every parish *maintaining its own highways,* at their first meeting in vestry for the nomination of overseers of the poor in every year, shall proceed to the election of one or more persons to serve the office of surveyor," &c.   That appears to be so clearly confined to parishes which maintain their own highways that it is difficult to understand how any doubt could have arisen whether a surveyor can be appointed for a parish which does not maintain any highway at all.   The power of appointment is conferred by sect. 11 of the same Act, " in case it shall appear on oath to the justices at a special sessions for the highways that the inhabitants of any parish have neglected or refused to nominate and elect a surveyor or surveyors in manner and for the purposes aforesaid," &c.   The

same section then authorizes and requires such justices, by writing under their hands, at their next succeeding special sessions,
"to appoint any person whom they may think fit to be a surveyor for such parish till the annual meeting then next ensuing
for the nomination of overseers or for the election of surveyors as
aforesaid, and with or without such salary as to the said justices
shall seem fit and proper."

The powers conferred by sect. 11 are so clearly confined to
parishes within the operation of sect. 6, that one is at a loss to
understand how any doubt can have been entertained whether
the power of *appointment* could apply to a parish in which the
election of a surveyor was clearly not authorized. Whatever
doubt, however, there may have been is now removed by this
section, which not only enables the justices to appoint, but authorizes the inhabitants in vestry assembled to elect. In point of
fact the section gives greater facilities for the appointment in
such a case than 5 & 6 Will 4, c. 50, s. 11, does. For, under the
latter section, the fact of the omission to elect must be brought
before the justices on oath at one special sessions, and the appointment cannot be made until the next special sessions (*Reg.* v. *Best,*
16 L. J. m. 102); whereas under the present section, although
the neglect or refusal must still be proved on oath, or at any rate
by legal evidence, the justices " at a special sessions for the highways or in petty sessions assembled," may, " at any time," exercise all the powers of the Highway Acts with respect to the
appointment of a surveyor, which, apparently, dispenses with
the necessity for making the appointment at the second special
sessions, or at any special sessions at all. It does not even appear that the justices must be assembled " at their usual place
of meeting," as required by 27 & 28 Vict. c. 101, s. 46.

BYE-LAWS BY COUNTY AUTHORITY.

26. A county authority (*g*) may from time to time
make, with respect to all or any main roads or other
highways within any highway area (*h*) in their county,
and when made alter or repeal, bye-laws (*i*) for all or
any of the purposes following ; that is to say :—

   (1.) For prohibiting or regulating the use of any
        waggon, wain, cart, or carriage drawn by
        animal power and having wheels of which
        the fellies or tires are not of such width (*k*)
        in proportion to the weight carried by, or to
        the size of, or to the number of wheels of

such waggon, wain, cart, or carriage, as may be specified in such bye-laws; and

(2.) For prohibiting or regulating the use of any waggon, wain, cart, or other carriage drawn by animal power not having the nails in its wheels countersunk (*l*) in such manner as may be specified in such bye-laws, or having on its wheels bars or other projections forbidden by such bye-laws; and

(3.) For prohibiting or regulating the locking of the wheel of any waggon, wain, cart, or carriage drawn by animal power when descending a hill, unless there is placed at the bottom of such wheel during the whole time of its being locked a skidpan (*m*), slipper, or shoe in such manner as to prevent the road from being destroyed or injured by the locking of such wheel; and

(4.) For prohibiting or regulating the erection of gates (*n*) across highways, and prohibiting gates opening outwards (*o*) on highways and

(5.) For regulating the use of bicycles (*p*).

Fines to be recovered summarily (*q*) may be imposed by any such bye-laws on persons breaking any bye-law made under this section, provided that no fine exceeds for any one offence the sum of two pounds, and that the bye-laws are so framed as to allow of the recovery of any sum less than the full amount of the fine.

(*g*) A county authority means "the justices of the county in general or quarter sessions assembled" (sect. 38, *infra*).

(*h*) Highway areas are defined by sect. 14, *ante*. It must, however, be borne in mind with respect to an urban sanitary district, which is one of those areas, that by sect. 38 no borough having a separate court of quarter sessions, and no part of any

such borough is deemed to be or to be included in any such dis- Act '78, s. 26.
trict.

(*i*) No bye-law will be of any validity until it has been submitted to and confirmed by the Local Government Board, under
sect. 35, *infra*. It cannot be confirmed until the expiration of
one month after notice of the intention to apply for confirmation
has been given in one or more local newspapers. (*Id.*)

(*k*) See 3 Geo. 4, c. 126, s. 7, and 4 Geo. 4, c. 95, s. 10, as to
regulations respecting the width of wheels on turnpike roads.

(*l*) See 4 Geo. 4, c. 95, s. 2, as to nails of tires of wheels being
countersunk on turnpike roads.

(*m*) See 3 Geo. 4, c. 126, s. 126, as to using skidpans or slippers
on turnpike roads.

(*n*) But see 2 & 3 Vict. c. 45, s. 1, requiring railway com-
panies whose line crosses a highway to make and maintain gates
across each end of the road.

(*o*) See 3 Geo. 4, c. 126, s. 125, prohibiting the making of gates,
&c., to open towards turnpike roads, and providing for their alteration if so made.

(*p*) In connection with this matter it may be mentioned, that
5 & 6 Will. 4, c. 50, s. 78, enacts that "if any person riding any
horse or beast, or driving any sort of carriage, shall ride or drive the
same furiously so as to endanger the life or limb of any passenger,"
he shall, on conviction, in addition to any civil action to which
he may make himself liable, forfeit not exceeding £5, " in case
such *driver* shall not be the owner of such waggon, cart, or other carriage, and in case the offender be the owner of such waggon, cart,
or other carriage, then any sum not exceeding £10," &c., &c. It
was held in *Williams* v. *Evans*, 1 Ex. D. (D. C. A.) 277, 41 J. P.
151, that the penalty applies to "*riders*," as well as to "*drivers*."
Under this section several convictions have been made by justices
for furiously riding a bicycle, and it is understood that the
question will shortly be raised before the High Court of Justice
as to whether a bicycle is or is not a "carriage" within the meaning of this section.

(*q*) It is presumed that this means "before a court of summary
jurisdiction," under sect. 36, *infra*.

SAVING FOR MINERALS.

27. Notwithstanding anything contained in section 68 To whom
of the Public Health Act, 1848, or in section 149 of the minerals under dis-
Public Health Act, 1875 (*r*), all mines and minerals of turnpiked roads to
any description whatsoever under any disturnpiked belong. 11 & 12 Vict.
road or highway which has or shall become vested in c. 63. 38 & 39 Vict.
an urban sanitary authority by virtue of the said sec- c. 55.

Act '78, s. 27. tions, or either of them, shall belong to the person who would be entitled thereto in case such road or highway had not become so vested, and the person entitled to any such mine or minerals shall have the same powers of working and of getting the same or other minerals as if the road or highway had not become vested in the urban sanitary authority, but so nevertheless that in such working and getting no damage shall be done to the road or highway.

This section shall extend to the Isle of Wight and to South Wales, as defined by the said Act, 23 & 24 Vict. c. 68, "An Act for the better management and control of the Highways in South Wales" (s).

(r) This section enacts that "all streets being, or which at any time become, highways repairable by the inhabitants at large within any urban district . . . . shall vest in and be under the control of the urban authority." In *Coverdale* v. *Charlton*, 3 Q. B. D. 376, 42 J. P. 517, it was held that under this section the soil of the highway vests in the urban authority. Consequently, but for special provision to the contrary, the mines and minerals under highways would also vest in the same authority, a result which was clearly never intended, and has, therefore, been rectified.

(s) This is the only portion of Part I. to which the saving in sect. 2 applies.

PART II.

AMENDMENT OF LOCOMOTIVE ACTS, 1861 AND 1865.

Weight of locomotives and construction of wheels.
24 & 25 Vict. c. 70.
28 & 29 Vict. c. 83.

28. Section 3 of the Locomotive Act, 1861, and section 5 of the Locomotive Act, 1865, are hereby repealed, so far as relates to England, and in lieu thereof be it enacted that it shall not be lawful to use on any turnpike road or highway a locomotive constructed otherwise than in accordance with the following provisions; that is to say:—

(1.) A locomotive (*t*) not drawing any carriage, and not exceeding in weight three tons, shall have the tires of the wheels thereof not less than three inches in width, with an additional inch for every ton or fraction of a ton above the first three tons; and

(2.) A locomotive drawing (*u*) any waggon or carriage shall have the tires of the driving wheels thereof not less than two inches in width for every ton in weight of the locomotive, unless the diameter of such wheels shall exceed five feet, when the width of the tires may be reduced in the same proportion as the diameter of the wheels is increased, but in such case the width of such tires shall not be less than fourteen inches; and

(3.) A locomotive shall not exceed nine feet in width or fourteen tons in weight, except as hereinafter provided (*v*); and

(4.) The driving (*w*) wheels of a locomotive shall be cylindrical and smooth-soled, or shod with diagonal cross-bars of not less than three inches in width nor more than three-quarters of an inch in thickness, extending the full breadth of the tire, and the space intervening between each such cross-bar shall not exceed three inches.

The owner of any locomotive used contrary to the foregoing provisions shall for every such offence be liable to a fine not exceeding £5 : Provided that the mayor, aldermen, and commons in the city of London, and the Metropolitan Board of Works in the metropolis, exclusive of the city of London, and the council of any borough which has a separate court of quarter sessions, and the county authority of any county, may, on the application of the owner of any locomotive exceeding nine feet in width or fourteen tons in weight, authorize such locomotive to be used on any turnpike road or highway within the areas (*x*) respectively above mentioned, or part of any such road or highway, under such conditions (if any) as to them may appear desirable. Provided also, that the owner of a locomotive used contrary to the provisions of sub-section two of this section shall not be deemed guilty of an offence under this section if he proves to the satisfaction of the court having cognizance of the case that such locomotive was constructed before the passing of this Act, and that the tires of the wheels thereof are not less than nine inches in width (*y*).

(*t*) By sect. 38 *infra*, "locomotive" means a locomotive propelled by steam or by other than animal power. This sub-section contains the same provisions as the 1st paragraph of 24 & 25 Vict. c. 70, s. 3, but in simpler language.

(*u*) The 2nd paragraph of 24 & 25 Vict. c 70, s. 3 provided that every such locomotive should have the tires of the wheels not less than 9 inches in width. This sub-section only applies to the *driving* wheels, and makes no provision as to the others.

(*v*) The 3rd paragraph of 24 & 25 Vict. c. 70, s. 3 provided that no locomotive should exceed seven feet in width or twelve tons in weight, except it were authorized by certain authorities similar to those mentioned in the proviso to this section. This was increased by 28 & 29 Vict. c. 83, s. 5 to nine feet and fourteen tons, subject to the same provisions.

(*w*) The 4th paragraph of the 24 & 25 Vict. c. 70, s. 3 enacted that "the wheels of every locomotive shall be cylindrical and smooth-soled, or used with shoes or other bearing surface of a width not less than nine inches." This part of the latter section came under discussion in *Stringer* v. *Sykes*, 2 Ex. D. 240, and *Body* v. *Jeffery*, 3 Ex. D. 95. But as it is now repealed the relevancy of those cases will only apply in case this part of the Act should at any time be allowed to expire. It will be observed that this sub-section only applies to the *driving* wheels of the locomotive, and that the alternative of not being smooth-soled differs materially from that given by 24 & 25 Vict. c. 70, s. 3.

(*x*) The areas in question, both in this and in sect. 31 *infra*, are the city of London, the Metropolis exclusive of the city of

London (but saying nothing about the liberties of the said city),
boroughs with a separate court of quarter sessions, and counties.
They are quite distinct from the "highway areas" under sect. 14
ante. It may be observed that so far as the county authority is
concerned, the application can only be made at general or
quarter sessions. Act '78, s. 28.

(y) In accordance with 24 & 25 Vict. c. 70, s. 3. *See* note (u)
supra.

29. The paragraph numbered "secondly" of section 3 Amendment of 28 & 29 Vict. c. 83, s. 3.
of the Locomotive Act, 1865, is hereby repealed, so far
as relates to England, and in lieu thereof the following
paragraph is hereby substituted; namely,—

> " Secondly, one of such persons, while the locomo-
> tive is in motion, shall precede by at least twenty
> yards the locomotive on foot, and shall in case
> of need assist horses, and carriages drawn by
> horses, passing the same."

30. Section 8 of the Locomotive Act, 1861, is hereby Steam locomotives to be constructed so as to consume their smoke. 24 & 25 Vict. c. 70.
repealed, so far as relates to England; and in lieu
thereof, be it enacted that every locomotive used on
any turnpike road or highway shall be constructed on
the principle of consuming its own smoke; and any
person using any locomotive not so constructed, or not
consuming, so far as practicable, its own smoke, shall
be liable to a fine not exceeding £5 for every (z) day
during which such locomotive is used on any such
turnpike road or highway.

(z) It would seem from the judgment of *Blackburn, J.,* in
Smith v. *Stokes,* 27 J.P. 535, in the case of a conviction under
5 & 6 Will. 4, c. 50, s. 70, for erecting a steam engine within 25
yards of a highway, that the penalty is incurred although the
locomotive is only used during part of the day. In that case his
lordship observed, "It is true that the penalty is said by that
section to be £5 a day for every day the engine is permitted to
remain; but I do not think it is necessary that it should remain
there for the whole day in order to incur the penalty."

Act '78, s. 31.

Power to
local autho-
rities to
make orders
as to hours
during which
locomotives
may pass
over roads.
·28 & 29 Vict.
·c. 83.

31. Section 8 of the Locomotive Act, 1865, is hereby repealed, so far as relates to England; and in lieu thereof, be it enacted that the mayor, aldermen, and commons in the city of London, and the Metropolitan Board of Works in the metropolis, exclusive of the city of London, and the council of any borough which has a separate court of quarter sessions, and the county authority of any county, may make bye-laws (a) as to the hours during which locomotives are not (b) to pass over the turnpike roads or highways situate within the areas (c) respectively above mentioned, the hours being in all cases consecutive hours and no more than the eight out of the twenty-four, and for regulating the use of locomotives upon any highway, or preventing such use upon every bridge where such authority is satisfied that such use would be attended with danger to the public; and any person (cc) in charge of a locomotive acting contrary to such bye-laws shall be liable to a fine not exceeding £5.

(a) These bye-laws will not be of any validity until they have been submitted to and confirmed by the Local Government Board under sect. 35. They cannot be confirmed until the expiration of one month after notice of the intention to apply for confirmation has been given in one or more local newspapers circulating in the county or district. (*Id.*) They can only be made by a county authority at general or quarter sessions.

(b) According to the marginal note, this section gives "power to local authorities to make orders as to hours during which locomotives *may pass* over roads." This, however, is not borne out by the body of the section which only enables them to "make bye-laws as to the hours during which locomotives *are not to pass* over turnpike roads or highways," &c. The authorities may prohibit the passing of locomotives during not exceeding eight specified consecutive hours out of the twenty-four; but beyond this they have no power whatever to regulate the hours of passing, but only the mode of user, or the prevention of user upon certain bridges where they are satisfied that it would be attended with danger to the public.

(c) See note (x) *ante*, p. 202.

(cc) The penalty under the bye-laws will be payable by the person in charge of the locomotive, and not by the owner as in the case of an offence against sect. 28.

32. A county authority may from time to time make, alter, and repeal bye-laws (*d*) for granting annual licenses to locomotives (*e*) used within their county, and the fee (not exceeding ten pounds) to be paid in respect of each license; and the owner of any locomotive for which a license is required under any bye-law so made who uses or permits the same to be used in contravention (*f*) of any such bye-law shall be liable to a fine not exceeding forty shillings for every (*g*) day on which the same is so used.

Act '78, s. 32.

Power of county authority to license locomotives.

All fees received under this section shall be carried to and applied as part of the county rate.

This section shall not apply to any locomotive used solely for agricultural purposes.

(*d*) See note (*a*), *supra.*
(*e*) The license, it will be observed, will be granted to the locomotive, and not to its owner. It will, consequently, pass with the locomotive, and will continue in force during the year, notwithstanding any number of changes in the ownership of the engine. It will not be required in the case of a locomotive used *solely* for agricultural purposes.
(*f*) Using the locomotive in contravention of the bye-law means, it is presumed, using it without a license.
(*g*) See sect. 30, note (*s*), *supra.*

33. This part of this Act shall remain in force so long only as the Locomotive Act, 1865, continues in force (*h*).

Duration of Part II. of Act.
28 & 29 Vict. c. 83.

(*h*) The Locomotive Act, 1865, is continued in force by 41 & 42 Vict. c. 70, up to 31st December, 1879.

PART III.

PROCEDURE AND DEFINITIONS.

Confirmation of provisional order.

34. It shall be lawful (*i*) for the Local Government Board to submit any provisional order made by them under this Act to Parliament for confirmation, and without such confirmation a provisional order shall not be of any validity.

(*i*) Although these words are permissive, it is nevertheless imperative on the Local Government Board to submit such orders to Parliament for confirmation, unless, perhaps, it can be shown that there are special reasons which, if known at the time of the making of the order, would have prevented its being made at all. (See *Maxwell* on the Interpretation of Statutes, pp. 218-224.) The 16th section is the only provision in the Act to which this section applies.

Confirmation of bye-laws.

35. A bye-law (*j*) made under this Act, and any alteration made therein and any repeal of a bye-law, shall not be of any validity until it has been submitted to and confirmed by the Local Government Board.

A bye-law made under this Act shall not, nor shall any alteration therein or addition thereto or repeal thereof, be confirmed until the expiration of one month (*k*) after notice of the intention to apply for confirmation of the same has been given by the authority making the same in one or more local newspapers circulating in their county or district.

(*j*) The only sections under which bye-laws can be made are the 26th, 31st, and 32nd.

(*k*) This means "calendar month" (13 & 14 Vict. c. 21, s. 4.)

Recovery of penalties and expenses.

36. All offences, fines, and expenses under this Act (*l*), or any bye-law made in pursuance of this Act (*l*), may be prosecuted, enforced, and recovered before a

court of summary jurisdiction in manner provided by Act 78, s. 35.
the Summary Jurisdiction Acts.

The expression "the Summary Jurisdiction Acts"
means the Act 11 & 12 Vict. c. 43, "An Act to facilitate the performance of the duties of justices of the
peace out of sessions within England and Wales with
respect to summary convictions and orders," inclusive
of any Acts amending the same.

The expression "court of summary jurisdiction"
means and includes any justice or justices of the peace,
metropolitan police magistrate, stipendiary or other
magistrate, or officer, by whatever name called, to
whom jurisdiction is given by the Summary Jurisdiction Acts: Provided that the court, when hearing and
determining an information or complaint under this
Act, shall be constituted either of two or more justices
of the peace in petty sessions, sitting at a place appointed for holding petty session, or of some magistrate
or officer sitting alone or with others at some court or
other place appointed for the administration of justice,
and for the time being empowered by law to do alone
any act authorized to be done by more than one justice
of the peace.

(*l*) This section is confined to offences, &c., "under this Act,"
and consequently is not applicable to offences, &c., under any
other Highway or Locomotive Act. There is no provision in
the Act, as in 27 & 28 Vict. c. 101, s. 2, and in 28 & 29 Vict. c. 83,
s. 13, requiring it to be construed as one Act either with the
Highways, or Locomotives Acts, and therefore, no difficulty can
arise on that account.

37. If any party thinks himself aggrieved by any
conviction or order made by a court of summary jurisdiction on determining any information or complaint
under this Act (*l*), the party so aggrieved may appeal

Form of ap-
peal to quar-
ter sessions.

Act '78. s. 87. therefrom, subject to the conditions and regulations following :—

(1.) The appeal shall be made to the next practicable court of quarter sessions for the county or place where the decision appealed from was given holden not less than twenty-one days after the decision of the court from which the appeal is made; and

(2.) The appellant shall, within ten days after the pronouncing by the court of the decision appealed from, give notice to the other party and to the court of summary jurisdiction of his intention to appeal and of the ground thereof; such notice of appeal shall be in writing signed by the person or persons giving the same, or by his, her, or their solicitor on his, her, or their behalf; and

(3.) The appellant shall, within three days after such notice, enter into a recognizance before a justice of the peace, with two sufficient sureties, conditioned personally to try such appeal, and to abide the judgment of the court thereon and to pay such costs as may be awarded by the court, or give such other security by deposit of money or otherwise as the justice may allow; and

(4.) Where the appellant is in custody the justice may, if he think fit, on the appellant entering into such recognizance or giving such other security as aforesaid, release him from custody.

(5.) The court of appeal may adjourn the appeal, and upon the hearing thereof they may confirm, reverse, or modify the decision of the

court of summary jurisdiction, or remit the Act 76, s. 37.
matter to the court of summary jurisdiction
with the opinion of the court of appeal
thereon, or make such other order in the
matter as the court thinks just, and if the
matter be remitted to the court of summary
jurisdiction the said last-mentioned court
shall thereupon re-hear and decide the information or complaint in accordance with
the opinion of the said court of appeal.
The court of appeal may also make such
order as to costs to be paid by either party
as the court thinks just.

(*l*) This section, like the 36th, is confined to proceedings
"under this Act," and does not apply to convictions or orders
made under the other Highway or Locomotives Acts.

38. In this Act— Interpreta-
"County" has the same meaning as it has in the tion. 25 & 26 Vict.
Highway Acts, 1862 and 1864, except that every c. 61. 27 & 28 Vict.
liberty not being assessable to the county rate of c. 101.
the county or counties within which it is locally
situate shall, for the purposes of this Act other
than those relating to the formation and alteration of highway districts, and the transfer of the
powers of a highway board, be deemed to be a
separate county :
"County authority" means the justices of a county
in general or quarter sessions assembled :
"Borough" means any place for the time being
subject to the Act 5 & 6 Will. 4, c. 76, "An Act
to provide for the regulation of municipal corporations in England and Wales," and the Acts
amending the same :
"Highway district" means a district constituted in

P

Act '78, s. 38.
pursuance of the Highway Act, 1862, and the
25 & 26 Vict.
c. 61.
27 & 28 Vict.
c. 101.
Highway Act, 1864, or one of such Acts :

"Highway board" means the highway board
having jurisdiction within a highway district :

"Highway parish" means a parish or place included or capable of being included in a highway
25 & 26 Vict.
c. 61.
27 & 28 Vict.
c. 101.
district in pursuance of the Highway Acts, 1862
and 1864, or one of such Acts :

"Highway authority" means as respects an urban
sanitary district the urban sanitary authority,
and as respects a highway district the highway
board, and as respects a highway parish the surveyor or surveyors or other officers performing
similar duties :.

"Rural sanitary district" and "rural sanitary
authority" mean respectively the districts and
authorities declared to be rural sanitary districts
38 & 39 Vict.
c. 55.
and authorities by the Public Health Act, 1875 :

"Urban sanitary district" and "urban sanitary
authority" mean respectively the districts and
authorities declared to be urban sanitary districts
38 & 39 Vict.
c. 55.
and authorities by the Public Health Act, 1875,
except that for the purposes of this Act no
borough having a separate court of quarter
sessions, and no part of any such borough, shall
be deemed to be or to be included in any such
district, and where part of a parish is included
in such district for the purpose only of the
repairs of the highways such part shall be
deemed to be included in the district for the purposes of this Act :

"The metropolis," means the parishes and places
mentioned in the Schedules A. B., and C.,
18 & 19 Vict.
c. 120.
annexed to the Metropolis Management Act,
1855, and any parish to which such Act may be

extended by order in council in manner in the Act '78, s. 28.
said Act provided; also the city of London and
the liberties of the said city :

" Quarter sessions " includes general sessions :

" Petty sessional division " means. any division for
the holding a special sessions formed or to be
formed under the provisions of the Act 9 Geo. 4,
c. 43, or any Act amending the same; also any
division of a county, or of a riding, division,
parts, or liberty of a county, having a separate
commission of the peace, in and for which petty
sessions or special sessions are usually held,
whether in one or more place or places, in
accordance with any custom, or otherwise than
under the said last-mentioned Act : but does not
include any city, borough, town corporate, or district constituted a petty sessional division by the
Act 12 & 13 Vict. c. 18, " An Act for the holding of petty sessions of the peace in boroughs,
and for providing places for the holding of such
petty session in counties and boroughs :"

" Locomotive " means a locomotive propelled by
steam or by other than animal power :

" Person " includes a body of persons corporate or
unincorporate.

CONSOLIDATED ABSTRACT

OF

THE LOCOMOTIVE ACTS, 1861 & 1865,

AND OF

THE HIGHWAYS AND LOCOMOTIVES (AMENDMENT) ACT, 1878,

SO FAR AS IT RELATES TO LOCOMOTIVES.

In this Abstract the following abbreviated expressions have been used, viz:—

Act '61, means "The Locomotive Act, 1861." (24 & 25 Vict. c. 70.)

Act '65, means "The Locomotives Act, 1865." (28 & 29 Vict. c, 83, *temporary*.)"

Act '78, means "The Highways and Locomotives (Amendment) Act, 1878." (41 & 42 Vict. c. 77, *temporary* as to Locomotives.)

PRELIMINARY.

Act '61, s. 14.
Short title.
The Act 24 & 25 Vict. c. 70, may be cited as "The Locomotive Act, 1861."

Act '65, s. 13.
Short title.
The Act 28 & 29 Vict. c. 83, may be cited as "The Locomotives Act, 1865."

Act '78, s. 1.
Short title.
The Act 41 & 42 Viet. c. 77, may be cited as "The Highways and Locomotives (Amendment) Act, 1878."

Act '65, s. 13.
Construction.
"The Locomotives Act, 1861," and "The Locomotives Act, 1865," are to be construed together as one Act.

Id. s. 1.
Duration.
"The Locomotives Act, 1865," shall cease and de-

termine on the 1st of September, 1867. (N. B., this
Act is continued by 41 & 42 Vict. c. 70, until the 31st
day of December, 1879). Act '65, s. 1.

The second part of the Act 41 & 42 Vict. c. 77
(amending the Locomotive Acts, 1861 and 1865), remains in force so long only as the Locomotive Act,
1865, continues in force Act '78, s. 38. Duration.

INTERPRETATION AND CONSTRUCTION
OF 41 & 42 VICT. CAP. 77.

" County " has the same meaning in the Highways
and Locomotives (Amendment) Act, 1878, as it
has in the Highway Acts, 1862 and 1864, except
that every liberty not being assessable to the
county rate of the county or counties within which
it is locally situate shall, for the purposes of this
Act other than those relating to the formation
and alteration of highway districts, and the
transfer of the powers of a highway board, be
deemed to be a separate county : Id. s. 38. County.

" County authority " means the justices of a county
in general or quarter sessions assembled : County authority.

" Borough " means any place for the time being
subject to the Act 5 & 6 Will. 4, c. 76, " An Act
to provide for the regulation of municipal corporations in England and Wales," and the Acts
amending the same : Borough.

" The metropolis " means the parishes and places
mentioned in the Schedules A., B., and C., annexed to the Metropolis Management Act, 1855,
and any parish to which such Act may be ex-
tended by order in council in manner in the said The Metro-polis.

Act provided; also the city of London and the liberties of the said city:

"Quarter sessions," includes general sessions.

"Locomotive" means a locomotive propelled by steam or by other than animal power:

"Person" includes a body of persons corporate or unincorporate:

The expression "The Summary Jurisdiction Acts," means the Act of 11 & 12 Vict. c. 43, "An Act to facilitate the performance of the duties of justices of the peace out of sessions within England and Wales with respect to summary convictions and orders," inclusive of any Acts amending the same.

The expression "court of summary jurisdiction" means and includes any justice or justices of the peace, metropolitan police magistrate, stipendiary or other magistrate, or officer, by whatever named called, to whom jurisdiction is given by the Summary Jurisdiction Acts: Provided that the court when hearing and determining an information or complaint under this Act, shall be constituted either of two or more justices of the peace in petty sessions, sitting at a place appointed for holding petty session or of some magistrate or officer sitting alone or with others at some court or other place appointed for the administration of justice, and for the time being empowered by law to do alone any act authorized to be done by more than one justice of the peace.

Where a turnpike road subject to one trust extends into divers counties, such road, for the purposes of this Act, shall be treated as a separate turnpike road in each county through which it passes.

LICENSING LOCOMOTIVES; AND TOLLS ON TURNPIKE ROADS, &c.

A county authority may from time to time make, alter, and repeal bye-laws for granting annual licenses to locomotives (not being locomotives used solely for agricultural purposes) used within their county, and the fee (not exceeding £10), to be paid in respect of each license.

The owner of any locomotive for which a license is required under any bye-law so made, who uses or permits it to be used in contravention of any such bye-law, is liable to a fine, not exceeding 40s., for every day on which it is so used.

All fees received under this section are to be carried to and applied as part of the county rate.

Trustees, corporations, commissioners, and other persons acting under and in execution of any general or local Turnpike Road Act, or Public Bridge Act existing on the 1st of August, 1861, shall demand and take tolls not exceeding the following; that is to say:

For every locomotive propelled by any power, containing within itself the machinery for its own propulsion, such a toll for every two tons weight, or fractional part of every two tons weight that such locomotive shall weigh as shall be equal to the toll or tolls by their respective Acts, made payable for every horse drawing any waggon, wain, cart, or carriage, with wheels of a width similar to those of such locomotive; or in the case of a toll charged on the horse or horses drawing any such waggon, wain, cart, or carriage, without reference to the width of the wheels thereof, then such a toll for every two tons or fractional part thereof, that such locomotive shall weigh, as shall be

Act '78, s. 28.
License to locomotives.

Act '61, s. 1.
Tolls to be taken for locomotives.

equal to one horse drawing such waggon, wain, cart, or carriage.

There tolls are payable so often as tolls made payable for such waggon, wain, cart, or carriage are payable at the same gate;

With a proviso that if the wheels of the locomotive rest upon any shoe or other bearing, the surface of which bears upon the ground so as to prevent the wheels coming in contact therewith, the same tolls only shall be payable as if the wheels thereof were of a width similar to such shoe or bearing.

For every waggon, wain, cart, or carriage drawn or propelled by any locomotive, for each pair of wheels thereof such a toll as shall not exceed the toll by the respective Acts made payable for two horses drawing any waggon, wain, cart, or carriage with wheels of a similar width, and for every additional wheel thereof one half toll in addition to the said toll.

Or in the case of a toll charged on the horse or horses drawing any such waggon, wain, cart, or carriage, without reference to the width of the wheels thereof, then such a toll for each wheel as shall be equal to one horse drawing such waggon, wain, cart, or carriage.

These tolls are payable so often as the toll made payable for such waggon, wain, cart, or carriage, drawn by horses is payable at the same gate.

With a proviso that in every case where the wheels of any waggon, wain, cart, or carriage are not 3 Geo. 4, c. 126, s. 9. cylindrical, as described in the Act 3 Geo. 4, c. 126, s. 9, the toll payable in respect thereof shall be one half more.

Act '61, s. 10. Exemptions from toll of waggons, &c., continued. All waggons, wains, carts, or carriages, drawn by any locomotive, and loaded with any materials such as on the 1st August, 1861, were exempt from toll under the provisions of any General or Local Act, are entitled to the same exemption as if drawn by animal power. Act '61, s. 10.

No waggon, wain, cart, or carriage drawn or propelled as aforesaid, not having cylindrical wheels, can carry any greater weight than is permitted by the General Turnpike Act. *Id.* s. 4.
Weight to be carried.

And no waggon, wain, cart, or carriage having cylindrical wheels can carry over and above the weight of the waggon, wain, cart, or carriage any greater weight than one ton and a half for each pair of wheels, unless the fellies, tires, or shoes are four inches or more in breadth; nor a greater weight than two tons for each pair of wheels, unless the fellies, tires, or shoes are six inches or more in breadth; nor a greater weight than three tons for each pair of wheels, unless the fellies, tires, or shoes are eight inches or more in breadth.

And for every single wheel one half of that permitted to be carried on a pair of wheels; nor in any case to carry a greater weight than four tons on each pair of wheels, or two tons on each wheel; but if such waggons, wains, or other carriages are built and constructed with springs upon each axle, then they may carry one sixth more weight in addition to the abovementioned weights upon each pair of wheels:

Provided that the regulation of weight herein mentioned shall not extend to any waggon, wain, cart, or other carriage carrying only one tree or one log of timber, or one block of stone, or one cable or rope, or one block, plate, roll, or vessel of iron or other metal, or compounded of any two or more metals, cast, wrought, or united in one piece. Exceptions.

INSUFFICIENCY OF BRIDGE TO CARRY WEIGHT;
AND COMPENSATION FOR DAMAGE.

Act '61, s. 6.
Restriction of use over suspension and other bridges.

No owner or driver of any locomotive can drive it over any suspension bridge, nor over any bridge on which a conspicuous notice has been placed by the authority of the surveyor or persons liable to the repair of the bridge that the bridge is insufficient to carry weights beyond the ordinary traffic of the district, without previously obtaining the consent of the surveyor of the road or bridgemaster under whose charge such bridge shall be for the time being, or of the persons liable to the repair of such bridge ;

And in case such owner of the locomotive and surveyor of the road or bridge, or bridgemaster differ in opinion as to the sufficiency of any bridge to sustain the transit of the locomotive, then the question shall be determined by an officer to be appointed, on the application of either party, by one of Her Majesty's principal Secretaries of State, whose certificate of sufficiency of such bridge shall entitle the owner of the locomotive to take the same over such bridge.

Id. s. 7.
Damage caused by locomotives to bridges to be made good by owners, &c.

Where any turnpike or other roads upon which locomotives are used, pass, or are carried over or across any stream or watercourse, navigable river, canal, or railway by means of any bridge or arch (whether stationary or moveable), and such bridge or arch, or any of the walls, buttresses, or supports thereof are damaged by reason of any locomotive or any waggon or carriage drawn or propelled by or together with a locomotive passing over the same or coming into contact therewith, none of the proprietors, undertakers, directors, conservators, trustees, commissioners, or other person interested in or having the charge of such navigable river, canal, or railway, or the tolls Act '61, s. 7. thereof, or of such bridge or arch, are liable to repair or make good any damage so occasioned, or to make compensation to any person for any obstruction, interruption, or delay which may arise therefrom to the use of such bridge or arch, navigable river, canal, or railway; but every such damage must be forthwith repaired to the satisfaction of the proprietors, undertakers, directors, conservators, trustees, commissioners, or other persons as aforesaid respectively interested in or having the charge of such river, canal, or railway, or the tolls thereof, or of such bridge or arch, by and at the expense of the owner or owners, or the person or persons having the charge of such locomotive at the time of the happening of such damage;

And all such owners and persons having the charge of such locomotive are also liable, both jointly and severally, to reimburse and make good as well to the proprietors, undertakers, directors, conservators, trustees, commissioners, and other persons interested in or having the charge of any such navigable river, canal, or railway, or the tolls thereof, or of such bridge or arch, as to all persons navigating on or using, or who but for such obstruction, interruption, or delay would have navigated on or used the same, all losses and expenses which they or any of them may sustain or incur by reason of any such obstruction, interruption, or delay, such losses and expenses to be recoverable by action at law; which action, in case of such proprietors, undertakers, directors, conservators, trustees, commissioners, or other persons so interested as aforesaid, may be brought in the name or names of their agent or agents, clerk or clerks for the time being, or by any person or persons legally authorized to act in their behalf.

WEIGHT AND CONSTRUCTION OF LOCOMOTIVES.

Weight of locomotives and construction of wheels.

It is unlawful to use on any turnpike road or highway in England a locomotive constructed otherwise than in accordance with the following provisions, that is to say :—

(1.) A locomotive not drawing any carriage, and not exceeding in weight three tons, shall have the tires of the wheels thereof not less than three inches in width, with an additional inch for every ton or fraction of a ton above the first three tons; and

(2.) A locomotive drawing any waggon or carriage shall have the tires of the driving wheels thereof not less than two inches in width for every ton in weight of the locomotive, unless the diameter of such wheels shall exceed five feet, when the width of the tires may be reduced in the same proportion as the diameter of the wheels is increased, but in such case the width of such tires shall not be less than fourteen inches; and

(3.) A locomotive shall not exceed nine feet in width or fourteen tons in weight, except as hereinafter provided; and

(4.) The driving wheels of a locomotive shall be cylindrical and smooth-soled, or shod with diagonal cross-bars of not less than three inches in width nor more than three-quarters of an inch in thickness, extending the full breadth of the tire, and the space intervening between each such cross-bar shall not exceed three inches.

Owner liable to fine of £5.

The owner of any locomotive used contrary to the

foregoing provisions shall for every such offence be ^{Act '78, s. 28.} liable to a fine not exceeding £5 :

Provided that the mayor, aldermen, and commons ^{Mayor, &c.} in the city of London, and the Metropolitan Board of ^{&c., &c.,} Works in the metropolis, exclusive of the city of ^{rise loco-} London, and the council of any borough which has a ^{motives ex-} separate court of quarter sessions, and the county ^{feet in width} authority of any county, may, on the application of the ^{weight to be} owner of any locomotive exceeding nine feet in width or ^{used.} fourteen tons in weight, authorize such locomotive to be used on any turnpike road or highway within the areas respectively above mentioned, or part of any such road or highway, under such conditions (if any) as to them may appear desirable.

Provided also, that the owner of a locomotive used ^{Owner not} contrary to the provisions of sub-section two of this ^{for using} section shall not be deemed guilty of an offence under ^{contrary to} this section if he proves to the satisfaction of the court ^{2 on proof} having cognizance of the case that such locomotive ^{constructed} was constructed before the passing of the Highways ^{ing of Act,} and Locomotives (Amendment) Act, 1878, and that ^{&c.} the tires of the wheels thereof are not less than nine inches in width.

Every locomotive used on any turnpike road or ^{Id. s. 30.} highway must be constructed on the principle of con- ^{to be con-} suming its own smoke; and any person using any ^{as to con-} locomotive not so constructed or not consuming, so ^{smoke.} far as practicable, its own smoke, is liable to a fine not exceeding £5 for every day during which such locomotive is used on any such turnpike road or highway.

RULES FOR WORKING LOCOMOTIVES.

Every locomotive propelled by steam or any other ^{Act '65, s. 3.} than animal power on any turnpike road or public

Act '65, s. 3. highway must be worked according to the following rules and regulations, viz. :—

    Firstly. At least three persons shall be employed to drive or conduct such locomotive, and if more than two waggons or carriages be attached thereto an additional person shall be employed, who shall take charge of such waggons or carriages:

Act '78, s. 29.   Secondly. One of such persons, while the locomotive is in motion, shall precede by at least twenty yards the locomotive on foot, and shall in case of need assist horses and carriages drawn by horses passing the same:

Act '65, s. 3.   Thirdly. The drivers of such locomotives shall give as much space as possible for the passing of other traffic:

    Fourthly. The whistle of such locomotive shall not be sounded for any purpose whatever; nor shall the cylinder taps be opened within sight of any person riding, driving, leading, or in charge of a horse upon the road; nor shall the steam be allowed to attain pressure such as to exceed the limit fixed by the safety valve, so that no steam shall blow off when the locomotive is upon the road:

    Fifthly. Every such locomotive shall be instantly stopped, on the person preceding the same, or any other person with a horse, or carriage drawn by a horse, putting up his hand as a signal to require such locomotive to be stopped:

    Sixthly. Any person in charge of any such locomotive shall provide two efficient lights, to be affixed conspicuously, one on each side on the front of the same, between the hours of one hour after sunset and one hour before sunrise:

Penalty on owner on non-com-   In the event of a non-compliance with any of the provisions of this section, the owner of the locomotive,

on summary conviction before two justices, is liable to Act '65, s. 3.
a penalty not exceeding £10; but the owner, on prov- pliance with
ing that he has incurred such penalty by reason of the rules.
negligence or wilful default of any person in charge of by owner
or in attendance on such locomotive, may recover sum- defaulter.
marily from such person the whole or any part of the
penalty he may have incurred as owner.

No locomotive can be driven along any turnpike *Id.* s. 4.
road or public highway at a greater speed than four speed.
miles an hour, through any city, town, or village at a
greater speed than two miles an hour;

Any person acting contrary thereto shall for every
such offence, on summary conviction, forfeit not exceeding £10.

The name and residence of the owner of every loco- *Id.* s. 7.
motive must be affixed thereto in a conspicuous manner. residence of
If it is not so affixed, the owner, on summary convic- affixed.
tion, is liable to a penalty not exceeding £2.

The mayor, &c., in the city of London, and the Me- Act '78, s. 31.
tropolitan Board of Works in the metropolis, exclusive to hours
of the city of London, and the council of any borough which loco-
which has a separate court of quarter sessions, and the not pass
county authority of any county, may make bye-laws over roads.
as to the hours during which locomotives are not to
pass over turnpike roads or highways situate within
the areas respectively above mentioned, the hours
being in all cases consecutive hours, and no more than
eight out of the twenty-four, and for regulating the
use of locomotives upon any highway, or preventing Preventing
such use upon every bridge where such authority is bridges.
satisfied that such use would be attended with danger
to the public.

Any person in charge of a locomotive acting contrary to such bye-laws is liable to a fine not exceeding
£5.

Act '51, s. 12. PROVISIONS IN GENERAL ACTS, AND SAVINGS.

Provisions
in Turnpike
Acts to
apply to
locomotives,
&c.

All clauses and provisions of any general or local Acts relating to turnpike roads or highways, so far as they are not altered or repealed by or are not inconsistent with the provisions of this Act, apply to all locomotives propelled by other than animal power, and to all waggons, wains, carts and carriages of any other description drawn by such locomotive, and to the owners, drivers and attendants thereof, in like manner as if drawn by animal power :

Weight and
owner's
name to be
affixed.

Provided the weight of every locomotive, and the name of the owner or owners thereof, be conspicuously and legibly affixed thereon :

Any owner not having affixed such weight and name shall upon conviction before two justices, forfeit not exceeding £5 :

Any owner who fraudulently affixes thereon any incorrect weight, shall upon conviction, forfeit not exceeding £10 :

Act '65, s. 6.
Restrictions
as to steam
engines
within 25
yards of
roads not to
apply to
locomotives
for plough-
ing purposes.

Any provision in any Act prohibiting under penalty the erection and use of any steam engine, gin, or other like machine, or any machinery attached thereto, within the distance of twenty-five yards from any part of any turnpike road, highway, carriageway, or cartway, unless such steam engine, gin, or other like engine or machinery be within some house or other building, or behind some wall, fence, or screen, sufficient to conceal or screen the same from such turnpike road, highway, carriageway, or cartway, shall not extend to prohibit the use of any locomotive steam engine for the purpose of ploughing within such distance of any turnpike road, highway, carriageway, or cartway :

Provided a person shall be stationed in the road, and employed to signal the driver when it shall be

necessary to stop, and to assist horses, and carriages Act '65, s. 6.
drawn by horses, passing the same, and provided the
driver of the engine do stop in proper time.

No person is authorized by the Locomotive Act, Act '61, s. 12.
Indictment
1861, to use upon a highway a locomotive engine so or action in
case of
constructed or used as to cause a public or private nui- nuisance.
sance; and every person so using such engine is liable
to indictment or action for such use, where, but for the
passing of that Act, such indictment or action could
be maintained.

No person is authorized by the Locomotives Act, Act '65, s. 12.
Actions for
1865, to use a locomotive so constructed or used as to nuisance
or damage.
be a public nuisance at common law; and nothing
therein contained shall affect the right of any person
to recover damages in respect of any injury he may
have sutsained in consequence of the use of a locomotive.

Bye-Laws.

The mayor, aldermen, and commons in the city of Act '78, s. 31,
Local autho-
London, and the Metropolitan Board of Works in the rities may
make bye-
metropolis, exclusive of the city of London, and the laws as to
hours during
council of any borough which has a separate court of which
locomotives
quarter sessions, and the county authority of any may not
pass over
county, may make bye-laws as to the hours during roads.
which locomotives are not to pass over the turnpike
roads or highways situate within the areas respectively
above-mentioned the hours being in all cases consecutive hours, and no more than 8 out of the 24, and for
regulating the use of locomotives upon any highway, or
preventing such use upon every bridge where such Preventing
use on
authority is satisfied that such use would be attended bridges.
with danger to the public;

Any person in charge of a locomotive acting con-

Q

Act '78, s. 31. trary to such bye-laws is liable to a fine not exceeding £5.

Id. s. 32.
County
authority
may make
bye-laws
for licensing
locomotives.
A county authority may from time to time make, alter, and repeal bye-laws for granting annual licenses to locomotives used within their county, and the fee (not exceeding £10) to be paid in respect of each license;

And the owner of any locomotive for which a license is required under any bye-law so made who uses or permits the same to be used in contravention of any such bye-law shall be liable to a fine not exceeding 40s. for every day on which the same is so used.

All fees received under this section are to be carried to and applied as part of the county rate.

This section does not apply to any locomotive used solely for agricultural purposes.

Id. s. 35.
Confirmation.
A bye-law made under the Highways and Locomotives (Amendment) Act, 1878, and any alteration made therein, and any repeal of a bye-law, is of no validity until it has been submitted to and confirmed by the Local Government Board.

Notice of
intention to
apply for
confirmation.
No such bye-law, nor any alteration, addition, or repeal, can be confirmed until the expiration of one month after notice of the intention to apply for confirmation of the same has been given by the authority making the same in one or more local newspapers circulating in their county or district.

RECOVERY OF PENALTIES AND APPEAL UNDER THE HIGHWAYS AND LOCOMOTIVES (AMENDMENT) ACT, 1878.

Id. s. 36.
Fines and
expenses
recoverable
before court
All offences, fines, and expenses under the Highways and Locomotives (Amendment) Act, 1878, or any bye-law made in pursuance of that Act, may be

prosecuted, enforced, and recovered before a court of summary jurisdiction in manner provided by the Summary Jurisdiction Acts. Act '78, s. 36, of summary jurisdiction.

If any party thinks himself aggrieved by any conviction or order made by a court of summary jurisdiction on determining any information or complaint under this Act, the party so aggrieved may appeal therefrom, subject to the conditions and regulations following:— *Id.* s. 37. Appeal to quarter sessions.

(1.) The appeal shall be made to the next practicable court of quarter sessions for the county or place where the decision appealed from was given holden not less than twenty-one days after the decision of the court from which the appeal is made; and Appeal to next practicable sessions holden not less than 21 days after decision.

(2.) The appellant shall, within ten days after the pronouncing by the court of the decision appealed from, give notice to the other party and to the court of summary jurisdiction of his intention to appeal and of the ground thereof; such notice of appeal shall be in writing signed by the person or persons giving the same, or by his, her, or their solicitor on his, her, or their behalf; and Written notice to be given within 10 days to the other party and to court of summary jurisdiction, of intention to appeal and of the ground thereof signed by appellant or solicitor.

(3.) The appellant shall, within three days after such notice, enter into a recognizance before a justice of the peace, with two sufficient sureties, conditioned personally to try such appeal, and to abide the judgment of the court thereon, and to pay such costs as may be awarded by the court, or give such other security by deposit of money or otherwise as the justice may allow; and Within 3 days after notice, appellant to enter into recognizance with 2 sureties, or give other security by deposit of money, &c.

Act '78, s. 37.

Appellant
may be
liberated
from custody
on entering
into recog-
nizance, &c

Court may
adjourn
appeal and
confirm, &c.,
the decision,
or remit the
matter to
court of
summary
jurisdiction
with opinion
of court of
appeal, &c.

If matter
remitted
court of
summary
jurisdiction
to rehear
and decide
according to
opinion of
court of
appeal.

Court of
appeal may
make order
as to costs.

(4.) Where the appellant is in custody the justice may, if he think fit, on the appellant entering into such recognizance or giving such other security as aforesaid, release him from custody :

(5.) The court of appeal may adjourn the appeal, and upon the hearing thereof they may confirm, reverse, or modify the decision of the court of summary jurisdiction, or remit the matter to the court of summary jurisdiction with the opinion of the court of appeal thereon, or make such other order in the matter as the court thinks just, and if the matter be remitted to the court of summary jurisdiction the said last-mentioned court shall thereupon re-hear and decide the information or complaint in accordance with the opinion of the said court of appeal. The court of appeal may also make such order as to costs to be paid by either party as the court thinks just.

N.B.—The foregoing provisions only apply to offences, &c., under 41 & 42 Vict. c. 77. Penalties incurred under 24 & 25 Vict. c. 70, s. 12, and 28 & 29 Vict. c. 83, ss. 3, 4, 7, must consequently still be recovered under 11 & 12 Vict. c. 43, and the Acts amending that Act; and there is no appeal from the conviction.

LOCOMOTIVES ACT, 1861.

24 & 25 VICT. c. 70.

*An Act for regulating the Use of Locomotives on
Turnpike and other Roads, and the Tolls to be
levied on such Locomotives and on the Waggons
and Carriages drawn or propelled by the same.*
[1st August, 1861.]

WHEREAS the use of locomotives is likely to become
common on turnpike and other roads: and whereas
the general Turnpike and Highway Acts and many
of the local Turnpike Acts do not contain any provisions for regulating the use of locomotives on the
roads to which they respectively apply, nor do they
authorize the levying of tolls upon or in respect of any
locomotive using the roads, or upon or in respect of
any waggon or carriage drawn by locomotives: and
whereas under and by virtue of certain local Turnpike Acts tolls may be levied upon locomotives and
other engines drawing or propelling waggons or
carriages, or upon the waggons or carriages so drawn
or propelled, which are or may be prohibitory of the
use of locomotives on the roads to which the said Acts
respectively apply: and whereas the weighing clauses
in the general Turnpike Acts have not been framed
in anticipation of traffic by locomotives, and are in
many respects ill adapted to the profitable carrying of
goods, or to the levying of just and adequate tolls
upon waggons or carriages drawn by locomotives:
and whereas it is desirable that the use of locomotives

on turnpike and other roads should be regulated by uniform general provisions, and that tolls should be levied upon such locomotives and the waggons or carriages drawn by such locomotives upon turnpike roads: Be it therefore enacted by the Queen's most Excellent Majesty, by and with the advice and consent of the Lords spiritual and temporal, and Commons, in this present Parliament assembled, and by the authority of the same, as follows:—

Scale of tolls to be taken after passing of this Act. 1 (*a*). From and after the passing of this Act all trustees, corporations, commissioners, and other persons acting under and in execution of any existing general or local Turnpike Road Act or public Bridge Act shall demand and take tolls not exceeding the tolls following; that is to say:—

> For every locomotive (*b*) propelled by any power containing within itself the machinery for its own propulsion, such a toll for every two tons weight or fractional part of every two tons weight that such locomotive shall weigh as shall be equal to the toll or tolls by their respective Acts made payable for every horse drawing any waggon, wain, cart, or carriage with wheels of a width similar to those of such locomotive; or in the case of a toll by any such Act made payable being charged on the horse or horses drawing any such waggon, wain, cart, or carriage, without reference to the width of the wheels thereof, then such a toll for every two tons or fractional part thereof that such locomotive shall weigh as shall be equal to one horse drawing such waggon, wain, cart, or carriage; which tolls respectively shall be payable so often as tolls made payable as aforesaid for such waggon, wain, cart, or carriage

shall be payable at the same gate: provided
always, that if the wheels of such locomotive
shall rest upon any shoe or other bearing the
surface of which shall bear upon the ground so
as to prevent the wheels coming in contact therewith, such and the same tolls only shall be
demanded and payable as if the wheels thereof
were of a width similar to such shoe or bearing:

For every waggon, wain, cart or carriage drawn (*b*)
or propelled by any locomotive, for each pair of
wheels thereof such a toll as shall not exceed the
toll by their respective Acts made payable for
two horses drawing any waggon, wain, cart, or
carriage with wheels of a similar width, and for
every additional wheel thereof one half toll in
addition to the said toll; or in the case of a toll
by any such Act made payable being charged on
the horse or horses drawing any such waggon,
wain, cart, or carriage, without reference to the
width of the wheels thereof, then such a toll for
each wheel as shall be equal to one horse drawing
such waggon, wain, cart, or carriage; which said
toll or tolls shall be payable so often as the toll
made payable as aforesaid for such waggon,
wain, cart, or carriage drawn by horses shall be
payable at the same gate :

Provided always that in every case where the wheels
of any waggon, wain, cart, or carriage shall not all be
cylindrical, as described in the Act 3 Geo. 4, c. 126,
s. 9, the toll payable in respect thereof shall be one
half more.

(*a*) This section, it will be observed, is confined to roads
which are governed by General or Local Turnpike Road Acts
or Public Bridge Acts. Consequently in all other cases locomo-

Act '61, s. 1. tives can be used on highways like any other description of
— traffic without any payment whatever. To meet in some degree
the injustice arising from this state of things, power is now
conferred upon the justices in quarter sessions by the 32nd
section of the recent Act, 41 & 42 Vict. c. 77 (*ante*, p. 205) to
license locomotives upon payment of a fee not exceeding £10,
which is to be carried to and applied as part of the county rate.
Locomotives used solely for agricultural purposes are, however,
excepted from this provision.

To a certain extent this, no doubt, is a palliation of the evil
arising from the unrestricted use of locomotives upon ordinary
highways. But it is obvious that the real sufferer, viz., the
parish or highway district, gets little or no benefit from the fee,
and consequently will practically be no better off than before,
unless it avails itself of the power conferred by the 23rd section
of the same Act of recovering compensation for extraordinary
expenses incurred in repairing the highway by reason of the
damage caused by excessive weight passing over it.

It must, however, be borne in mind that both the power to
license locomotives and that of recovering compensation are
temporary, and merely remain in force so long as the Locomotive Act, 1865, continues in force, viz., until the 31st December,
1879 (see 41 & 42 Vict. c. 77, s. 33). And it may also be re-
marked that the license applies to any locomotive "propelled by
steam or by any other than animal power" (*Id.* s. 38), whereas
toll is only payable under sect. 1 of the Locomotive Act, 1861,
upon every locomotive "propelled by any power containing
within itself the machinery for its own propulsion," whatever
that may mean.

(*b*) See sect. 10 as to the exemption from toll of waggons, &c.,
"*drawn* by any locomotive;" and sect. 12 as to the application
of the provisions of general Acts to "locomotives propelled by
other than animal power, and to all waggons . . . *drawn* by
such locomotive." Neither of these provisions applies to
waggons, &c., "*propelled* by any locomotive." They are consequently not co-extensive with the provision in this section,
whilst the description of the power of propulsion in sect. 12 also
varies from that contained in the 1st section.

Repeal of former enactments as to tolls to be taken for locomotives.

2. All clauses and provisions in any local or general
Turnpike Road Act or public Bridge Act authorizing
tolls to be demanded or taken upon locomotives or carriages drawn by steam or any other than animal power,
different to the tolls herein provided for, shall so far as
the same relate to such tolls, be and the same are
hereby repealed: Provided always, that this enact—

ment shall not be deemed or construed to extend to Act 61, s. 2. any tolls authorized to be taken in respect of any private roads or private bridges, or to the roads comprised in "The *Commercial* Roads Continuation Act, 1849" (c).

(c) 12 & 13 Vict. c. lxxvi. See also *Rapley* v. *Richards*, 28 J.P. 486, as an instance of a local turnpike Act authorizing toll to be demanded for a locomotive different from that mentioned in sect. 1 *supra*.

3 (d) * * * * *

(d) This section is repealed as to Scotland by 41 & 42 Vict. c. 58, s. 3, and as to England by 41 & 42 Vict. c. 77, s. 28. But as that part of the latter Act which amends the Locomotive Acts, 1861 & 1865, is only operative so long as the Locomotive Act, 1865, continues in force, viz., until the 31st December, 1879, the repeal is only temporary. In all probability, however, that part of the Act will be further continued, and as it contains substituted provisions as to England for those in 24 & 25 Vict. c. 70, s. 3, there seems to be no other reason for printing the latter section than that it still applies to Ireland.

Two decisions have been given on the provisions of the section, viz., *Stringer* v. *Sykes*, 2 Ex. D. 240, and *Body* v. *Jeffery*, 3 Ex. D. 95. But as they relate to provisions which have been altered by the recent Act and are, no longer operative in England, it is considered sufficient to refer to them in general terms.

4. It shall not be lawful for any waggon, wain, cart, As to the weight on each pair of wheels. or other carriage so drawn or propelled as aforesaid, not having cylindrical wheels, to carry any greater weight than is permitted in such waggon, wain, cart, or carriage by the general Turnpike Act (e); and it shall not be lawful for any waggon, wain, cart, or other carriage having cylindrical wheels to carry over or above the weight of the waggon, wain, cart, or carriage, any greater weight than one ton and a half for each pair of wheels, unless the fellies, tires, or shoes are four inches or more in breadth; nor to carry a greater weight than two tons for each pair of wheels, unless the fellies, tires, or shoes are six inches or more in breadth; nor to

Act '61, s. 4. carry a greater weight than three tons for each pair of
wheels, unless the fellies, tires, or shoes are eight
inches or more in breadth; and for every single
wheel one-half of that permitted to be carried on a pair
of wheels; nor in any case to carry a greater weight than
four tons on each pair of wheels, or two tons on each
wheel; but if such waggons, wains, or other carriages
are built and constructed with springs upon each axle,
then they shall be allowed to carry one-sixth more
weight in addition to the above mentioned weights
upon each pair of wheels: Provided (f) always, that
the regulation of weight herein mentioned and provided
shall not extend to any waggon, wain, cart, or other
carriage carrying only one tree, or one log of timber,
or one block of stone, or one cable or rope, or one block,
plate, roll, or vessel of iron or other metal, or compounded of any two or more metals cast, wrought, or
united in one piece.

(e) 3 Geo. 4, c. 126, ss. 12-16, both inclusive.
(f) The exemptions contained in the proviso are the same as
in 3 Geo. 4, c. 126, s. 16, and 4 Geo. 4, c. 95, s. 21.

5. (g)   *   *   *   *   *

(g) The 5th, 9th, 11th, and 15th sections of this Act are
repealed by 28 & 29 Vict. c. 83, s. 2, so long as that Act continues in force. Originally the duration of the latter Act was
limited to the 1st September, 1867; but the Act has since been
continued by the 41 & 42 Vict. c. 70, and previous continuance
Acts, to the 31st December, 1879.

Use of
locomotives
restricted
over suspen-
sion and
other
bridges.

6. It shall not be lawful for the owner or driver of
any locomotive to drive it over any suspension bridge
nor over any bridge on which a conspicuous notice has
been placed, by the authority of the surveyor or
persons liable to the repair of the bridge, that the
bridge is insufficient to carry weights beyond the
ordinary traffic of the district, without previously ob-

taining the consent of the surveyor of the road or
bridgemaster under whose charge such bridge shall be
for the time being, or of the persons liable to the repair
of such bridge; and in case such owner of the locomotive and surveyor of the road or bridge, or bridgemaster, shall differ in opinion as to the sufficiency of
any bridge to sustain the transit of the locomotive,
then the question shall be determined by an officer to
be appointed, on the application of either party, by
one of Her Majesty's principal Secretaries of State,
whose certificate ot sufficiency of such bridge shall
entitle the owner of the locomotive to take the same
over such bridge.

7. (*h*) Where any turnpike or other roads, upon Damage caused by locomotives to bridges to be made good by owners.
which locomotives are or hereafter may be used, pass
or are or shall be carried over or across any stream or
watercourse, navigable river, canal, or railway, by
means of any bridge or arch (whether stationary or
moveable), and such bridge or arch, or any of the
walls, buttresses, or supports thereof, shall be damaged
by reason of any locomotive or any waggon or carriage
drawn or propelled by or together with a locomotive
passing over the same or coming into contact therewith, none of the proprietors, undertakers, directors,
conservators, trustees, commissioners, or other person
interested in or having the charge of such navigable
river, canal, or railway, or the tolls thereof, or of such
bridge or arch, shall be liable to repair or make good
any damage so to be occasioned, or to make compensation to any person for any obstruction, interruption,
or delay which may arise therefrom to the use of such
bridge or arch, navigable river, canal or railway,
but every such damage shall be forthwith repaired to
the satisfaction of the proprietors, undertakers, direc-

Act '61, s. 7. tors, conservators, trustees, commissioners, or other persons as aforesaid respectively interested in or having the charge of such river, canal, or railway, or the tolls thereof, or of such bridge or arch, by and at the expense of the owner or owners or the person or persons having the charge of such locomotive at the time of the happening of such damage; and all such owner and owners, person and persons, having the charge of such locomotive as aforesaid, shall also be liable, both jointly and severally, to reimburse and make good as well to the proprietors, undertakers, directors, conservators, trustees, commissioners, and other persons interested in or having the charge of any such navigable river, canal, or railway, or the tolls thereof, or of such bridge or arch, as to all persons navigating on or using, or who but for such obstruction, interruption, or delay would have navigated on or used the same, all losses and expenses which they or any of them may sustain or incur by reason of any such obstruction, interruption, or delay, such losses and expenses to be recoverable by action at law, which action, in case of such proprietors, undertakers, directors, conservators, trustees, commissioners, or other persons so interested as aforesaid, may be brought in the name or names of their agent or agents, clerk or clerks for the time being, or by any person or persons legally authorized to act in their behalf.

(*h*) This section does not apply to county bridges, *Reg.* v. *Kitchener*, L. R. 2 C. C. 88, 34 J. P. 134. It is confined to bridges in the nature of private property.—*Id.*

8. (*i*)   *   *   *   *   *

(*i*) Repealed by 41 & 42 Vict. c. 77, s. 30, so far as relates to England, and other provisions made on the same subject as to England. The substituted provisions, however, are only temporary. But, for reasons already mentioned, *ante* p. 233, sect. 3,

note (*d*), it has been considered unnecessary to print the section, Act '61, s. 8.
although it still applies to Ireland.

9. (*j*)   *   *   *   ●   *

(*j*) See note (*g*) to sect. 5, *ante* p. 234.

10. All waggons, wains, carts, or carriages, as Exemption from tolls of
hereinbefore described, drawn (*k*) by any locomotive, waggons,
and loaded with any materials such as are now exempt &c., now ex-
from toll under the provisions of any general or local or local Act.
Act, shall be entitled to the same exemption as they
would be if drawn by animal power.

(*k*) The waggons, &c., here referred to are those described in
the 3rd par. sect. 1, *ante*, p. 231. That section, however, includes
waggons, &c., "drawn *or propelled*" by a locomotive; whereas
sect. 10 only applies to waggons, &c., "*drawn*" by a locomotive.
Consequently waggons which are propelled by a locomotive seem
to be excluded from the benefit of the exemption which would
attach to them if they were drawn, instead of being propelled,
by it.

11. (*l*)   *   ●   *   ●   *

(*l*) See note (*g*) to sect 5, *ante*, p. 234.

12. All the clauses and provisions of any general or Provisions of general
local Acts relating to turnpike roads or highways shall, Acts relating
so far as the same are not expressly altered or repealed Roads to
by or are not inconsistent with the provisions of this apply to lo-
Act, apply to all locomotives propelled by other than comotives.
animal power (*m*), and to all waggons, wains, carts,
and carriages of any other description drawn (*n*) by
such locomotive, and to the owners, drivers, and attendants thereof, in like manner as if drawn by animal
power : provided (*o*) always, that the weight of every
locomotive and the name of the owner or owners
thereof, shall be conspicuously and legibly affixed
thereon ; and any owner not having affixed such
weight and such name shall, upon conviction thereof

Act '61, s. 12. before two justices, forfeit any sum not exceeding £5;
and any owner who shall fraudulently affix thereon
any incorrect weight shall, upon conviction thereof,
forfeit any sum not exceeding £10.

(*m*) The locomotives on which toll is imposed by sect. 1, are
those " propelled by any power, containing within itself the
machinery for its own propulsion." Sect. 12 extends beyond
this, and applies the provisions of the Turnpike Acts to all locomotives whatsoever propelled " by other than animal power," no
matter whether that power does or does not " contain within itself
the machinery for its own propulsion." In point of fact, it seems
difficult to understand how the *power* can contain within itself
the machinery for its own propulsion, although one could have
well understood how the *locomotive* might have contained such
machinery.

A locomotive, propelled by its own steam power, having on it
gear necessary for working a plough, passed through a turnpike
gate on its way to a farm not occupied by the owner of the engine, and more than three miles from the gate, to drive a plough
which, from its construction, could not be used without a steam
engine and gear. And it was held that the locomotive was liable
to toll, under sect. 1, being only exempt under 3 Geo. 4, c. 126,
s. 32, like a horse, when it had not gone more than two miles on
the road : *Skinner* v. *Visger*, L. R. 9 Q. B. 199, 24 J.P. 534.

The case of *Reg.* v. *Matty*, 22 J.P. 575, 27 L. J. *m.* 59, illus-
trates the state of the law before the passing of this section. In
that case the keeper of a turnpike gate had been convicted of
taking toll in respect of a moveable steam engine exclusively
employed for the purpose of working a threshing machine. The
steam engine was drawn by horses, and was following a threshing machine, also drawn by horses, and both were going along a
turnpike road to a farm, to be employed there in threshing corn.
Exemption was claimed for both as implements of husbandry,
but the toll taker demanded and received the toll in respect of
the steam engine, demanding none in respect of the threshing
machine.

The sessions, having on appeal, confirmed the conviction, subject to a case, it was *held* by the Court of Queen's Bench, that as
the steam engine was to be employed to work the threshing machine, it must be considered as part of the threshing machine,
and therefore was free from toll, and consequently that the conviction was right.

And Lord *Campbell*, C. J., added, that " if the steam engine
had been going along the road by itself for the sole purpose of
working the threshing machine, it may be that it would also
be exempt. If it had been going along the road for the purpose of being employed for some other purpose as well as

moving a threshing machine, it may be that it would not be Act '61, s. 12.
exempt."

(n) The power to take toll under sect. 1, extends to waggons,
&c. " drawn or *propelled* " by any locomotive, but this section
only applies to those which are *drawn* by locomotives.

(o) Affixing the weight of the locomotive and the name of the
owner appears to be a condition precedent to the application of
the clauses and provisions of the general Turnpike Acts. The
liability to the penalty for default seems to be a cumulative
punishment which attaches to the owner independently of the
non-applicability of such clauses and provisions. The name and
residence of the owner are also required to be affixed to the locomotive under a penalty not exceeding £2 (See 28 & 29 Vict. c.
83, s. 7.)

13. Nothing in this Act contained shall authorize Right of ac-
any person to use upon a highway a locomotive engine of nuisance.
which shall be so constructed or used as to cause
a public or private nuisance; and every such person
so using such engine shall notwithstanding this Act,
be liable to an indictment or action, as the case
may be, for such use, where, but for the passing of
this Act, such indictment or action could be maintained.

14. This Act may be cited as the " Locomotive Short title.
Act, 1861."

15. (p) *   *   *   *   *   *

(p) See note (g) to sect. 5, *ante*, p. 234.

LOCOMOTIVES ACT, 1865.

28 & 29 Vict. c. 83.

An Act for further regulating the Use of Locomotives on Turnpike and other Roads for agricultural and other Purposes.

[5th July, 1865.]

24 & 25 Vict. c. 70. WHEREAS by the Locomotives Act, 1861, certain provision was made for regulating the use of locomotives on turnpike and other roads, and it is expedient that further and fuller provision should be made for that object: Be it therefore enacted by the Queen's most excellent Majesty, by and with the advice and consent of the Lords spiritual and temporal, and Commons, in this present Parliament assembled, and by the authority of the same as follows:—

Commencement of Act. 1. This Act shall not come into operation till the 1st September, 1865, which day is hereinafter referred to as the commencement of the Act, and shall cease and determine on the 1st September, 1867 (*a*).

(*a*) The Act has since been continued by the 41 & 42 Vict. c. 70, and previous continuance Acts, to the 31st December, 1879.

Certain sections of 24 & 25 Vict. c. 70 repealed. 2. After the commencement of this Act, and so long as the same shall continue in force, the 5th, 9th, 11th, and 15th sections of the said recited Act, and all orders made in pursuance of the said 5th section, are hereby repealed.

3. Every locomotive propelled by steam or any Act '65, s. 8.
other than animal power on any turnpike road or Rules for the manner
public highway shall be worked according to the of working locomotives
following rules and regulations, viz. :— on turnpike roads and

> 1st. At least three persons shall be employed to drive highways herein stated.
> or conduct such locomotive, and if more than
> two waggons or carriages be attached thereto,
> an additional person shall be employed, who shall
> take charge of such waggons or carriages :

> 2nd. (*b*) * * * * * *

> 3rd. The drivers of such locomotives shall give as
> much space as possible for the passing of other
> traffic :

> 4th. The whistle of such locomotive shall not be
> sounded for any purpose whatever : nor shall
> the cylinder taps be opened within sight of any
> person riding, driving, leading or in charge of
> a horse upon the road ; nor shall the steam be
> allowed to attain a pressure such as to exceed
> the limit fixed by the safety valve, so that no
> steam shall blow off when the locomotive is
> upon the road :

> 5th. Every such locomotive shall be instantly
> stopped on the person preceding the same, or
> any other person with a horse or carriage drawn
> by a horse, putting up his hand as a signal to
> require such locomotive to be stopped :

> 6th. Any person in charge of any such locomotive
> shall provide two efficient lights to be affixed
> conspicuously, one at each side on the front of
> the same, between the hours of one hour after
> sunset and one hour before sunrise :

Penalty on non-compliance with rules.
In the event of a non-compliance with any of the
provisions of this section, the owner of the locomotive

R

Act '55, s. 3. shall, on summary conviction thereof before two justices, be liable to a penalty not exceeding £10; but it
shall be lawful for such owner on proving that he has
incurred such penalty by reason of the negligence or
wilful default of any person in charge of or in attendance on such locomotive, to recover summarily from
such person the whole or any part of the penalty he
may have incurred as owner.

(*b*) This paragraph is repealed, as to Scotland by 41 & 42 Vict.
c. 58, s. 4; and as to England, by 41 & 42 Vict. c. 77, s. 29, and
another paragraph substituted for it (*ante*, p. 203). As it now
only applies to Ireland, it has been omitted as inapplicable to an
edition intended merely for the use of English readers.
It should, however, be mentioned that the repeal is only temporary, as that part of 41 & 42 Vict. c. 77, which amends the
Locomotive Acts, 1861 and 1865, is only operative so long as
this Act continues in force, viz., until the 31st December, 1879.
(See 41 & 42 Vict. c. 77, s. 33.)

Limit of
speed of
locomotives
on turnpike
roads and
highways.

4. Subject and without prejudice to the regulations
hereinafter authorized to be made by local authorities,
it shall not be lawful to drive any such locomotive along
any turnpike road or public highway at a greater speed
than four miles an hour, or through any city, town or
village at a greater speed than two miles an hour; and
any person acting contrary thereto shall for every
such offence, on summary conviction thereof, forfeit
any sum not exceeding £10.

5. (*c*) *   *   *   *   *   *

(*c*) This section is repealed as to Scotland by 41 & 42 Vict.
c. 58, s. 3; and as to England by 41 & 42 Vict. c. 77 s. 28, and
other provisions substituted for it. Similar remarks to those
already made in note (*b*), *supra*, apply to this section and account
for its omission.

Restrictions
as to the use
of steam en-
gines within
25 yards of
roads not to
apply to

6. Any provision in any Act contained (*d*) prohibiting,
under penalty, the erection and use of any steam engine,
gin, or other like machine, or any machinery attached
thereto within the distance of twenty-five yards from

any part of any turnpike road, highway, carriageway,
or cartway, unless such steam engine, gin, or other
like engine or machinery be within some house or
other building, or behind some wall, fence, or screen
sufficient to conceal or screen the same from such
turnpike road, highway, carriageway, or cartway, shall
not extend to prohibit the use of any locomotive steam
engine for the purpose of ploughing within such distance of any such turnpike road, highway, carriageway, or cartway, provided a person shall be stationed
in the road, and employed to signal the driver when it
shall be necessary to stop and to assist horses, and carriages drawn by horses, passing the same, and provided
the driver of the engine do stop in proper time.

(*d*) The provisions here referred to are contained in 5 & 6
Will. 4, c. 50, s. 70, with regard to highways ; and in 27 & 28 Vict.
c. 75, s. 1, which made similar but amended provisions, with
respect to turnpike roads.

In *Smith* v. *Stokes*, 32 L. J., *m.*, 199, 27 J. P., 535, it was held
that a portable engine on wheels drawn by horses from place to
place and used to drive a threshing machine within a barn
without being fixed into the ground, is a steam engine within
the meaning of 5 & 6 Will. 4, c. 50, s. 70. But the owner of such
an engine let out to hire cannot be convicted if he was not
present and took no part in fixing the engine within the prohibited distance (*Harrison* v. *Leaper*, 26 J. P., 373).

7. The name and residence of the owner of every
locomotive shall be affixed thereto in a conspicuous
manner. If it is not so affixed the owner shall, on
summary conviction, be liable to a penalty not exceeding £2 (*e*).

(*e*) The 12th section of 24 & 25 Vict. c. 70 also requires the
owner to affix the weight of the engine and his own name, under
a penalty of £5 in case of failure to do so.

8. (*f.*)   *   *   *   *   *   *

(*f*) This section is repealed as to Scotland by 41 & 42 Vict.
c. 58, s. 5 ; and as to England by 41 & 42 Vict. c. 77, s. 31, and

Act 88, s. 8. other provisions substituted for it. Similar remarks to those already made in note (*b*), *supra*, apply to this section, and account for its omission.

9. (*g.*)   *   *   *   *   *   *

10. (*g.*)   *   *   *   *   *   *

(*g*) This section applies to Ireland only, and is consequently omitted.

Sect. 41 of 25 & 26 Vict. c. 93, not to be affected.

11. Nothing in this Act contained shall repeal, alter, or in any way affect the provisions of the 41st section of the Thames Embankment Act, 1862.

Saving as to actions at law.

12. Nothing in this Act contained shall authorize any person to use a locomotive which may be so constructed or used as to be a public nuisance at common law, and nothing herein contained shall affect the right of any person to recover damages in respect of any injury he may have sustained in consequence of the use of a locomotive (*h*).

(*h*) In *Watkins* v. *Reddin*, 2 F. & F. 629, an action was maintained by a person who had sustained an injury through his horse being frightened by a traction engine used on a highway, under 24 & 25 Vict. c. 70, the jury finding that the engine was likely to frighten horses, and that the defendant knew it: and *semb.* the scienter is not material. In instructing the jury, Erle, C. J., said—"The plaintiff is entitled to your verdict, if the engine was calculated by its noise or appearance to frighten horses, so as to make the use of the highway dangerous to persons riding or driving horses. For the defendant has clearly no right to make a profit at the expense of the security of the public."

Short title.

13. This Act may be cited as The Locomotives Act, 1865; and The Locomotives Act, 1861, and this Act, shall be construed together as one Act.

INDEX.

Highways—*continued.*

board may contract for materials, 41, 160 ; may contract to repair highways repairable by other parties, 41, 135 ; may permit landowner to erect fences without his incurring liability to repair, 42, 119.

default by highway authority in maintaining, 42, 175 ; on complaint, county authority to make order on defaulting authority, 42, 175 ; on non-compliance, to appoint some one to perform the duty, and order payment of expenses and costs, 42, 175 ; person appointed has powers of defaulting authority, 43, 176 ; on notice that defaulting authority declines to comply until liability determined, county authority to cancel or modify order, or submit question to jury, 43, 176 ; if question submitted to jury, indictment to be preferred to assizes, 43, 176 ; order suspended, 43, 176 ; operative, if defendants guilty, 44, 176; void, if defendants acquitted, 44, 177 ; costs, as court directs, 44, 177 ; out of what funds payable, 44, 177.

main roads, disturnpiked roads to become, 44, 180 ; half expense of maintenance to be paid out of county rate, 45, 180 ; proviso as to metropolis and municipal corporations, 45, 180 ; county authority may order ordinary highway to become, 45, 183 ; may apply for provisional order that disturnpiked roads ought not to become, 46, 185 ; or that main road has become an ordinary highway, 46, 185 ; Local Government Board may make provisional order, 46, 185.

discontinuance of unnecessary highways. *See* Unnecessary Highways, 50, 53.

widening, diverting, and stopping up, provisions of Principal Act applicable to highways under local or personal Acts, 76, 118 ; borough councils may adopt parish roads and highways, and apply rates for their repair, 76, 118 ; provisions as to cattle found straying, &c., on highways, 77, 136 ; encroachment, penalty and proceedings, 78, 158 ; mines and minerals under, belong to former owner of land, 79, 199.

Hundred bridges, expense of repairing main roads over, how repayable, 48, 188.

Improvements, definition, 55, 157 ; board may make, and borrow money with approval of quarter sessions, 53, 154 ; estimate must be made, and two months' notice given, before application for approval, 53, 154 ; contents of notice, 53, 155 ; service and publication of notice, 54,

Ratione tenuræ—continued.

a penalty, 57, 109 ; sums exceeding £50 to be invested and interest applied towards maintenance of highways, 58, 109 ; smaller sums to be applied in like manner, 58, 110 ; appeal to quarter sessions upon written notice within fourteen days, and recognizance seven days before sessions, 58, 110 ; after order, &c., highway repairable by parish, 58, 110 ; board may apply to make highway repairable *ratione tenuræ* repairable by parish, 59, 136.

Receipt and expenditure, statement of, to be sent to members of board and overseers, 68, 147 ; clerk to furnish copy to ratepayers and owners, 68, 147.

Regulations, as to orders for forming districts, 9, 84 ; on making provisional order, subsequent court to be appointed for confirmation, 9, 84 ; clerk of peace to send notice with notice of holding sessions, 10, 84 ; justices may quash or confirm order, or respite to subsequent sessions, 10, 84 ; provisional order to state parishes to be united, &c., 10, 85 ; construction of order including more than one district, 11, 122 ; jurisdiction of justices as to union of parishes in different counties, 11, 129 ; first meeting of board to be held at time appointed by order, 11, 126 ; day appointed for first meeting deemed day of formation of district, 12, 126 ; justices may appoint day for first election of waywardens, 12, 127.

as to proceedings of highway board, 23, 24, 25, 161, 162, 163.
as to working locomotives, 221, 241.

Removal of parish from district, costs of application, 19, 130.

Repair, of highways, 39-59, 97, 98, 101. *See* Highways.

Restriction of use of locomotives over bridges, 218, 234.

Rules for working locomotives, 221, 241 ; penalty on non-compliance, 223, 241.

Rural sanitary authority, definition, 5, 210 ; application to exercise powers of highway board, 36, 167 ; county authority may declare that it shall exercise such powers, 36, 167 ; consequences, 37, 38, 169, 170.

Rural sanitary district, definition, 5, 210 ; highway districts to be made coincident with, 9, 166.

Seal, highway board to have common, 21, 89.

Separation of townships, &c., consolidated by previous order, 19, 130.

Service, of notices, &c., *by* board, 25, 138 ; by post, proof of, 25, 138 ; on overseers or waywardens, 25, 138 ; of notices, summonses, &c., *on* board, 31, 116.

London : Printed by SHAW & SONS, Fetter Lane, E.C

Lightning Source UK Ltd.
Milton Keynes UK
UKHW020908100822
407113UK00006BB/1353